THE
RAY "CRASH"
CORRIGAN
FILMOGRAPHY

Ray "Crash" Corrigan

The
Ray "Crash" Corrigan
Filmography

by Jerry L. Schneider

Corriganville Press
California

A Corriganville Press
First Edition
June 2014

Published by
Corriganville Press

For a list of our books, please visit our web site at
www.CorriganvillePress.com

Hardcover ISBN: 978-0-9831972-8-7
Soft Cover ISBN: 978-0-6922308-8-6

TABLE OF CONTENTS

THE TELEVISION SHOWS

THE
RAY "CRASH" CORRIGAN
CORRIGAN
FILMOGRAPHY

Metro Goldwyn Mayer
Metro-Goldwyn-Mayer
TARZAN
THE APE MAN
Johnny Weissmuller Neil Hamilton
C. Aubrey Smith Maureen O'Sullivan
Directed by
W. S. VAN DYKE
Based upon the characters created
EDGAR RICE BURROUGHS
CYRIL HUME
IVOR NOVELLO
DOUGLAS SHEARER
CEDRIC GIBBONS
HAROLD ROSSON
CLYDE DE VINNA
TOM HELD
Film Editor
Western Electric
SOUND SYSTEM
CAST
Harry Holt NEIL HAMILTON
MAUREEN O'SULLIVAN
C. AUBREY SMITH
DORIS LLOYD
Beamish
IVORY WILLIAMS
JOHNNY WEISSMULLER as TARZAN

TARZAN
JOHNNY WEISSMULLER
NEIL HAMILTON
C. AUBREY SMITH
MAUREEN O'SULLIVAN
A Metro-Goldwyn-Mayer
Picture

Tarzan, the Ape Man

Produced and Released by Metro-Goldwyn-Mayer Picture on March 12, 1932. Copyright March 14, 1932, Metro-Goldwyn-Mayer Distributing Corp., LP2913, renewed March 5, 1959, Loew's Inc., R233163. Running time 99, 101, or 104 minutes, ten reels. Passed by the National Board of Review. *Directed by* W. S. Van Dyke; *produced by* Bernard H. Hyman; *based upon the characters created by* Edgar Rice Burroughs; *adaptation by* Cyril Hume; *dialogue by* Ivor Novello; *recording director,* Douglas Shearer; *art director,* Cedric Gibbons; *photographed by* Harold Rosson and Clyde de Vinna; *film editors,* Ben Lewis and Tom Held; *sound,* Western Electric Sound System; *production manager,* Joseph J. Cohn; *animal supervision,* George Emerson, Bert Nelson, Louis Roth, and Louis Goebel; *photographic effects,* Warren Newcombe; *additional cinematography,* William Snyder, ASC; *music by* George Richelavie, Fritz Stahlberg, and P. A. Marquardt; *composite effects by* Dunning Process Company and Williams Composite Laboratories.

Cast:

Neil Hamilton	. . . . .	Harry Holt
Maureen O'Sullivan	. . . . .	Jane Parker
C. Aubrey Smith	. . . . .	James Parker
Doris Lloyd	. . . . .	Mrs. Cutten
Forrester Harvey	. . . . .	Beamish
Ivory Williams	. . . . .	Riano
Johnny Weissmuller	. . . . .	Tarzan
Ray Benard	. . . . .	Ape
Bert Nelson	. . . . .	Animal Stunts
Louis Goebel	. . . . .	Animal Stunts
Flying Cordonas	. . . . .	Aerial Stunts
Picchiani Troupe	. . . . .	Aerial Stunts

Synopsis:

James Parker, owner of a General Store/Trading Post in Africa and his young friend, Harry Holt are questioning an elderly native about the Mutia Escarpment and the elephant hunting ground, but he refuses to answer their questions.

Jane Parker, daughter of James Parker, is met at the port by Mrs. Cutten and Harry Holt, the latter of whom take Jane to her father at the trading post.

The subject of the Mutia arises and Jane questions her father and Holt. They explain that when an elephant knows it is near death, the animal heads to the ceremonial burial ground, a secret graveyard, where they perish—and where there would be thousands of dollars worth of ivory.

When she learns that her father and Holt are heading there on safari, Jane persists until she convinces them to take her along. It is quite apparent that Holt is falling in love with her.

While on safari, one night a mortally wounded native stumbles into camp and is questioned by Parker and Holt who learn the direction of the Mutia escarpment. Almost immediately, the sound of the native's tribe assails their ears. Quickly hiding the native, his tribe arrives, seeking him as he has been sentenced to death for viewing the Mutia.

Holt convinces them that they have not seen the native and the others depart.

The next day, the safari arrives at the Mutia and begin to scale it. Part way up, Jane nearly loses her life when she falls off. Luckily, Holt had tied a rope to her that saves her from falling to her death thousands of feet below.

Atop the escarpment, they hear a human yell, Tarzan's, but they do not see him.

They soon reach a river infested with hippopotamuses and the safari boys make two rafts for the crossing. The rafts are attacked by the hippos and Holt's is

overturned. Holt and a few of the natives are saved, but others are killed. The survivors make it to sure and the hippos follow them, ready to attack, when Tarzan's yell causes the hippos to retreat to the water.

They see Tarzan in the trees, but he disappears. Within moments, pygmies attack and Tarzan kidnaps Jane. The safari staves off the attack and discover that Jane is missing.

After defeating a leopard, Tarzan takes Jane to his abode in the trees.

The next morning, Tarzan and Jane introduce themselves in the famous "Me Tarzan, You Jane" routine where the dialogue actually says "Tarzan, Jane" and

4

nothing more.

While Tarzan is searching for breakfast, he aids an elephant to escape from an elephant pit. The safari finds Jane in the trees and Holt shoots an ape. Tarzan appears and he is shot at by Holt and is narrowly missed. Jane returns to her father and Holt.

In revenge for the death of the ape, Tarzan follows the safari and begins killing the natives. Holt finally sees the apeman and shots at him, striking him in the head. Wounded, Tarzan attempts to escape and is attacked by a lioness and lion in succession, each killed by the apeman. Finally, he sinks into unconsciousness. An elephant comes to his aid and carries him away until he is taken by the apes who attempt to administer to his needs. They also bring Jane to his aid.

When Tarzan has recovered, he and Jane are happy and swim together. Finally, he takes her back to her father, then the apeman departs in dejection.

Dwarfs attack the safari and capture the members. Cheetah sees this and hurries away to tell Tarzan. After Tarzan has been informed, he speeds off to the safari's rescue while Cheetah gets the elephants to aid Tarzan.

In the dwarf's village, the safari members are being sacrificed to a huge gorilla. With Jane in his arms and Parker and Holt attempting to save her, Tarzan arrives and defeats the gorilla. The elephants attack the dwarfs and Tarzan saves Jane, Parker, and Holt.

They arrive at the elephant's burial ground, but Parker, seriously wounded by the gorilla, dies. Tarzan and Jane accompany Holt to an area of the escarpment where Holt can descend. Tarzan and Jane remain behind.

Production Notes:
Filmed from October 31, 1931 to late December 1931, at a cost of $652,675. A majority of the film was shot utilizing the sound stages and Lot 1 at Metro-Goldwyn-Mayer Studios in Culver City, California. At the west end of Lot 1 were the river/lake and the Mutia Escarpment rocks (aka "Tarzan" rocks). Other location sites included Lake Sherwood and Sherwood Forest, and the Iverson Movie Location Ranch. The Indian elephants used in the film were fitted with African elephant sized ears. The little people in the film were mentioned in the October 20, 1931, issue of *Variety*: "Railroad companies are cooperating with Charles Hatch, RKO's outdoor booker, in digging up midgets, animals and freaks for Metro's 'Tarzan' and 'Freaks'... Studio needs about 150 smallies..."

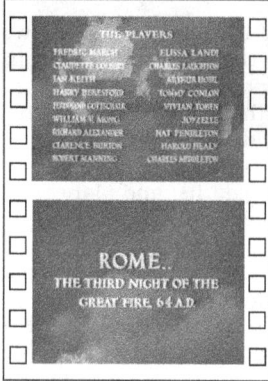

The Sign of the Cross

Produced and Released by Paramount Publix Corp. on November 30, 1932. Running time, 123-125 Minutes, 14 reels. *Directed by* Cecil B. De Mille; *screen play by* Waldemar Young and Sidney Buchman; *from the play by* Wilson Barrett; *photographed by* Karl Struss; *costumes by* Mitchell Leisen.

Cast:

Fredric March	Marcus
Elissa Landi	Mercia
Claudette Colbert	Poppaea
Charles Laughton	Nero
Ian Keith	Tigellinus
Arthur Hohl	Titus
Harry Beresford	Flavius
Tommy Conlon	Stephanus
Ferdinand Gottschalk	Glabrio
Vivian Tobin	Dacia
William V. Mong	Licinius
Joyzelle	Ancaria
Richard Alexander	Viturius
Nat Pendleton	Strabo
Clarence Burton	Servilius
Harold Healy	Tibal
Robert Manning	Philodemus
Charles Middleton	Tyros

Also featuring: Joseph Bonomo, Ynez Seabury, Lillian Leighton, Otto Lederer, Lane Chandler, Wilfred Lucas, Jerome Storm, Florence Turner, Gertrude Norman, Horace B. Carpenter, Carol Holloway, Wynne Gibson, and Ray Benard.

Synopsis:
In Rome in the year 66 A.D., Emperor Nero burns the city and blames it on the Christians. Marcus falls in love with Mercia. They are condemned to death.

Production Notes:
Filming began on July 25, 1932. While there was a gorilla scene in the film, but cut from the final release print, Corrigan was not the actor in the suit. He had a bit part, which means he is in the background of one or more scenes.

WHISTLING
IN THE DARK

ERNEST TRUEX · UNA MERKEL
JOHN MILJAN · JOHNNY HINES
EDWARD ARNOLD
Directed by ELLIOTT NUGENT

Whistling in the Dark

Produced and Released by Metro-Goldwyn-Mayer Corp. on January 21, 1933. Copyright Metro-Goldwyn-Mayer Corp., January 30, 1933, LP3608. Running time, 76 or 78 Minutes, 8 reels. *Directed by* Elliott Nugent; produced by Lucien Hubbard; *screen play by* Elliott Nugent; *based upon the play by* Laurence Gross and Edward Childs Carpenter; *presented on the stage by* Alexander McKaig; *recording director*, Douglas Shearer; *art director*, Cedric Gibbons; *photographed by* Norbert Brodine; *film editor*, Ben Lewis.

Cast:

Ernest Truex	Wallace Porter
Una Merkel	Toby Van Buren
John Miljan	Charlie Shaw
Johnny Hines	Slim Scanlon
Edward Arnold	Jake Dillon
C. Henry Gordon	Ricco Lombardo
Joseph Cawthorn	Otto Barfuss
Nat Pendleton	Joe Salvatore
Tenen Holtz	Herman Lefkowitz
Marcelle Corday.	Hilda
Ray Benard	Policeman

Synopsis:

"What an assignment!" groans Wally Porter, successfule writer of mystery stories. It was an assignment calculated to bring anybody up short. Inadvertently walking into a household of crooks, Porter found himself arbitrarily faced by the job of creating a "perfect crime": The murder of one Barfuss, legalized brewer by the racketeering ring he has opposed—a murder to be managed in such a way that it will not seem like murder at all, but death from causes unknown. Porter had his work cut out for him. For sympathy he had Toby Van Buren with whom he happened to be eloping when his car broke down. What scheme he finally hit upon, and what it led to, consume the major footage of the film.

Production Notes:

Filming began on December 3, 1932, and was based on the play "Whistling in the Dark" by Laurence Gross and Edward Childs Carpenter, as presented by Alexander McKaig in New York in January 1932. Remade in 1941 with Red Skelton and Ann Rutherford.

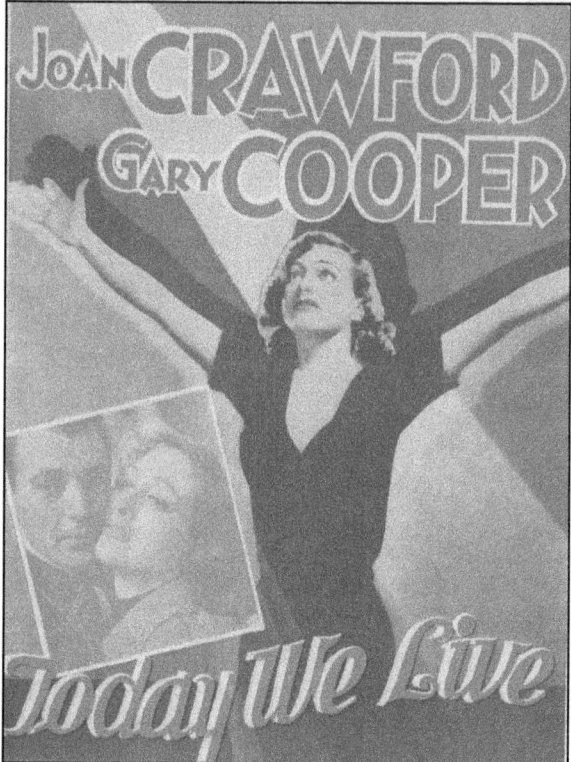

Today We Live

Produced and Released by Metro-Goldwyn-Mayer on April 21, 1933. Copyright Metro-Goldwyn-Mayer Corporation, April 28, 1933, LP3904. Running time 110-115 minutes, eleven reels. *Directed by* Howard Hawks; *story and dialogue*, William Faulkner; *screen play by* Edith Fitzgerald and Dwight Taylor; *co-director*, Richard Rosson; *recording director*, Douglas Shearer; *art director*, Cedric Gibbons; *gowns by* Adrian; *photographed by* Oliver T. Marsh; *film editor*, Edward Curtiss..

Cast:

Joan Crawford	. . . . .	Diana
Gary Cooper	. . . . .	Bogard
Robert Young	. . . . .	Claude
Franchot Tone	. . . . .	Ronnie
Roscoe Karns	. . . . .	McGinnis
Louise Closser Hale	. . . . .	Applegate
Rollo Lloyd	. . . . .	Major
Hilda Vaughn	. . . . .	Eleanor

Also featuring: Murray Kinnell, Eily Malyon, and Ray Bernard.

Synopsis:
In 1916, while England is at war with Germany, American Bogard buys an estate in Kent and displaces its longtime occupant, Diana. Although she has just learned that her father has been killed in action, Diana treats Bogard with brave graciousness and moves to the guest cottage without complaint. She then prepares to say goodbye to her brother Ronnie and childhood friend and neighbor, Claude, both newly trained naval officers on their way to France. Claude is blinded at war and returns to England with Ronnie. They soon learn that Diana has fallen in love with Bogard. Ronnie and Claude volunteer for a dangerous mission at sea. While Claude mans the torpedo, Ronnie steers their boat directly into a German battleship, and both officers die in a spectacular explosion. Free to love, Diana and Bogard return to their home in Kent,

Production Notes:
Based on the short story "Turn About" by William Faulkner which appeared in *The Saturday Evening Post* on March 5, 1932. Aerial sequences were filmed at March Field in California. Main production began in late December 1932. The original preview Running time of the film was 135 minutes.

Hell Below

Produced and Released by Metro-Goldwyn-Mayer Corp. on June 9, 1933. Copyright May 12, 1933, Metro-Goldwyn-Mayer Corp., LP3893. Running time, 105 Minutes, 10 reels. *Directed by* Jack Conway; *adapted by* Laird Doyle and Raymond L. Schrock; *from the book "Pigboats" by* Commander Edward Ellsberg; *dialogue by* John Lee Mahin and John Meehan; *technical advisor,* Lt. Comdr. MOrris D. Gilmore, U.S.N. (ret); *recording director,* Douglas Shearer; *art director,* Cedric Gibbons; *photographed by* Harold Rosson; *film editor,* Hal C. Kern; *assistant director,* John Waters; *mixer,* Ralph Shugard.

Cast:

Robert Montgomery	. . . . Lieut. Thomas Knowlton
Walter Huston	. . . . Lieut. Comdr. T. J. Toler
Madge Evans	. . . . Joan Standish
Jimmy Durante	. . . . "Ptomaine", ship's cook
Eugene Pallette	. . . . MacDougal, chief torpedo man
Robert Young	. . . . Lieut. (JG) "Brick" Walters
Edwin Styles	. . . . Herbert Standish, flight comdr.
John Lee Mahin	. . . . Lieut. (JG) "Speed" Nelson
David Newell	. . . . Lieut. (JG) Radford
Sterling Holloway	. . . . Seaman Jenks
Charles Irwin	. . . . Buck teeth sergeant
Maude Eburne	. . . . Lady Higby
Ray Benard	. . . . Sailor

Also featuring: Matt McHugh, James Donlan, Frank Marlowe, Bradley Page.

Synopsis:

In 1918, at the Allied Naval Base in Taranto, Italy, Lieutenant Commander T. J. Toler takes over command of an American submarine from Lieutenant Commander Thomas Knowlton. Immediately after assuming command, Toler imposes his tough and exacting personality on his sailors and orders his officers, including Knowlton and his best friend, Lieutenant Commander "Brick" Walters, to attend an officer's dance while on shore leave. Bored by the dance, Knowlton and Walters are about to sneak away when Knowlton spots pretty young Joan Standish, Toler's daughter, in a crowd of fat matrons. After the two officers compete for Joan's attention, Knowlton finally gets her alone and, while startled to discover that she is married, convinces her to accompany him to a local carnival. During the festivities, the town is attacked by German bombers, and the couple flees to safety in Knowlton's apartment. There Knowlton confesses to Joan that he loves her, but she resists his advances and is relieved when he is called suddenly to his submarine. While at sea, the submarine sinks two German battleships, and Toler orders several men, including Walters, to rescue the German survivors in a dinghy. Before the dinghy reaches the ship, however, German airplanes attack the exposed submarine, forcing Toler to dive without rescuing Walters. Although damaged by the bombing, the submarine survives and returns to the base for another shore leave. While seamen like MacDougal and "Ptomaine," the ship's cook and an aspiring dentist, cavort with boxing kangaroos and fiesty British sailors, Knowlton finds Joan working in a military hospital. There Joan introduces Knowlton to her husband Herbert, a British flight commander who was paralyzed in an airplane crash. Stunned by the introduction, Knowlton rushes off but is followed to his apartment by Joan, who finally confesses her love. After the couple pledges to remain together in spite of Herbert, Toler shows up and subtly warns Knowlton to stay away from his daughter. During the next sea patrol, Toler confronts Knowlton about the affair and forcefully advises him to terminate the romance. Later, as the submarine approaches a small fleet of German battleships, Knowlton spots Walter's dinghy in the periscope and asks that a rescue be attempted. When Toler refuses his request and orders his men only to watch the battleships, Knowlton countermands his superior and begins to bomb the Germans with torpedoes. Although two battleships are sunk, two others survive and immediately attack the submarine. The submarine is badly damaged and is forced to submerge to a dangerous depth. Although confined to the brig, Knowlton rushes to the control room when he discovers a chlorine gas leak. As the deadly gas seeps through the submarine, the sailors crowd into the control room and, using water-soaked cloth to delay the gas's effects, work frantically to start up the damaged motor. With only moments to spare, the engine is started by the surviving men, and the submarine maneuvers to safety. On shore, Knowlton is dishonorably discharged, but Joan is undeterred by the scandal and insists that Herbert be told the truth. When Knowlton learns that his rival has just been operated on and probably will walk again, however, he leaves the hospital without telling Herbert about the affair. Knowlton then returns to Joan and, in front of Toler, pretends to be drunk and callous. Shocked by Knowlton's behavior, Joan, who is unaware of Herbert's successful operation, dismisses him and prepares to return to her marriage. Before Toler's submarine leaves on a dangerous mission, Knowlton slips on board and, after revealing his sacrifice to Toler, is allowed to rejoin the crew. During the fierce battle, the submarine is hit while attacking a German fort. As the submarine sinks, Knowlton throws Toler overboard and then, while spraying the enemy with a final round of bullets, goes down with the ship.

Production Notes:
Filming began in late November 1932. The film was "Produced with the co-operation of the Navy Department" and was "Dedicated to those officers and men of the United States Navy, who, in peace and war, volunteer their lives in one of the most hazardous branches of its service: SUBMARINES." Some scenes were shot in Honolulu and Pearl Harbor, Hawaii, and along the coast of California.

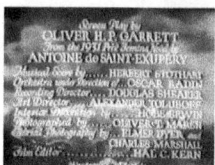

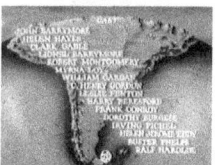

Night Flight

Produced and Released by Metro-Goldwyn-Mayer Corp. on October 6, 1933. Copyright Metro-Goldwyn-Mayer Corp., October 2, 1933, LP4156. Running time 89-91 Minutes, 9 reels. *Directed by* Clarence Brown; *produced by* David O. Selznick; *screenplay by* Oliver H. P. Garrett; *musical score by* Herbert Stothart; *orchestra under direction of* Oscar Radin; *recording director*, Douglas Shearer; *art director*, Alexander Toluboff; *interior decoration by* Hobe Erwin; *photographed by* Oliver T. Marsh; *aerial photography by* Elmer Dyer and Charles Marshall; *film editor*, Hal C. Kern; *assistant director*, Charles Dorian.

Cast:

John Barrymore	A. Riviere
Helen Hayes	Simone Fabian
Clark Gable	Jules Fabian
Lionel Barrymore	Inspector Robineau
Robert Montgomery	Auguste Pellerin
Myrna Loy	Brazilian pilot's wife
William Gargan	Brazilian pilot
C. Henry Gordon	Daudet
Leslie Fenton	Radio operator
Harry Beresford	Roblet
Frank Conroy	Radio operator
Dorothy Burgess	Pellerin's girl friend
Irving Pichel	Dr. Decosta
Helen Jerome Eddy	Worried mother
Buster Phelps	Sick child
Ralf Harolde	Pilot no. 5
Marcia Ralston	Nightclub vamp

Synopsis:

As a worried mother comforts her desperately ill son in Rio de Janeiro, the child's physician, Dr. Decosta, assures her that, thanks to the new night flying schedule of the Trans-Andean European Air Mail, which is being inaugurated that evening, they will receive a life-saving serum the next day. The treacherous night flying over the Andes is shown with scenes alternating between the pilot's dilemmas and their spouse's worries. However, the serum reaches Dr. Decosta in time and the child is saved.

Production Notes:

Based on the novel *Vol de nuit* by Antoine de Saint-Exupery, production began in late April 1933 and lasted through late July 1933.

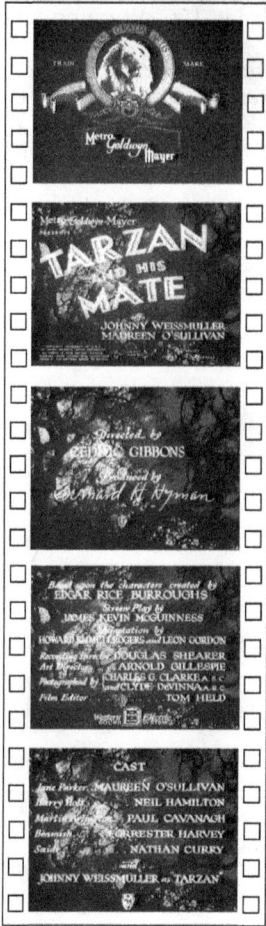

Tarzan and His Mate

Produced and Released by Metro-Goldwyn-Mayer on April 13, 1934. Copyright April 13, 1934, Metro-Goldwyn-Mayer Distributing Corp., LP4647, renewed April 14, 1961, Loew's Inc., R274614. Running time 92 or 105 minutes, 116 or 117 minutes for preview version, eleven reels. *Directed by* Cedric Gibbons; *produced by* Bernard H. Hyman; *based upon the characters created by* Edgar Rice Burroughs; *scree nplay by* James Kevin McGuinness; *adaptation by,* Howard Emmett Rogers and Leon Gordon; *recording director,* Douglas Shearer; *art director,* Arnold Gillespie; *photographed by* Charles G. Clarke, a.s.c., and Clyde deVinna, a.s.c.; *film editor,* Tom Held.

Cast:

Johnny Weissmuller	. . . . .	Tarzan
Maureen O'Sullivan	. . . . .	Jane Parker
Neil Hamilton	. . . . .	Harry Holt
Paul Cavanagh	. . . . .	Martin Arlington
Forrester Harvey	. . . . .	Beamish
Nathan Curry	. . . . .	Saidi

Also featuring: Doris Lloyd, William Stack, Desmond Roberts, Paul Porcasi; Evertt Brown, and Ray Bernard.

Synopsis:

Harry Holt returns to Africa with a friend, Arlington, for the purpose of bringing Jane back to civilization, if possible, and to seize upon a fortune in ivory in the secret burial ground of the elephants. Their safari has unbelievable hardships and dangers to endure, and at the last moment having reached the Mutia escarpment that guards the elephant country, they are barely rescued by Tarzan and Jane. At first the ape man is quite willing to guide Holt and Arlington to the elephants' graveyard, but he will not countenace their taking away the ivory, even bringing a herd of elephants to block their departure. In the end, Holt and Arlington are killed endeavoring to protect Jane from a murderous band of savages, and Tarzan, whom Arlington had endeavored to kill, is left master of the jungle with Jane still beside him.

Production Notes:

Initial filming of underwater scenes with Johnny Weissmuller were undertaken during the early part of May 1933 at the Metro-Goldwyn-Mayer Culver City lot, but the regular production filming began on August 2, 1933. After about three and a half weeks of shooting, the first unit shut down. The director and four of the actors were replaced—the reason for the change is not known. Production resumed in early September 1933. Filming officially ended March 10, 1934, but re-takes and other shots were filmed until late in the month. Total negative cost was $1,279,142. Location work of a scene or two were shot at China Flats in Hidden Valley, Big Tujunga, and the Pico Rivera swamplands (the current Woodland Park is a part of the original swamps). More extensive filming was done

19

at Lake Sherwood and Sherwood Forest. On the M-G-M backlot, the Mutia Escarpment rocks on Lot 1 were once again utilized as well as the river on Lot 2, the top of the escarpment on Lot 2, the *Red Dust* boat and house, the rhino arena on Lot 2, and the underwater tank on Lot 1. Because of the Production Code Office, the nude underwater scene of Tarzan and Jane (she was doubled by Josephine McKim) was scrapped and two alternate versions filmed: a topless Jane and a fully clothed Jane.

Hollywood Party

Produced and Released by Metro-Goldwyn-Mayer Corp. on June 1, 1934. Copyright Metro-Goldwyn-Mayer Corp., June 14, 1934, LP4716. Running time, 68-70 minutes, 7 reels. *Screen play by* Howar Dietz and Arthur Kober; *recording director,* Douglas Shearer; *art director,* Fredric Hope; *interior decoration by* Edwin B. Willis; *costuming by* Adrian; *photographed by* James Wong Howe, a.s.c.; *film editor,* George Boemler; *music and lyrics by* Richard Rodgers, Lorenz Hart, Walter Donaldson, Gus Kahn, Nacio Herb Brown, and Arthur Freed; *dance numbers arranged by* Symour Felix, George Hale, and David Gould; *animated cartoon sequence by* Courtesy of Walt Disney Productions, Ltd; *color sequence photographed by* Technicolor Process.

Cast:

Stan Laurel	. . . . .	Stan Laurel
Oliver Hardy	. . . . .	Oliver Hardy
Jimmy Durante	. . . . .	Jimmy Durante/Schnarzan
Jack Pearl	. . . . .	Baron Munchausen
Polly Moran	. . . . .	Henrietta Clemp
Charles Butterworth	. . . . .	Harvey Clemp
Eddie Quillan	. . . . .	Bob Benson
June Clyde	. . . . .	Linda Clemp
Mickey Mouse	. . . . .	Mickey Mouse
Lupe Velez	. . . . .	Lupe Velez, Jaguar Woman, Jane
George Givot	. . . . .	Liondora
Richard Carle	. . . . .	Knapp
Ray Benard	. . . . .	Gorilla

Also featuring: Ernie Alexander, Frank Austin, Ben Bard, Harry Barris, George Beranger, Billy Bletcher, Sidney Bracey, Pauline Brooks, Jack Byron, Ben Carter, Nora Cecil, Ruth Channing, Baldwin Cooke, ay Cooke, Richard Cramer, Walt Disney, Jay Eaton, Celeste Edwards, Bill Elliott, Muriel Evans, Larry Fine, Bess Flowers, Greta Garbo, Kay Gordon, Ferdinand Gottschalk, Julia Griffith, Sherry Hall Ted Healy, Tom Herbert, Irene Hervey, Tenen Holtz, Curly Howard, Moe Howard, Arthur Jarrett, Tom Kennedy, The King's Men, Leonid Kinskey, Iris Lancaster, Tom London, Edwin Maxwell, Florine McKinney, Claire Meyers, Jeanne Olsen, Jed Prouty, Marcia Ralston, Henry Roquemore, Shirley Ross, Martha Sleepe, Larry Steers, Eddie Tamblyn, Edward Thomas, Arthur Treacher, Frances Williams, Clarence Wilson, Florence Wix, Robert Young.

Synopsis:

Jimmy Durante is jungle star Schnarzan, but the public has tired of his fake lions. When Baron Munchausen comes to town with real man-eating lions, Durante throws a big party so that he might use the lions in his next movie. His film rival, Liondora, sneaks into the party to buy the lions before Durante can.

Production Notes:

The film was completed in mid-March 1934. No director was listed in the on-screen credits, but modern sources indicate that Allan Dwan, Richard Boleslawski, George Stevens, and Charles Riesner directed different sections of the film.

HAT WAVING NEWS! ATLANTA WINS WORLD PREMIERE of GIANT MUSICAL FUN SHOW!

METRO-GOLDWYN-MAYER'S TOP EFFORT SINCE "GRAND HOTEL" and "DINNER at EIGHT"

HOLLYWOOD PARTY

Loew's STATE Starts

Four-Col. Ad Mat No. 601-44

COMPLETE AD MATS

The ads in this campaign have the type incorporated in the mats. The copy is unusually striking—giving a good idea of the gayety, surprise and production value of "Hollywood Party." The references to "World Premiere" and Atlanta can be routed out of the mats, with the name of your city substituted.

A NEW FEATURE OF M-G-M AD SERVICE

To those theatres making their own ad engravings, M-G-M is offering a new service. . . . This consists of photos of retouched art work and drawings, used in campaign-book ads, just as they are prepared for the engraver.

With this service, a good layout letterer becomes a one-man agency equipped to turn out work of agency quality.

The photos are 8 x 10 in size, and are available singly or in sets.

ORDER THESE ART PHOTOS
from your
M-G-M EXCHANGE

Loew's STATE Starts

"IT'S A WHOOPENSOCKER!"

If the Greeks had a name for a music-splashed fun show like "Hollywood Party"... they kept it a secret!

"IT'S A WHOOPENSOCKER!"

WORLD PREMIERE

HOLLYWOOD PARTY

2000 IN THE CAST

Four-Col. Ad Mat No. 601-45

Murder in the Private Car

Produced and Released by Metro-Goldwyn-Mayer Corp. on June 29, 1934. Copyright Metro-Goldwyn-Mayer Corp., June 27, 1934, LP4807. Running time, 60-65 minutes, 7 reels. *Directed by* Harry Beaumont; *produced by* Lucien Hubbard; *screen play by* Ralph Spence, Edgar Allan Woolf, and Al Boasberg; *from the play "The Rear Car" by* Edward E. Rose; *adaptation by* Harvey Thew; *recording director*, Douglas Shearer; *art director*, Cedric Gibbons; *associates*, David Townsend and Edwin B. Willis; *photographed by* James Van Trees, a.s.c. and Leonard Smith, a.s.c.; *film editor*, William S. Gray.

Cast:

Charles Ruggles	. . . . . Godfrey D. Scott
Una Merkel	. . . . . Georgia Latham
Mary Carlisle	. . . . . Ruth Raymond/Ruth Carson
Russell Hardie	. . . . . John Blake
Porter Hall	. . . . . Alden Murray
Willard Robertson	. . . . . Hanks aka Elwood Carson
Berton Churchill	. . . . . Luke Carson
Cliff Thompson	. . . . . Allen
Snowflake	. . . . . Titus
Ray Benard	. . . . . Gorilla

Also featuring: Harry Semels, Akim Tamiroff, Ray Brown, Sterling Holloway, Charles Dunbar, John David Horsley, Lee Phelps, Ernie Adams, William Nye, Wilfred Lucas, Jack Baxley, Hooper Atchley, James Warwick, Standing Bear, Nick Copeland, Jack Cheatham, Bud Ernest, Olaf Hytten, James P. Burtis, Walter Brennan, John Kelly, Art Beery Sr.

Synopsis:

Ruth Raymond believes herself an orphan and works as a telephone girl for a Los Angeles brokerage house. Georgia Latham works with her, and is her devoted friend. Suddenly a lawyer appears who reveals Ruth to be the missing daughter of a multi-millionaire railroad president. He takes her out of her job, and she takes Georgia. They all start East together. Almost at once it is apparent that some sinister influence menaces the newly-found heiress. Clutching hands in the dark warn her she has eight hours to live. A man is murdered. A giant gorilla, escaped from a wrecked circus train, swings aboard the car in the night and adds to the terror. Hourly, Ruth receives a note warning her that her end is near.

Production Notes:

Filmed between May 8 and mid June 1934. Charlie Ruggles was on loan from Paramount Studios. An ad for the film credits Naba as playing the gorilla. This was the name which Corrigan used for his first gorilla costume.

28

Midland—"Murder in the Private Car."

Scott	Charlie Ruggles
Georgia	Una Merkel
Ruth	Mary Carlisle
Blake	Russell Hardie
Murray	Porter Hall
Hanks	Willard Robertson
Carson	Berton Churchill
Allen	Cliff Thompson

Fine thrills, fair laughs, bad mystery.

THIS picture contains the oddest assortment of entertainment and faults that it has been the lot of this reviewer to inspect.

As was remarked in Thursday's tabloid review, the climax is a thriller. The mad flight of a railroad car loaded with explosives careening, with its frightened passengers down from the Continental Divide, is a thing to make your hair stand on end. Fortunately it is photographed so expertly and worked out so ingeniously that it makes your logic stand on end, too. You arrive at the finish so breathless that you have no time or inclination to question the events that lead up to it.

With the increased interest in detective stories, there has been built up in the last twenty years a certain code by which the good mystery writer obliges himself to play fair with the reader. In neither the original dramatic version nor in the silent picture version, "Red Lights," did the authors obey this code. Things are included simply to mystify the spectator. If he has a filing cabinet mind he is in a bad way for most of these mysteries never are cleared up.

For some unrevealed reason a comedy detective begins hanging around a brokerage office. Soon one of the phone girls is recognized as the long lost daughter of a railroad magnate. The office manager, who has been making passes at her, acts suspiciously. So does the lawyer who carries the glad tidings. A bodyguard attempts to kidnap her. Her boy friend is attacked and captured. He escapes and breaks through a police line, saying he must warn her, but when he gets to her he never delivers the warning. His misadventures never are explained. In a private car, heading east, the office manager appears, and acts suspiciously. We never are told his connection with the plot. The lawyer is found murdered. We never find out by whom or why. The villain is the girl's uncle and although she says she remembers his telling her about her father she fails to recognize him. At the proper time the villain is found dead but we are not told how or why his demise occurs. Verily this is a mystery drama for the incurious. Beside such a picture as "The Mystery of Mr. X" it is third rate mystery stuff.

M.-G.-M. evidently appalled at the task of straightening it out, decided to make the absurd ridiculous. Hokum is added with a free hand. The wreck of a circus train provides a gorilla (or at least a man in a gorilla suit) to stalk the characters. Charlie Ruggles gets some good laughs and strains for others in the character of an unbelievable detective. He belongs to that tribe born of a playwright's efforts to be funny. Una Merkel scores some real laughs and Mary Carlisle shows many signs of improvement as the ingenue.

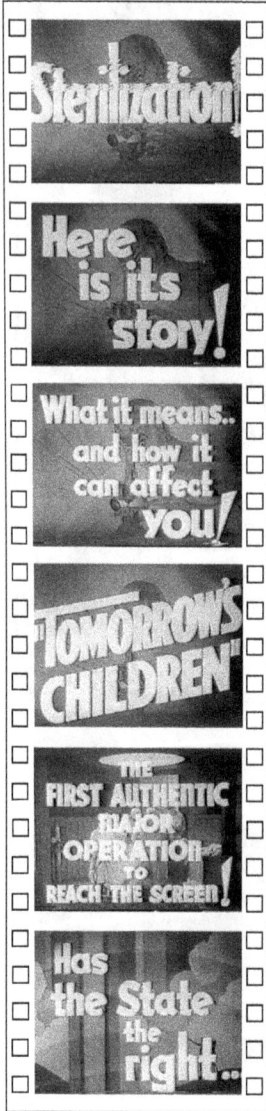

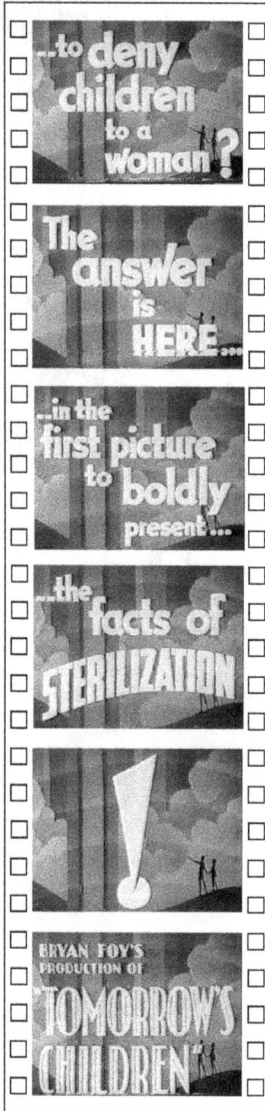

Tomorrow's Children

Produced by Foy Productions, Ltd. Distributed by State Rights. No Copyright. Released in May 1934. Running time, 70 Minutes. *Directed by* Crane Wilbur; *screenplay by* Wallace Thurman and Crane Wilbur; *story by* Wallace Thurman; *photography*, William Thompson.

Cast:

Diane Sinclair	Alice Mason
Don Douglas	Dr. Brooks
John Preston	Dr. Crosby
Carlyle Moore, Jr.	Jim Baker
Sterling Holloway	Dr. Dorsey
W. Messenger Bellis	Dr. McIntyre
Hiram Hoover	Spike
Constance Kent	Nurse
Lewis Gambart	Jeff
Crane Wilbur	Father O'Brien
Arthur Wanzer	Mr. Mason
Sarah Padden	Mrs. Mason
Ray Benard	Newspaper reporter

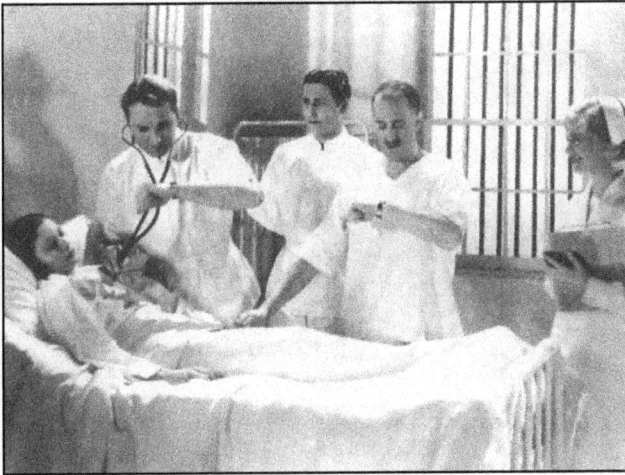

Synopsis:

Alice Mason, apparently the daughter of poor people who have brought feeble-minded and crippled children into the world, is ordered legally sterilized along with other adults in the family. It is pointed out early in the production that the young lady is a foster daughter, having no blood relation with the others, and this fact eventually saves her from the operation, but just in the nick of time, for she is

31

on the talbe when her recuers arrive with the saving court order.

A young surgeon, Dr. Brooks, is interested in charity cases and plays the hero of the story and due to his perseverance in the matter, the girl escapes the knife. She is a perfectly normal, healthy person, in love with a clean, upright boy and the closing scene shows the happy couple on the way to get married.

Production Notes:
Filmed in late March or early April 1934 at the Bryan Foy Studio at 9077 Venice Blvd., in the city of Palms, California, and in the neighborhoods of the area. In January 1938, fire destroyed the studio. Among the few items saved from the fire was the negative for this film.

'TOMORROW'S CHILDREN' A DRAMA OF HUMAN STERILIZATION WITH STERLING HOLLOWAY AND DIANE SINCLAIR NOW PLAYING AT PARAMOUNT

Yesterday, hundreds of Paramount theater patrons were amazed at the frank and timely facts revealed in "Tomorrow's Children," a drama of human sterilization, featuring Sterling Holloway, Dianne Sinclair and Sarah Padden. which is now playing last times Wednesday at the Paramount theater.

"Tomorrow's Children" is a gripping, dramatic story based on one of the world's greatest and most timely problems, and has the distinction of being the first motion picture ever made which shows an actual sterilization operation being performed. "Tomorrow's Children" is not a clinical lecture on sterilization, but a frank vivid story of a modern day family, picturing their existence, their hardships, and their passions.

You must see "Tomorrow's Children." It answers the great question of "What Is Human Sterilization?" Due to the vital social problem involved this picture is being shown to adults only.

FOY PRODUCTIONS LTD.
PRESENT

TOMORROW'S
CHILDREN
A·DRAMA·OF
HUMAN·STERILIZATION

PHONE HAMMOND 8188
Where the Best Attractions Play First!

25c
Daily
Til
2:00 p.m.

25c
Balcony
After
5:00 p.m.

Paramount
THEATRE · COMPANY

NOW PLAYING
LAST TIMES
WEDNESDAY

ADULTS
ONLY!

Yesterday hundreds of Paramount Theatre patrons were amazed at the frank revelations of this timely, vivid drama . . .

"Tomorrow's Children" is not a silly lecture, but a real human drama of a modern-day family . . . their hardships . . . their existence . . . their passions!

YOU MUST
SEE . . .

TOMORROW'S
CHILDREN
A DRAMA OF HUMAN STERILIZATION

With an Cast including All-Star Hollywood

DIANE SINCLAIR
STERLING HALLOWAY
SARAH PADDEN

EXTRA
HAL KEMP
Musical Novelty
"No Other One"

PARAMOUNT
PICTORIAL

Sunday Only · On the Stage
ALL-STAR MUSICAL
— with an —
25 · MUSICAL STARS · 25
YOUTH · BEAUTY · RHYTHM!

33

Love, Music In Movie Of Modern Cinderella

One of the most colorful and brilliant motion picture scenes ever filmed is the Cinderella Ball in Universal's "Romance in the Rain," a romantic comedy with music, which will open an engagement at the Orpheum theatre starting today.

More than 500 people were employed in this single scene, which features an enormous pumpkin that unfolds in beautiful display, disclosing an array of singing and dancing beauties who characterize the ancient story of Cinderella. In this scene may be seen the traditional witches on broomsticks, the coach and mice and all the other famous characters in the tale.

The role of Cinderella is portrayed by Heather Angel, beautiful young English actress, who is featured with Roger Pryor. He is actually a new Roger Pryor in this picture, following the acquisition of a moustache and a new style hair dress. This picture is not the legendary story of Cinderella, but that of a modern Cinderella, the product of the popularity contest and radio age, whose experiences paraphrase those of her predecessoress. Much comedy and romantic interest is supplied by Pryor and Miss Angel, aided by the splendid trouper, Victor Moore, Esther Ralston, Ruth Donnelly and others.

Climaxing an unending series of fast-moving and amazing situations is a public radio wedding staged in one of the largest stadiums of the country during a nationally famous football game.

Romance in the Rain

Produced and Released by Universal Pictures Corp. on August 13, 1934. Copyright Universal Pictures Corp., October 8, 1934, LP4886. Running time 73-76 Minutes, 8 reels. *Directed by* Stuart Walker; *produced by* Carl Laemmle; *screenplay by* Barry Trivers; *photography by* Charles Stumar; *art direction*, Albert S. D'Agostino; *film editor*, Edward Curtiss; *costumes by* Vera West; *music by* Edward Ward; *sound*, Gilbert Kurland; *special effects*, John P. Fulton; *dance*, Harold Hecht.

Cast:

Roger Pryor	Charles Denton
Heather Angel	Cynthia Brown
Esther Ralston	Gwen de la Rue
Victor Moore	J. Franklin Blank
Ruth Donnelly	Miss Sparks
Henry Armetta	Tulio
Paul Kaye	Rex Bruce
Christian Rub	Mr. Slotnik
Frank Parker	Master of ceremonies
Georgia Caine	Mrs. Brown
Betty Francisco	Julia
Lita Chevret	Jennie
Gay Seabrook	Gloria
Clara Kimball Young	Mlle. Fleurette Malevinsky
King Baggott	Milton McGillicuddy
John T. Murray	Melville O'Grunion
Francesca Rotoli	Fanny Pilkington
Grace Hayle	Mrs. Crandall
"Big Boy" Williams	Panya Mankiewicz
David Worth	Hedgwick
Baxter Gamble	Eskimo
Verna Hillie	Cinderella girl
Rosalind Culli	Cinderella girl
Wanda Perry	Cinderella girl
Julie Kingdon	Cinderella girl
Margaret Nearing	Cinderella girl
Tom Hanlon	Radio announcer
Frankie Adams	Slotnick's son
Marcia Remy	Sbo sister
Earl Eby	Reporter
Jessie Arnold	Switchboard operator

Also featuring: Scotty Becket, Georgia Bark, Dean Benton, Anne Darling, Fifteen Universal Beauties, and Raymond Benard.

Synopsis:

35

Charles Denton, head writer for *Livid Love Tales* , a romance magazine owned by J. Franklin Blank, conceives a stunt to boost sales when he meets Cynthia Brown after she drops a shoe on his head on a rainy day. Seeing the way her stepmother and two stepsisters order her around, Charlie proposes a contest in which each entrant must write an essay on the subject, "Why I am the modern Cinderella," and subscribe to the magazine.

Production Notes:
Production began on June 7, 1934, and ended on July 2, 1934.

A Paramount Picture
ADOLPH ZUKOR
A CECIL B. DeMILLE PRODUCTION
with
CLAUDETTE COLBERT
WARREN WILLIAM
HENRY WILCOXON
GERTRUDE MICHAEL
JOSEPH SCHILDKRAUT
IAN KEITH
C. AUBREY SMITH
CLEOPATRA
directed by
CECIL B. DeMILLE
SCREEN PLAY BY
WALDEMAR YOUNG AND
VINCENT LAWRENCE
BARTLETT CORMACK
PHOTOGRAPHED BY VICTOR MILNER, A.S.C.
TRAVIS BANTON

THE PLAYERS
WARREN WILLIAM
CAESAR, HAVING CONQUERED HALF
THE WORLD, TURNED HIS AMBITIOUS
EYES TOWARD THE SPLENDOR OF
EGYPT, WHERE PTOLEMY AND HIS
SISTER, CLEOPATRA, STRUGGLED
FOR THE SOLE POSSESSION OF THE
WORLD'S RICHEST THRONE.

Cleopatra

Produced and Released by Paramount Productions, Inc. on October 5, 1934. Copyright Paramount Productions, Inc., October 5, 1934 LP4995. Running time, 95-102 Minutes, 11 reels. *Directed by* Cecil B. DeMille; *produced by* Adolph Zukor; *screen play by* Waldemar Young and Vincent Lawrence; *from an adaptation of historical material by* Bartless Cormack; *music by* Rudolph Kopp; *photographed by* Victor Milner, a.s.c.; *Miss Colbert's costumes designed by* Travis Banton.

Cast:

Claudette Colbert	Cleopatra
Warren William	Julius Caesar
Henry Wilcoxon	Marc Antony
Joseph Schildkraut	Herod
Ian Keith	Octavian
Gertrude Michael	Calpurnia
C. Aubrey Smith	Enobarbus
Irving Pichel	Apollodorus
Arthur Hohl	Brutus
Edwin Maxwell	Casca
Ian MacLaren	Cassius
Eleanor Phelps	Charmion
Leonard Mudie	Pothinos
Grace Durkin	Iras
Claudia Dell	Octavia
Harry Beresford	Soothsayer
Jane Regan	Lady Vesta
William Farnum	Lepidus
Lionel Belmore	Fidius
Florence Roberts	Lady Flora
Dick Alexander	General Philodemas
Celia Ryland	Lady Leda
William V. Mong	Court physician
Robert Warwick	General Schillas

Also featuring: George Walsh, Jack Rutherford, Kenneth Gibson, Wedgewood Nowell, Bruce Warren, Robert Manning, Ed Deering, John Rutherford, Charles Morris, Margerie Bonner, Leon Beauman, Colonel Nicholai Kolovaloss, Colonel Tim Lonergan, John Roy Marsilio, Gil Barry, Bob Hall, Carl Saxe, Ernie Smith, Bryant Washburn, Mary MacLaren, Jack Mulhall, Julanne Johnston, Phillips Smalley, Edmund Jones, Inez Seabury, Wilfred Lucas, Bryant Washburn Jr., Carlyle Blackwell Jr., Reuben Schaffer, Horace B. Carpenter, Jilda Keeling, Mary Fahmey, and Ray Benard.

Synopsis:
In 48 BC, Cleopatra, facing palace revolt in her kingdom of Egypt, welcomes the arrival of Julius Caesar as a way of solidifying her power under Rome. When

Caesar is killed, she transfers her affections to Marc Antony and dazzles him on a barge full of splendor.

Production Notes:
Filmed between March 13 and May 2, 1934. Exteriors were partially shot near Muroc and the sand dunes at El Segundo. Corrigan had a bit part as a background player.

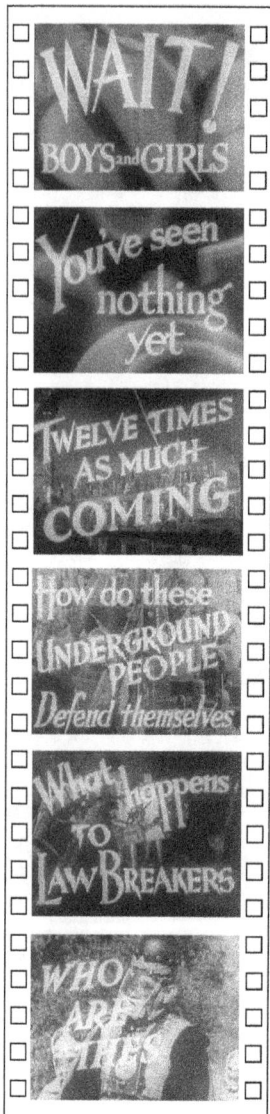

A Nation
20000 feet
underground
NAT
LEVINE
presents
The PHANTOM EMPIRE
A
MASCOT
MASTER SERIAL
with GENE AUTRY
FRANKIE DARRO
BETSY KING ROSS
Directed by OTTO BROWER & B. REEVES EASON
Supervised by ARMAND SCHAEFER

A NATION
20,000 FEET
UNDERGROUND
The PHANTOM EMPIRE
5 BENEATH
THE EARTH
GENE AUTRY
FRANKIE DARRO
BETSY KING ROSS
A MASCOT
MASTER SERIAL

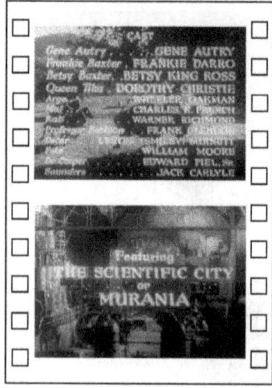

The Phantom Empire

Produced and Released by Mascot Pictures Corp. on February 23, 1935. Copyright Mascot Pictures Corp., Chapters 1-6, February 23, 1935, L5358, Chapters 7-12, February 23, 1935, L5412. Running time, 245 minutes, 12 Chapters, 13 reels. *Directed by* Otto Brower and Breezy Eason; *produced by* Nat Levine; *supervised by* Armand Shaeffer; *story by* Wallace McDonald, Gerald Gerahty, and H. Freedman; *continuity by* John Rathmell and Armand Schaefer; *photography by* Ernest Miller and William Nobles; *edited by* Earl Turner; *sound engineer*, Terry Kellum; *featuring The Scientific City of Murania.*

Cast:

Gene Autry	. . . . . Gene Autry
Frankie Darro	. . . . . Frankie Baxter
Betsy King Ross	. . . . . Betsy Baxter
Dorothy Christie	. . . . . Queen Tika
Wheeler Oakman	. . . . . Argo
Charles K. French	. . . . . Mal
Warner Richmond	. . . . . Rab
Frank Glendon	. . . . . Professor Beetson
Lester (Smiley) Burnett	. . . . . Oscar
William Moore	. . . . . Pete
Edward Piel, Sr.	. . . . . Dr. Cooper
Jack Carlyle	. . . . . Saunders

Also featuring: Wally Wales, Jay Wilsey, Stanley Blystone, Richard Talmadge, Frank Ellis, Peter Potter, Bob Burns, Bob Card, Bruce Mitchell, "Champion", and Ray Benard.

Episode Titles:

1. The Singing Cowboy
2. The Thunder Riders
3. The Lightning Chamber
4. Phantom Broadcast
5. Beneath the Earth
6. Disaster from the Skies
7. From Death to Life
8. Jaws of Jeopardy
9. Prisoners of the Ray
10. The Rebellion
11. A Queen in Chains
12. The End of Murania

Synopsis:

When the ancient continent of Mu sank beneath the ocean, some of its inhabitants survived in caverns beneath the sea. Cowboy singer Gene Autry stumbles upon the civilization, now buried beneath Radio Ranch. The Muranians have developed technology and weaponry such as television and ray guns. Their rich supply of radium draws unscrupulous speculators from the surface.

Production Notes:
Radio Ranch was located on the west side of the Morrison Agoura Ranch. The entrance to Murania was at the Bronson Canyon Caves. Murania exteriors were shot at the newly built Griffith Park Observatory.

Corrigan portrayed a Thunder Rider. In the above scene, his voice was dubbed in for the actor at the door to the shed and it may well be him.

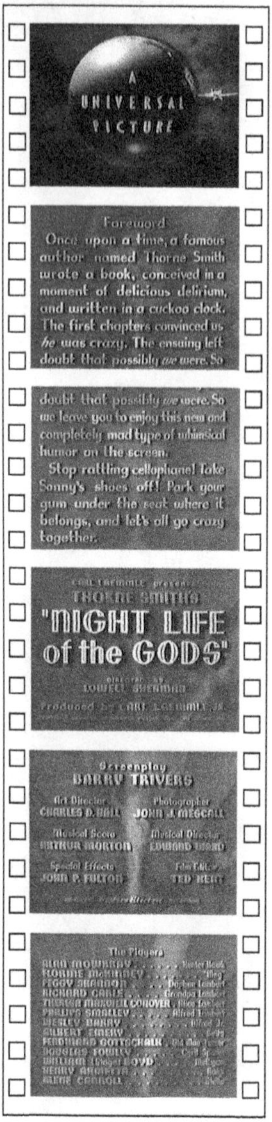
A
UNIVERSAL
PICTURE
Foreword
Once upon a time, a famous author named Thorne Smith wrote a book, conceived in a moment of delicious delirium, and written in a cuckoo clock. The first chapters convinced us *he* was crazy. The ensuing left doubt that possibly *we* were. So
doubt that possibly *we* were. So we leave you to enjoy this new and completely mad type of whimsical humor on the screen.
Stop rattling cellophane! Take Sonny's shoes off! Park your gum under the seat where it belongs, and let's all go crazy together.
THORNE SMITH'S
"NIGHT LIFE of the GODS"
Screenplay
BARRY TRIVERS
Art Director
CHARLES D. HALL
Photographer
JOHN J. MESCALL
Special Effects
JOHN P. FULTON
The Players
ALAN MOWBRAY
FLORINE McKINNEY
PEGGY SHANNON
RICHARD CARLE . . . . . Grandpa Lambert
THERESA MAXWELL CONOVER
PHILLIPS SMALLEY
WESLEY BARRY
GILBERT EMERY
FERDINAND GOTTSCHALK
DOUGLAS FOWLEY
HENRY ARMETTA
IRENE CARROLL

The Gods
RAYMOND BENARD . . . . . Apollo
GEORGE HASSELL . . . . . Bacchus
IRENE WARE . . . . Diana
GENEVA MITCHELL . . . . Hebe
PAUL KAYE . . . . Mercury
ROBERT WARWICK . . . . . Neptune
PAT DE CICCO . . . . Perseus
MARDA DEERING . . . . Venus

Night Life of the Gods

Produced and Released by Universal Pictures Corp. on March 11, 1935. Copyright Universal Pictures Corp., February 15, 1935, LP5331. Running time, 73-80 minutes, 8 reels. *Directed by* Lowell Sherman; *produced by* Carl Laemmle, Jr.; *screenplay by* Barry Trivers; *art director,* Charles D. Hall; *photographer,* John J. Mescall; *musical score,* Arthur Morton; *musical director,* Edward Ward; *special effects,* John P. Fulton; *film editor,* Ted Kent.

Cast:

Alan Mowbray	Hunter Hawk
Florine McKinney	"Meg"
Peggy Shannon	Daphne Lambert
Richard Carle	Grandpa Lambert
Theresa Maxwell Conover	Alice Lambert
Phillips Smalley	Alfred Lambert
Wesley Barry	Alfred, Jr.
Gilbert Emery	Betts
Ferdinand Gottschalk	Old Man Turner
Douglas Fowley	Cyril Sparks
William "Stage" Boyd	Mulligan
Henry Armetta	Roigi
Alene Carroll	Stella

The Gods

Raymond Benard	Apollo
George Hassell	Bacchus
Irene Ware	Diana
Geneva Mitchell	Hebe
Paul Kaye	Mercury
Robert Warwick	Neptune
Pat De Cicco	Perseus
Marda Deering	Venus

Also featuring: May Beatty, Alan Davis, Leo McCabe, Bert Roach, Maidel Turner, Fredrick Santly, Maude Turner Gordon, Ruth Cherrington, Tyler Brooke, Lee Moran, G. Pat Collins, Wade Boteler, Don Douglas, Harry Cornell, Joseph Young, Dick Winslow, Harold Nelson, Beatrice Roberts, Claire Meyers, Madlyn Talcot, William L. Thorne, Velma Gresham, Al Hill, Anne Darling, Russ Clark, Larry Wheat, Jean Warwick, Ann Doran, Lu Ann Meredith, Ruth Page, Lois January, Charles Irwin, Phyllis Crane, Lillian Castle, James Burtis.

Synopsis:

One day Hunter Hawks, a young scientist with a sense of humor, while working in his laboratory discovers a light ray by which he can turn people into stone and bring images to life. This gives him the chance he has longed for, to make some use out of his worthless, quarrelsome relatives. He transforms them into garden statuary, all but Daphne. Then he meets Meg, an exquisitely beautiful girl whom her extraordinary father describes as "a howling hellion who has been alive for nine hundred years." Meg and Hawks become fast friends and companions. They go to the Museum of Art together, of all places, and there Hawks brings the statues of the ancient pagan divinities, Neptune, Bacchus, Venus, Mercury, Hebe, Perseus, Apollo and Diana to life. They set out for Broadway. This is only the beginning of that perfectly mad Odyssey of Olympus gone.

Production Notes:
Filmed between August 13 and October 15, 1934 at the Universal Studios. Director Lowell Sherman in December 1934, prior to the release of the film. Twenty sculptors were brought to Universal City to create sixty-seven statues, each weighing at least 600 pounds, at a cost of $25,000. A $75,000 swimming pool was constructed, and an equally expensive museum set was built.

Fifty Statues Being Made For "Night Life of the Gods"

TWENTY sculptors started work at Universal City this week. Their job is to make fifty statues for "Night Life of the Gods." There are fifty characters in this unique comedy novel by Thorne Smith and all of them at one time or another are either statues or living people. An inventor in this story has discovered a way of making statues come to life and making human beings into statues. Universal is spending $25,000 for this item alone, because the statues have to look like their living prototypes and the best sculptors in the west have been employed on this work.

Lowell Sherman has gathered a cast which is of imposing proportions. Here are a few of the names, and the list is growing every week: Alan Mowbray, Florine McKinney, Peggy Shannon, Robert Warwick, Richard Carle, Irene Ware, Gilbert Emery, Ray Bernard, Henry Armetta, May Beatty, Pat De Cicco, George Hassell, Paul Kaye, William (stage) Boyd, Theresa Maxwell Conover, Phillips Smalley, Wesley Barry, Alene Carroll, Marda Deering, Douglas Fowley and Geneva Mitchell. "Night Life of the Gods" went into production last week and will require four more weeks before completion.

Coming To The Frederick

FLORINE McKINNEY
AND
ALAN MOWBRAY
in "NIGHT LIFE OF THE GODS"

UNIVERSAL

"Night Life Of The Gods" centers about Florine McKinney and Alan Mowbray as it shows today and Tuesday at the Frederick theater.

51

THE NUTTIEST NIGHTMARE
MAN EVER CONCEIVED AND
THE NERVIEST, SAUCIEST,
SASSIEST, FUNNIEST, MOST
COLOSSAL COMEDY HOLLY-
WOOD HAS EVER DARED
PRODUCE!

CARL LAEMMLE
presents
LOWELL SHERMAN'S
Uproarious Production of Thorne Smith's
Amazing Novel

"NIGHT LIFE OF THE GODS"

With
ALAN MOWBRAY · PEGGY SHANNON
RICHARD CARLE · FLORINE McKINNEY
WESLEY BARRY · HENRY ARMETTA
WILLIAM (Stage) BOYD · ROBERT WARWICK

PRODUCED BY CARL LAEMMLE, JR.
A UNIVERSAL PICTURE

53

THE PLAYERS

Hunter Hawk . . . . Alan Mowbray
"Meg" . . . . Florine McKinney
Daphne Lambert . . . . Peggy Shannon
Grandpa Lambert . . . . . . Richard Carle
Alice Lambert. . . . . . Theresa M. Conover
Alfred Lambert . . . . Phillips Smalley
Alfred, Jr. . . . . Wesley Barry
Betts . . . . Gilbert Emery
Old Man Turner . . . Ferdinand Gottschalk
Cyril Sparks . . . . Douglas Fowley
Mulligan . . . . William (Stage) Boyd
Roigi . . . . Henry Armetta
Stella . . . . Arlene Carroll

●

THE GODS AND GODDESSES

Apollo . . . . Raymond Benard
Bacchus. . . . . George Hassell
Diana . . . . Irene Ware
Hebe . . . . Geneva Mitchell
Mercury. . . . . Paul Kaye
Neptune. . . . . Robert Warwick
Perseus . . . . Pat De Cicco
Venus . . . . Marda Deering

Produced by CARL LAEMMLE, Jr.

A THREE COLOR 8 TO 15 FOOT STREAMER

A handsome die-cut, five piece streamer lithographed in three colors. Makes an attractive addition to your lobby or marquee displays. Comes complete ready for hanging. Can be used in spot eight feet long or can be stretched to suit fifteen foot space.

STREET BALLYHOO

A man, or woman, face whitened to marble paleness, dressed in costume, suggested by the stills, to represent one of the gods or godesses. Parades about streets and in front of theatre with signs, carrying copy as shown in the sketch.

COMIC MODERN COSTUME CONTEST

CONTACT students of art school to make statues of Mercury, Apollo, Diana and Venus. If this is not practical make compo-board cut-outs. Put them on display in lobby with offer of prizes for best designs of comic costumes made up and draped on the statues. They will add materially to your displays. See sketch for copy on placards.

A FEW SUGGESTIONS IN TABLOID

SCULPTURE IN LOBBY—Contact art schools for students willing to give exhibition of sculpturing in lobby. Let them work on gods and godesses in picture. Tie-up line is: We Can Make Statues of Humans—But We Can't Make Humans of Statues—If You Want to See This Trick Done see "Night Life of the Gods"—more surprising than "The Invisible Man."

TREASURE HUNT—18 merchants, each offering a letter to spell out the title, with a designated bargain item, co-operate with you on this. Contestants follow foot-prints (of the gods and godesses) leading from theatre to stores. The first to return to theatre with title receive pass or special prize.

VENUS AND ADONIS ON BIKE—Secure an old tandem bike and have boy and girl dressed like Venus and Adonis in the picture, pedal around the streets. On the frame of the bike mount a sign advertising picture.

SET OF 4 ADVANCE TEASER SNIPES — 14" x 21"

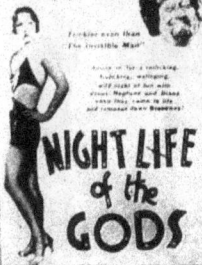

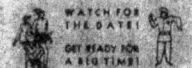

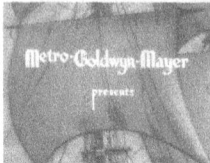

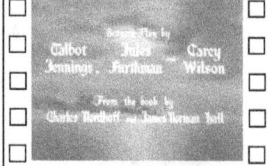

Mutiny on the Bounty

Produced and Released by Metro-Goldwyn-Mayer Corporation on August 23, 1935. Distributed by Loew's Inc. Copyright April 11, 1935, Metro-Goldwyn-Mayer Corp., LP5986. Running time, 130-132 minutes, 13 reels. *Directed by* Frank Lloyd; *associate producer*, Albert Lewin; *screenplay by* Talbot Jennings, Jules Furthman, and Carey Wilson; *from the book by* Charles Nordhoff and James Norman Hall; *musical score by* Herbert Stotbart; *recording director*, Douglas Shearer; *art director*, Cedric Gibbons; *associate art director*, Arnold Gillespie; *marine director*, James Havens; *photographed by* Arthur Edeson, a.s.c.; *film editor*, Margaret Booth; *second unit director*, J. Walter Ruben; *producers*, Frank Lloyd and Irving G. Thalberg; *photographed by* Charles G. Clarke, Sidney Wagner, and Glenn Strong; *costumes*, Western Costume Company; *sound*, William Steinkamp; *technical advisor*, Alfred Alexander; *unit manager*, Ulrich Busch; *production assistants*, Bob Roberts and John Waters; *technical advisor*, Major Oscar Bagley; *press agent*, Howard Dietz.

Cast:

Charles Laughton	. . . . . Captain William Bligh
Clark Gable	. . . . . Fletcher Christian
Franchot Tone	. . . . . Roger Byam
Herbert Mundin	. . . . . Smith
Eddie Quillan	. . . . . Thomas Ellison
Dudley Digges	. . . . . Bacchus
Donald Crisp	. . . . . Thomas Burkitt

Also featuring: Henry Stephenson, Francis Lister, Spring Byington, Movita, Mamo, Byron Russell, Percy Waram, David Torrence, John Harrington, Douglas Walton, Ian Wolfe, DeWitt Jennings, Ivan Simpson, Vernon Downing, William Bambridge, Marion Clayton, Stanley Fields, Wallis Clark, Crauford Kent, Pat Flaherty, Alec Craig, Charles Irwin, Dick Winslow, Robert Livingston, Hal LeSueur, David Thursby, John Powers, King Mojave, Doris Lloyd, Lucy Chavarria, William Stack, Robert Adair, Harold Entwistle, Eric Wilton, Lotus Thompson, Lilyan Irene, Vivien Oakland, Will Stanton, Harry Allen, Lionel Belmore, Harry Cording, Nadine Beresford, Mary Gordon, Winter Hall, and Ray Benard.

Synopsis:

The Bounty, a British warship, sails from London to the South Seas, its crew composed of men who are either products of the slums or jailbirds, or torn from their homes and families. Captain Bligh, a perfect symbol of vicious naval discipline, is in command; Fletcher Christian is executive officer and Byam, steeped in the tradition of Britain's sea power, a midshipman. At once Bligh, recognizing that only through fear and cruelty can his riffraff crew be made competent seamen, starts his continued rounds of floggings, starvings, spread-eaglings and killings that rouse his desperate crew to terrorized fury. Christian, openly and secretively, has tried to soften Bligh's harshness. In Tahiti the crew revels in association with native women and there is a semblance of legitimate

59

romance between Byam and Movita. Christian through the kindly offices of the Chief, is permitted to land. His association with Mamo, a glorious dream to her, is that of passion of a man long confined. The Bounty again sails. Bligh's cruelty becomes more vicious. Part of the crew, led by Christian, mutinies. Bligh and his loyal but still fearful supporters, are set adrift in a small boat.

Production Notes:
Filmed from May 8 to September 11, 1935. It received an Academy Award for Best Picture of 1935. Background shots of Tahiti were filmed prior to production. Two replicas of the Bounty were constructed—one was an exact and seaworthy copy, the other a stationary set used mostly for interiors. Filming took place at Papette, Tahiti, Pitcairn Island, Santa Catalina Island, and San Miguel Island.

Corrigan is on left, with a girl in his arms

She

Produced and Released by RKO Radio Pictures, Inc. on July 12, 1935. Copyright December 7, 1935, RKO Radio Pictures, Inc., LP5696. Running time, 94-101 Minutes, 11 reels. *Directed by* Irving Pichel and Lansing C. Holden; *produced by* Merian C. Cooper; *screenplay by* Ruth Rose; *additional dialogue by* Dudley Nichols; *from the novel by* H. Rider Haggard; *music by* Max Steiner; *production associate*, Shirley Burden; *dance director*, Benjamin Zemach; *photograph by* J. Roy Hunt, a.s.c.; *photographic effects by* Vernon Walker, a.s.c.; *sound effects by* Walter Elliott; *art director*, Van Nest Polglase; *art director associate*, Al Herman; *costumes by* Aline Bernstein and Harold Miles; *music recorded by* P. J. Faulkner; *recorded by* John L. Cass; *edited by* Ted Cheesman.

Cast:

Helen Gahagan	. . . .	She
Randolph Scott	. . . .	Leo Vincey
Helen Mack	. . . .	Tanya Dugmore
Nigel Bruce	. . . .	Horace Holly
Gustav von Seyffertitz	. . . .	Prime Minister Billali
Samuel Hinds	. . . .	John Vincey
Noble Johnson	. . . .	Amahagger chief
Lumsden Hare	. . . .	Dugmore
Jim Thorpe	. . . .	Captain of the guards
Ray Benard	. . . .	Palace guard and stunts

Synopsis:
The story describes the pilgrimage of two modern scientists and a young girl who set out over uncharted icy wastes in search of the secret of eternal youth. After hazardous adventures they reach the kingdom of Kor. Captured by Korish soldiers, they are taken before She, an important woman who rules the kingdom. One of the party, resembling a man She loved 500 years before, is thought to be a reincarnation of her lover. There in the magnificent splendor of her palace hewn from a solid mountain, She tells him that he will be bathed in the sacred flame and become an immortal.

Production Notes:
Filmed between March 12 and early May 1935 at the Prudential Studios.

Dante's Inferno

Produced by Fox Film Corp. Released by Twentieth Century-Fox Film Corp. on August 23, 1935. Copyright Twentieth Century-Fox Film Corp., August 8, 1935, LP5781. Running time, 88-90 minutes, 8,000 feet, 11 reels. *Directed by* Harry Lachman; *produced by* Sol M. Wurtzel; *screen play by* Philip Klein and Robert M. Yost; *cinematography*, Rudolph Maté, a.s.c.; *sound*, George Leverett; *film editor*, Al DeGaetano; *art direction*, Duncan Cramer and David S. Hall; *technical staff*, Fred M. Sersen, Ralph Hammeras, Louis J. Witte, and Willy Pogany; *gowns*, Royer; *danced staged by* Sammy Lee; *musical director*, Samuel Kaylin.

Cast:

Spencer Tracy	. . . . .	Jim Carter
Claire Trevor	. . . . .	Betty McWade
Henry B. Walthall	. . . . .	Pop McWade
Alan Dinehart	. . . . .	Jonesy
Scott Beckett	. . . . .	Alexander Carter
Robert Gleckler	. . . . .	Dean
Rita Cansino	. . . . .	Dancer
Gary Leon	. . . . .	Dancer
Willard Robertson	. . . . .	Inspector Harris
Morgan Wallace	. . . . .	Captain Morgan

Also featuring: Joe Brown, George Humbert, Maidel Turner, Nella Walker, Lita Chevret, Richard Tucker, Edward Pawley, Ruthelma Stevens, Harry Woods, Ruth Clifford, Dorothy Dix, Hal Boyer, J. Lloyd, Jayne Regan, Gardner James, Jerry Gamble, Edward McWade, Patricia Caron, John George, Harry Schultz, John Carpenter, George Chan, Gertrude Astor, Tiny Jones, Frank Austin, Frank Moran, Kenneth Gibson, Harold Miller, Barrett Whitelaw, Jean Fenwick, Warren Hymer, Ray Benard, Paul Schwegler, Aloha Porter, Noble Johnson, Lorna Lowe, Elinor Johnson, Andre Johnson, Leona Lane, Juana Sutton, Marion Strickland, Gale Goodson, Eva Kimberly, Margaret McCrystal, Dorothy Stockmar, Jay Eaton, Reginald Sheffield, Maude Truax, Oscar Apfel, Charles C. Wilson, John McGuire, Bob Reel McKee, Hale Hamilton, George Meeker, Barbara Pepper, Lloyd Pantages, Eddie Tamblyn, Jack Norton, Robert Graves, Harry Holman, Harry Strang, George Magrill, Paul Palmer, Bud Geary, Billie Huber, Paddy O'Flynn, Antoinette Lees, Robert Ross, Russell Hicks, George Irving, Frank Conroy, Georgia Caine, Mary Ashcraft, Paul Power, Marion Ladd, Laya Joy, and Gloria Roy.

Synopsis:

The story opens with Jim Carter in the stoke hole of a liner, working his way back to America after a reverse of fortunes abroad. He chances into a concession depicting "Dante's Inferno", operated by Pop and Betty McWade. Befriended by Pop, Carter remains to put the inferno concession on a paying basis, continues to climb until he becomes the operating head of all concessions. Carter's ruthless climbing over all obstacles can have but one result—retribution, which introduces the big spectacle of the picture.

Production Notes:

Filmed from December 3, 1934 to late January 1935. According to a *New York Times* article, 14,000 people worked on the film. Dancer Rita Cansino would go on to screen greatness under her stage name of Rita Hayworth. During the long sequence in the middle of the film, the interest suddenly shifts from the 20th century plot to a description of the terrors of hell. According to a newspaper article in the Boston Herald on August 11, 1935, "Thirteen thousand extras were used in filming this sequence. As a result the problem of making them up suitably so that the right sort of effect could be gained was extraordinarily difficult."

REPUBLIC PICTURES

REPUBLIC PICTURES
presents
GENE AUTRY
in
THE SINGING
VAGABOND
with
ANN RUTHERFORD

Directed by
CARL PIERSON

Supervised by
ARMAND SCHAEFER

Screen Play . . . . OLIVER DRAKE and
BETTY BURBRIDGE
Story by . . . . OLIVER DRAKE
Supervising Editor . . . . JOSEPH H. LEWIS
Photography . . . . WILLIAM NOBLES
Sound Engineer . . . . TERRY KELLUM
Sound Effects . . . . ROY GRANVILLE
Film Editor . . . . LESTER ORLEBECK
Songs by
GENE AUTRY and SMILEY BURNETTE
OLIVER DRAKE and HERBERT MYERS

GENE AUTRY

ANN RUTHERFORD

SMILEY BURNETTE

BARBARA PEPPER

CHAMPION

And
NILES WELCH
GRACE GOODALL
ALLAN SEARS
WARNER RICHMOND
HENRY ROQUEMORE
FRANK LARUE

The Singing Vagabond

Produced and Released by Republic Pictures Corp. on December 16, 1935. Copyright December 26, 1935, Republic Pictures Corp., LP6200. Running time, 52-55 minutes, 6 reels. *Directed by* Carl Pierson; *produced by* Nat Levine; *supervised by* Armand Schaefer; *screen play,* Oliver Drake and Betty Burbridge; *story by* Oliver Drake; *supervising editor,* Joseph H. Lewis; *photography,* William Nobles; *sound engineer,* Terry Kellum; *sound effects,* Roy Granville; *film editor,* Lester Orlebeck; *songs by* Gene Autry and Smiley Burnette, Oliver Drake and Herbert Myers.

Cast:

Gene Autry	Captain Tex Autry
Ann Rutherford	Lettie Morgan, aka Mary Varden
Smiley Burnette	Frog
Barbara Pepper	Honey
Champion	Champion
Niles Welch	Judge Forsythe Lane
Grace Goodall	Hortense
Allan Sears	Utah Joe
Warner Richmond	Buck LaCrosse
Henry Rocquemore	Otto
Frank LaRue	Colonel Seward

Also featuring: Tom Brower, Robinson Neeman, Ray Benard, Robert Burns, Charles King, Chief Big Tree, Chief Thunder Cloud, June Thompson, Janice Thompson, Marion O'Connell, Marie Quillan, Elaine Shepherd, Edmund Cobb, George Letz.

Synopsis:
Captain Tex Autry is the singing head of a troop of singing cavalry men convoying a wagon train of which runaway girl Lettie Morgan is a member. Bandits attack it and Autry's troop rides to the rescue. Romance which has a triangle complex develops for Tex, Lettie, and LaCrosse. Arriving at the fort, horses are stolen and Tex suspected is arrested and convicted and sentenced to death. The wagon train moves on. Aided by his buddies, Frog and Buffalo, Tex escapes. He catches up with the train just as marauding Indians attack it. Driving off the raiders, Tex puts the finger on Utah Joe as the culprit in the crime of which he is charged. Exonerated, he wins Lettie.

Production Notes:
Ray Benard portrayed Private Hobbs. According to press material, among the Native American tribes represented in the film included the Apache, Black Feet, Cherokee, Choctaw, Creek, Hopi, Mission, Navajo, Nez Perce, Osage, Ojibway, Pawnee, Penobscot, Pueblo and Sioux. Filmed on location at Kernville, California, and the Republic Studios backlot.

Town Has Autry.

Gene Autry is "The Singing Vagabond" in a civil war western heading the bill at the Town starting Sunday. Indian battles provide much of the excitement while Autry's singing is featured. Barbara Pepper, Ann Rutherford and Smiley Burnette support him.

Adventure along unexplored trails of...
"DARKEST AFRICA"
with CLYDE BEATTY
World's greatest wild animal trainer.
MANUEL KING
his bare hands!
as they go to the rescue of...
a Beautiful Blonde Goddess..
COME TO THIS THEATRE
for 15 weeks of...
the most sensational thrills...
World's youngest wild animal trainer.
BAT MEN
See these two pals and BONGA the fierce ape..
BATTLING the Tiger Men...
See a man...
conquer the kings of the jungle with...

Darkest Africa

Produced and Released by Republic Picture Corp. on February 15, 1936. Copyright Republic Pictures Corp., Chapters 1-5, February 15, 1936, L6431, Chapters 6-10, February 15, 1936, L6440, Chapters 11-15, February 15, 1936, L6460. Running time, 269 minutes, 15 chapters, 31 reels. *Directed by* B. Reeves Eason and Joseph Kane; *supervised by* Barney Sarecky; *screen play by* John Rathmell, Barney Sarecky, and Ted Parsons; *original story*, John Rathmell and Tracy Knight; *supervising editor*, Joseph H. Lewis; *photography*, William Nobles and Edgar Lyons; *film editor*, Dick Fantl; *sound engineer*, Terry Kellum; *sound effects*, Roy Granville.

Cast:

Clyde Beatty	. . . . .	Clyde Beatty
Manuel King	. . . . .	Baru Tremaine
Elaine Shepard	. . . . .	Valerie Tremaine
Lucien Prival	. . . . .	Dagna
Bonga (Ray Benard)	. . . . .	Bonga
Wheeler Oakman	. . . . .	Durkin
Tiger Men	. . . . .	Tiger Men
Bat Men	. . . . .	Bat Men
Edward McWade	. . . . .	Gorn
Edmund Cobb	. . . . .	Craddock
Ray Turner	. . . . .	Hambone
Donald Reed	. . . . .	Negus

Also featuring: Harrison Greene, Joe De La Cruz, Joseph Byrd, Prince Modupe, Henry Sylvester, and Eddie Parker.

Episode Titles:
1. Baru – Son of the Jungle
2. The Tiger-Men's God
3. Bat-Men of Joba
4. The Hunter Lions of Joba
5. Bonga's Courage
6. Prisoners of the High Priest
7. Swing for Life
8. Fang and Claw
9. When Birdmen Strike
10. Trial by Thunder-Rods
11. Jars of Death
12. Revolt of the Slaves
13. Gauntlet of Destruction
14. The Divine Sacrifice
15. The Prophecy of Gorn

Synopsis:
Clyde Beatty goes to Africa to rescue the Goddess of Joba, who is being held by the high priest.

Production Notes:
Filmed from November 29, 1935 to December 28, 1935, at a cost of $119,343. Locations included King's Jungleland in Brownsville, Texas, the Iverson Movie Ranch in Chatsworth, California, and the Republic Studio backlot. Clyde Beatty is billed as the "world's greatest wild animal trainer", and Manuel King as the "world's youngest wild animal trainer". The film was the first extensive use of Corrigan's gorilla costume. Ray Benard had two parts in the film: as the gorilla Bonga and as Samabi, one of the Bat Men. The serial was re-released on November 10, 1948, as "King of Jungleland". A 73 minutes feature version was released on May 21, 1936. A 100 minute feature version, entitled "Bat Men of Africa", was part of the Republic television Century 66 line. Both Beatty and Elaine Shepard were hospitalized for a couple of days after the director had a smoke bomb tossed into a scene without telling the cast. The bomb was overcharged with black powder and Beatty was knocked unconscious and suffered burns.

REPUBLIC PICTURES presents

Clyde BEATTY in 'DARKEST AFRICA'
WORLD'S GREATEST WILD ANIMAL TRAINER

WITH
MANUEL KING
WORLD'S YOUNGEST
WILD ANIMAL TRAINER

A REPUBLIC SERIAL IN 15 EPISODES
Chapter 9 WHEN BIRDMEN STRIKE

The Leathernecks Have Landed

Produced and Released by Republic Pictures Corp. on February 22, 1936. Copyright Republic Pictures Corp., May 13, 1936, LP6346. Running time, 67 minutes, 7 reels. *Directed by* Howard Bretherton; *supervised by* Ken Goldsmith; *screen play,* Seton I. Miller; *original story,* Wellyn Totman and James Gruen; *supervising editor,* Joseph H. Lewis; *photography,* Ernest Miller and Jack Marta; *film editor,* Robert Jahns; *sound engineer,* Terry Kellum.

Cast:

Lew Ayres	. . . .	Woody Davis
Isabel Jewell	. . . .	"Brooklyn"
Jimmy Ellison	. . . .	"Mac" MacDonald
James Burke	. . . .	Corrigan
J. Carrol Naish	. . . .	Drenov
Clay Clement	. . . .	Captain Halstead
Maynard Holmes	. . . .	"Tubby" Waters
Ward Bond	. . . . .	"Tex"
Paul Porcasi	. . . .	Enrico "Rico" Venetzi
Claude King	. . . .	British agent
Christian Rub	. . . .	Schooner captain
Joseph Sawyer	. . . .	Sergeant Regan
Henry Mowbray	. . . .	British army major
John Webb Dillion	. . . . .	Marine colonel
Louis Vincenot	. . . . .	Chinese officer
Lal Chand Mehra	. . . . .	Sikh sergeant

Also featuring: Frank Tang, Beal Wong, Victor Wong, Ray Benard, Robert Strange, Montague Shaw.

Synopsis:

Woody Davis has a way with the women and also a way of getting himself and his pals "Mac" MacDonald and "Tubby" Waters into difficulties.

Although he promises Mac he will not start anything—the next day finds all three in a Cuban jail—as the result of a cafe brawl. At the last moment Sergeant Regan bails the boys out just as the ship sails for China.

In Shanghai, Woody and Tubby meet Brooklyn in a barroom. Tubby goes on the make for her but she falls for Woody.

Drenov comes into the saloon, stumbles over Woody's feet and when the Russian starts making insulting remarks about Americans, the two are soon in a fight. Drenov pulls a gun, and when Tubby tries to stop him from shooting Woody, he is killed, and the murderer escapes.

As a result of the brawl, Woody is dismissed from the service, vowing to get Drenov.

Sympathetic Brooklyn offers her aid, but when Woody locates Drenov, the Russian is killed with his own gun when he tries to shoot Woody.

Embittered, Woody takes Drenov's old job, that of gun-runner for the rebels.

Meanwhile, Drenov's body has been found and when Brooklyn learns that the authorities are after Woody, she sets out for the interior to warn him.

The smashing climax comes when the rebels make a raid on a village where there is an American Oil Co. The Marines are sent for, but before they land, Woody, with Mac and Tex, who have come to arrest Woody, turn the contraband guns on the rebels and hold them off until the Marines break through.

For his valor, Woody is taken in the service again.

Brooklyn, realizing that she could only be a hindrance to his career, promises to meet him at the dock in Shanghair, but fails to show up, and Woody sails away with his pals.

Production Notes:

Filmed from late November 1935 to February 1936 on the Republic Studios backlot and sound stages. According to the New York Times review, the film was based partly on Chinese Warlord General Chang Tso-lin: "There seems to have been an honest doubt in the minds of those responsible for the picture over whether the forces of General Chang should be called bandits or rebels, but, under either label, the Leathernecks disposed of a lot of them in the process of protecting an oil company and a mining company in the interior of China." A dedication precedes the film's credits: "Republic Pictures respectfully dedicates this picture to 13th Battalion F. M. C. R. United States Marine Corps United States Marine Corps Reserve and extends its appreciation for their advice and cooperation." Ray Benard portrayed the Officer of the Day.

FLAMING...
SMASHING...
ACTION!
THE LEATHERNECKS HAVE LANDED
A RE-RELEASE
Lew AYRES • Isabel JEWELL
JIMMY ELLISON • JAMES BURKE • J. CARROL NAISH
Directed by
Screenplay by
A REPUBLIC PICTURE
Supervised by
Ken Goldsmith

INSPIRING THEME KEYNOTE
OF "LEATHERNECKS" PICTURE

Devotion to the Marine Corps, a spirit which transcends all personal considerations on the part of its present and former personnel, provides the inspiring theme of "The Leathernecks Have Landed," the Republic re-release production which comes to the .... Theatre for a .... day run starting ....

Lew Ayres is starred as a Marine who has a way with the women and also a way of getting himself and his best friends into trouble. Isabel Jewell will be seen in the leading feminine role with Jimmy Ellison featured in the part of Ayres' buddy.

The exotic seaports of Havana and Shanghai and the interior of China furnish the background over which the story moves. Seton I. Miller, who has had such screen successes as "Scarface," "The Crowd Roars," "The Last Mile," "Two Years Before the Mast" and "Here Comes Mr. Jordan," to his credit, wrote the screenplay.

Summed up in a few words, "The Leathernecks Have Landed" is the story of what happened to Woody Davis after he was kicked out of the service as the result of the death of a buddy in a cafe brawl, and the long hard road he had to take to make a comeback, aided by Brooklyn, the girl who had "missed too many boats."

Among the other well known names in the large cast are James Burke, J. Carrol Naish, Ward Bond, Maynard Holmes, Clay Clement, Ray Benard, Claude King and Paul Porcasi.

Howard Bretherton directed for producer Nat Levine.

Oriental Scenes Prove Difficult

One of the high points of the exciting Republic re-release production, "The Leathernecks Have Landed," now on the screen at the .... Theatre, is the Chinese funeral which suggested the ruse used by Lew Ayres, who stars in the production, to run a load of guns out of the International Settlement of Shanghai.

According to Louis Vincenot, the Chinese Technical director, this funeral differs somewhat from the old style that was the custom before China became a Republic.

In the old days a first class funeral had to have a full Chinese band playing the funeral dirge.

Added mourners are always hired by those families that can afford them, and a procession of a millionaire may take hours and hours to pass a given point. Today's funeral for a person of wealth very much resembles an American Naval or Military funeral. Either automobile or horse drawn hearses are used.

Played Banjo

Lew Ayres, whose screen career has been distinguished by many noteworthy performances, and who can be seen in the starring role of "The Leathernecks Have Landed," thrilling Republic re-release which opened .... at the .... Theatre, came to the cinema world from the bandstand, where he played banjo for some of the best known orchestras in the country.

Special Permit for Machine Guns

Machine guns play a prominent part in the Republic re-release production, "The Leathernecks Have Landed" which comes to the .... Theatre on .... with Lew Ayres in the starring role and Isabel Jewell and Jimmy Ellison, and unusual precautions had to be taken both in their usage, and in guarding them against theft.

Before Republic Pictures could use a gun, a special government permit had to be obtained. After this formality had been complied with, the sheriff's office detailed a deputy to stand guard over the guns while they were transported to and from the vaults in which they were stored, and, at all times, when they were in use.

"THE LEATHERNECKS HAVE LANDED" (2A)
Action Scene — Lew Ayres

Flash Gordon

Produced and Released by Universal Pictures on April 6, 1936. Copyright 1936 by Universal Pictures (see below). Running time 245 minutes, 13 Chapters, 2 reels each. A Henry MacRae Production. *Directed by* Frederick Stephani; *produced by* Henry MacRae; *screenplay,* Frederick Stephani, George Plympton, Basil Dickey, and Ella O'Neill; *art director,* Ralph Berger; *photography,* Jerry Ash, a.s.c. and Richard Fryer, a.s.c.; *electrical effects,* Norman Dewes; *special properties,* Elmer A. Johnson; *edited by* Saul Goodkind, Edward Todd, Alvin Todd, and Louis Sackin; *based on the newspaper feature entitled "Flash Gordon" owned and copyrighted by* King Features Syndicate.

Cast:

Buster Crabbe	Flash Gordon
Jean Rogers	Dale Arden
Priscilla Lawson	Princess Aura
Charles Middleton	Emperor Ming
Frank Shannon	Doctor Zarkov
Richard Alexander	Prince Barin
John Lipson	King Vultan
Theodore Lorch	High Priest
Richard Tucker	Professor Gordon
George Cleveland	Professor Hensley
James Pierce	Prince Thun
Duke York, Jr.	King Kala
Muriel Goodspeed	Zona
Earl Askam	Officer Torch
House Peters, Jr.	Shark Man
Ray Corrigan	Orangopoid

Episode Titles:

1.	Planet of Peril	copyright March 18, 1936 L6220
2.	The Tunnel of Terror	copyright March 23, 1936 L6229
3.	Captured by Shark Men	copyright April 9, 1936 L6262
4.	Battling the Sea Beast	copyright April 17, 1936 L6278
5.	The Destroying Ray	copyright April 23, 1936 L6298
6.	Flaming Torture	copyright April 30, 1936 L6319
7.	Shattering Doom	copyright May 6, 1936 L6338
8.	Tournament of Death	copyright May 14, 1936 L6354
9.	Fighting the Fire Dragon	copyright May 20, 1936 L6369
10.	The Unseen Peril	copyright May 27, 1936 L6379
11.	In the Claws of the Tigron	copyright June 3, 1936 L6386
12.	Trapped in the Turret	copyright June 10, 1936 L6397
13.	Rocketing to Earth	copyright June 17, 1936 L6420

Synopsis:

A rogue planet is rushing madly toward the earth. Impending doom creates worldwide pandemonium. Scientist Dr. Zarkov hopes to stop disaster by travelling to the new planet in his experimental rocket. Two chance-met strangers, athletic Flash Gordon and damsel in distress Dale Arden, go with him. Arrived, the trio find Mongo to be a planet of wonders, warring factions, and deadly perils, its orbit controlled by Emperor Ming who has his own sinister plans for Earth.

Production Notes:
Filmed at the Bronson Canyon Caves and Universal Studios backlot.

"FLASH GORDON" — Universal's Greatest Chapter Play   PRINTED IN U.S.A.

DIVE to the BOTTOM of the OCEAN.. in a Rocket Submarine...!
COME ALONG
With these BRAVE Explorers...
See them encounter the Strangest ADVENTURES
Ever Experienced by CIVILIZED MAN...!
"THE UNDERSEA KINGDOM"
Republic's MOST THRILLING Serial...
ACTION
SUSPENSE
a Serial that has
Everything YOU want...
Mechanical MEN...
Who have harnessed the
DISINTEGRATOR RAY...
A FORCE which destroys
EVERYTHING it touches...
ROCKET SUBMARINES...

ROCKET AEROPLANES...
EARTHQUAKES...
And it all takes place in A CITY Beneath THE SEA...
REPUBLIC PICTURES presents "THE UNDERSEA KINGDOM"
a 12 Chapter Serial
Coming to THIS THEATRE Soon
WATCH FOR IT!

12 AMAZING EPISODES
REPUBLIC PICTURES presents
Undersea Kingdom
with RAY "CRASH" CORRIGAN
Ep. 1. "BENEATH THE OCEAN FLOOR"
A REPUBLIC SERIAL
Produced by NAT LEVINE

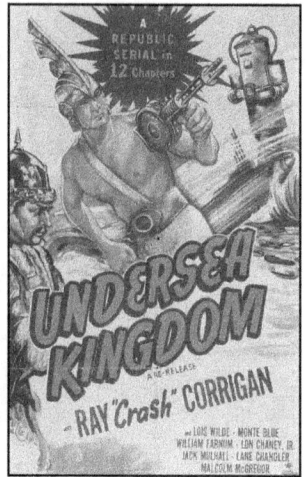

Undersea Kingdom

Produced and Released by Republic Pictures Corp. on May 30, 1936. Copyright Republic Pictures Corp., Chapters 1-6, May 30, 1936 L6451, Chapters 7-12, May 30, 1936, L6545. Running time, 226 minutes, 12 chapters, 25 reels. *Directed by* B. Reeves Eason and Joseph Kane; *produced by* Nat Levine; *supervised by* Barney Sarecky; *screen play,* John Rathmell, Maurice Geraghty, and Oliver Drake; *original story,* Tracy Knight and John Rathmell; *supervising editor,* Joseph H. Lewis; *photography,* William Nobles and Edgar Lyons; *film editors,* Dick Fantl and Helene Turner; *sound engineer,* Terry Kellum; *musical supervision,* Harry Grey.

Cast:

Ray (Crash) Corrigan	Crash Corrigan
Lois Wilde	Diana Compton
Monte Blue	Unga Khan
William Farnum	Sharad
Boothe Howard	Ditmar
Raymond Hatton	Gasspom
C. Montague Shaw	Norton
Lee Van Atta	Billy Norton
Smiley Burnette	Briny Deep
Frankie Marvin	Salty
Lon Chaney, Jr.	Hakur
Lane Chandler	Darius
Jack Mulhall	Andrews
John Bradford	Joe
Malcolm McGregor	Zogg
Ralph Holmes	Martos
John Merton	Moloch
Ernie Smith	Gourck
Lloyd Whitlock	Clinton

Also featuring: Everett Kibbons, Millard McGowan, William Stahl, Bill Yrigoyen, Kenneth Lawton, Eddie Parker, Al Seymour, George DeNormand, Alan Curtis, Tom Steele, Wes Warner, Dan Rowan, Rube Schaeffer, David Horsley, Jack Ingram, Tracy Layne.

Episode Titles:
1. Beneath the Ocean Floor
2. The Undersea City
3. Arena of Death
4. Revenge of the Volkites
5. Prisoners of Atlantis
6. The Juggernaut Strikes
7. The Submarine Trap
8. Into the Metal Tower
9. Death in the Air

Synopsis:

Professor Norton, renowned specialist in secret weapons, one day following a suspicious earthquake, and detecting a series of signals from an unusual direction, from the depths of the ocean exactly where Atlantis, thousands of years ago, had once sunk. Norton leads an expedition, including Lieutenant Crash Corrigan, Reporter Diana Compton, and his son Billy Joe, in his Rocket Submarine to the suspected location of Atlantis. Finding the lost continent beneath the sea, they become embroiled in an Atlantean civil war between Sharad (with his White Robes) and the usurper Unga Khan (with his Black Robes) who wishes to conquer Atlantis and then destroy the upper world with earthquakes generated by his Disintegrator Machine. Thus he will rule the world unless he can be stopped in time.

Production Notes:

Filmed from March 3 to March 28, 1936, at a cost of $99,222, with location scenes taken at the Iverson Movie Ranch in Chatsworth and on the Republic Studio backlot. Ray Benard was christened by Republic Pictures Corp, "Crash" Corrigan for this serial, in direct competition with Universal Pictures "Flash Gordon" serial which was released the month prior. Until the end of his career, the former Ray Benard would be known to the world as Ray "Crash" Corrigan. The serial was re-released on February 15, 1950. As "Sharad of Atlantis", it became a part of the Century 66 features (at 100 minutes) for television.

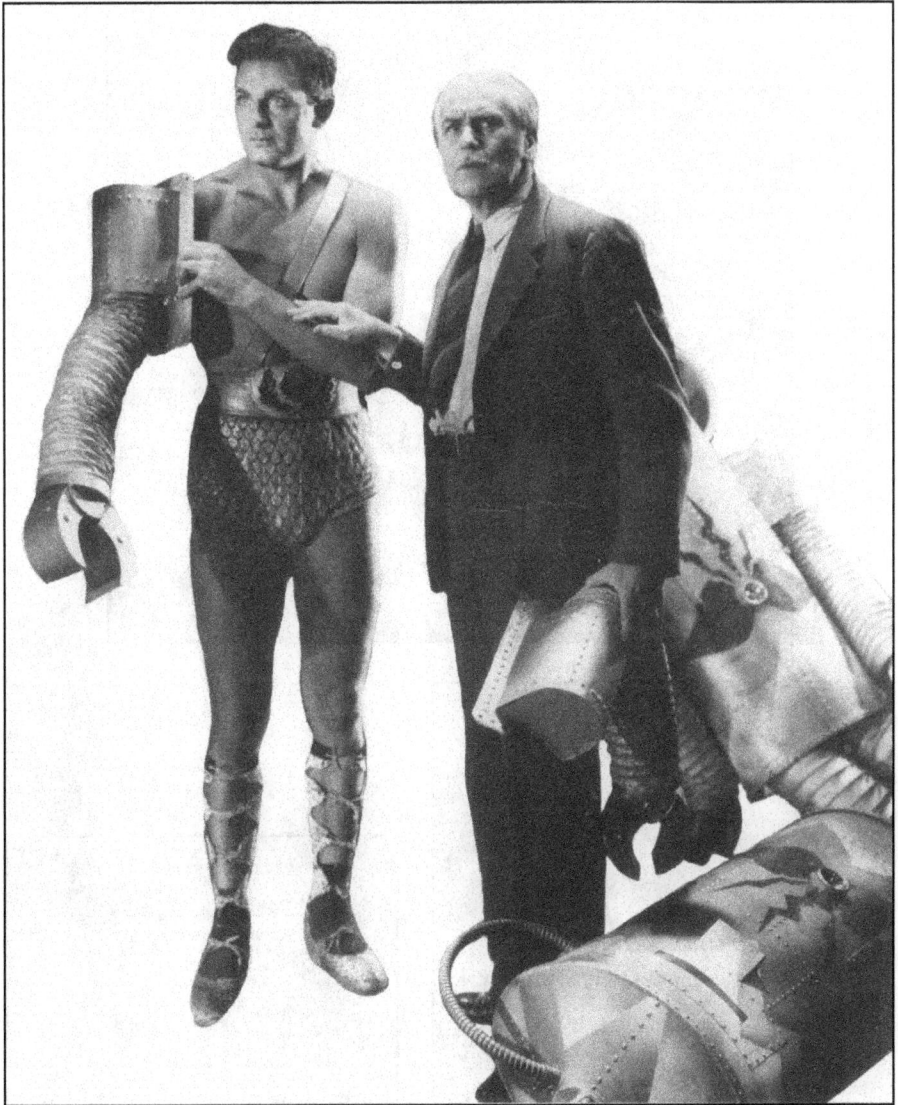

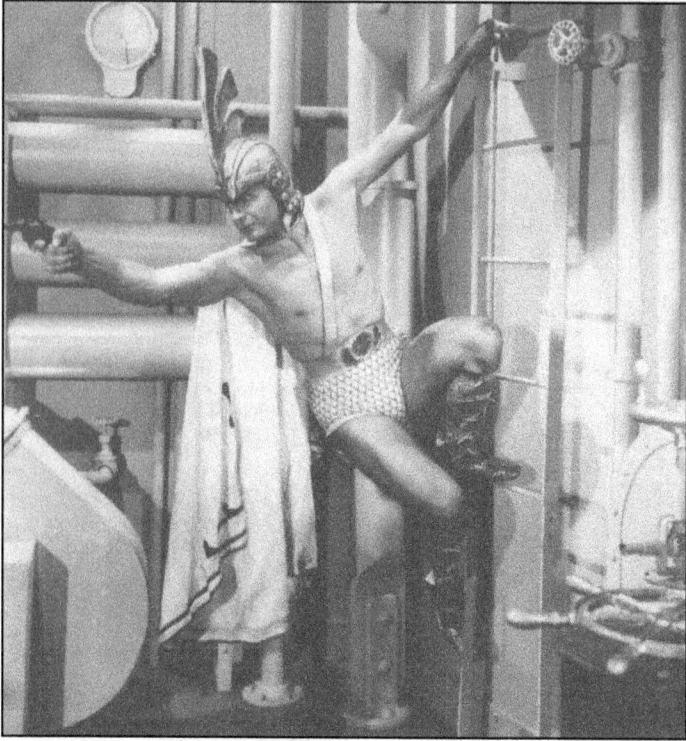

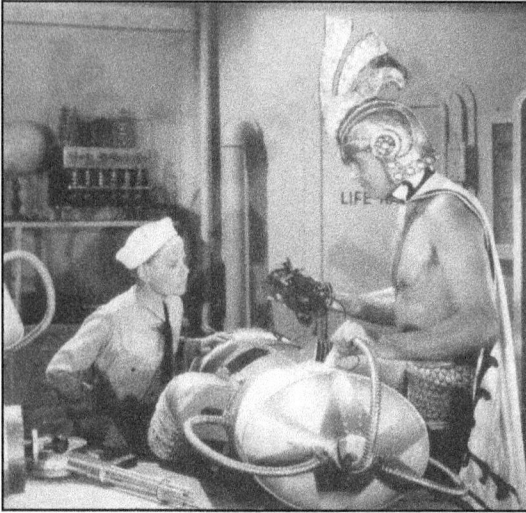

A REPUBLIC SERIAL in 12 AMAZING EPISODES

REPUBLIC PICTURES presents

UNDERSEA KINGDOM

with

RAY (CRASH) CORRIGAN

LOIS WILDE · MONTE BLUE · WILLIAM FARNUM
LON CHANEY JR. · LANE CHANDLER
JACK MULHALL · MALCOLM McGREGOR

PRODUCED by NAT LEVINE

Chapter 10 ATLANTIS DESTROYED

TRADE MARK
Metro Goldwyn Mayer
KELLY THE SECOND
GUS MEINS

FULL LENGTH FEATURE—90 MINUTES OF LAUGHS!
HAL ROACH PRESENTS
KELLY THE SECOND
WITH PATSY KELLY
CHARLIE CHASE
GUINN "BIG BOY" WILLIAMS
PERT KELTON
A METRO-GOLDWYN-MAYER PICTURE

HAL ROACH presents
KELLY THE SECOND
A FULL LENGTH COMEDY
PATSY KELLY
CHARLIE CHASE
GUINN "BIG BOY" WILLIAMS
PERT KELTON
GUS MEINS
90 MERRY MINUTES OF SCREEN JOY

Kelly the Second

Produced by Hal Roach Studios. Released by Metro-Goldwyn-Mayer Corp. on August 21, 1936. Copyright Metro-Goldwyn-Mayer Corp., July 27, 1936, LP6500. Running time: 70-71 minutes, 7 reels. *Directed by* Gus Meins; *screen play,* Jeff Moffitt and William Terhune; *adaptation,* Jack Jevne and Gordon Douglas; *dialogue,* Tom Bell and Arthur V. Jones; *photography by* Art Lloyd, a.s.c; *film editor,* Jack Ogilvie; *sound,* William Randall; *musical director,* Marvin Hatley; *photographic effects,* Roy Seawright.

Cast:

Patsy Kelly	. . . .	Mollie (Patricia Kelly)
Guinn "Big Boy" Williams	. . . .	Cecil Callahan
Charley Chase	. . . .	Dr. J. Willoughby Klum
Pert Kelton	. . . .	Gloria
Edward Brophy	. . . .	Ike Arnold
Harold Huber	. . . .	Spike
Maxie Rosenbloom	. . . .	Butch Flynn
DeWitt C. Jennings	. . . .	Judge
Syd Saylor	. . . .	Dan

Also featuring: Billy Gilbert, Carl "Alfalfa" Switzer, Robert E. O'Connor, and Ray Corrigan.

Synopsis:
Mollie Kelly, the sweetheart trainer of Cecil Callahan, a truck driver turned to the boxing ring, forces her employer, a druggist, to act as Cecil's manager, and they set out to build up a champion. Gloria provides an attractive menace as the gold-digging girl friend of Ike Arnold, a racketeer.

Production Notes:
Filmed from June 15, 1935 to late February 1936, at the Hal Roach Studio in Culver City, California. The original film length was reported by *Variety* at 82 to 85 minutes, but that "about fifteen minutes" were trimmed. Corrigan portrayed a ticket taker outside an arena.

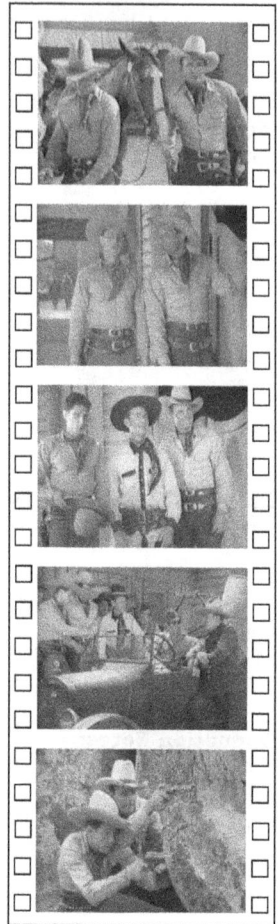

The Three Mesquiteers

Produced and Released by Republic Pictures Corp. on September 21, 1936. Copyright Republic Pictures Corp., September 22, 1936, LP6612. Running time, 56, 58, or 60-61 minutes, 6 reels. *Directed by* Ray Taylor; *produced by* Nat Levine; *screen play by* Jack Natteford; *associate producer*, Sol C. Siegel; *supervised by* Mack V. Wright; *original story*, Charles Condon; *based on idea by* William Colt MacDonald; *supervising editor*, Murray Seldeen; *photography*, William P. Nobles; *film editor*, William Thompson; *musical supervisor*, Harry Grey; *sound engineer*, Terry Kellum.

Cast:

Robert Livingston	Stony Brook
Ray Corrigan	Tucson Smith
Syd Saylor	Lullaby Joslin
Kay Hughes	Marian Brian
J. P. McGowan	Brack Canfield
Al Bridge	Olin
Frank Yaconelli	Pete
John Merton	Bull
Gene Marvey	Bob Brian
Milburn Stone	John
Duke York	Chuck
Nena Quartaro	Rosita
Allen Connor	Milt

Also featuring: Stanley Blystone, Ralph Bucko, Roy Bucko, Jack Evans, Oscar Gahan, Jack Hendricks, John Ince, Tracy Layne, Bert Lindley, Cactus Mack, George Plues, Rose Plumer, Rudy Sooter, and Wally West.

Synopsis:
Led by Lullaby Joslin, hundreds of World War I veterans and families rush to San Juan Basin, New Mexico, to file on homesteads just opened by the government. The army vets meet a lot of opposition from the cattle owners, especially the Canfield brothers, who want to keep the land for grazing purposes. Coming to the aid of Lullaby and the homesteaders are Stony Brooke and Tucson. When Bob Brian is killed, Stony and Tucson organize the veterans as a fighting unit and go into action against the Canfields.

Production Notes:
Corrigan signed a two-year contract with Republic Pictures Corp. which ran from May 25, 1936 to May 24, 1938. The Three Mesquiteers was his first film under the contract. Filming began on July 21, 1936, with location work at Kernville and the Republic Studios backlot. A *Daily Variety* news item stated that the production crew was at Lone Pine, but no scenes of Lone Pine are in the film. Robert Livingston was shot in the leg during filming and production was delayed.

Three Mesquiteers

Max Terhune   Bob Livingston   Ray Corrigan

REPUBLIC PICTURES
presents
THE THREE MESQUITEERS
BOB LIVINGSTON *as Stony Brooke*
RAY CORRIGAN *as Tucson Smith*
SYD SAYLOR *as Lullaby Joslin*
in

"The 3 MESQUITEERS"

Directed by RAY TAYLOR
Supervised by MACK V. WRIGHT
Screen Play by JACK NATTEFORD
Original Story by CHARLES CONDON
Based on idea by Wm. COLT MacDONALD

Produced by NAT LEVINE

A REPUBLIC PICTURE

"COUNTRY GENTLEMEN"

Sunday, Monday and Tuesday at the Wood theater, Olsen and Johnson, a rollicking, roistering comedy team of stage and radio fame, make their bid for screen fame in the Republic comedy, "Country Gentlemen."

The Scandinavian duo portray the shady characters of phoney stock promoters, bill jumpers, kidnapers, confidence men, forgers and scoundrels who in the end prove that their intentions were noble all along and not a widow or an orphan could condemn them.

The plot unfolds merrily, disclosing Olsen and Johnson in preposterously funny situations brought about by their efforts to fleece the public in a thoroughly nice way. Joyce Compton portrays the oh-so-dumb young lady who adds to the complications by trying to prove Olsen and Johnson wolves in sheeps' clothing—when they're really just a couple of little lambs at heart!

Lila Lee, former star of the silent screen, is pleasing in her comeback role. Others in the cast include Sammy McKim, Joe Cunningham, Olin Howard, Wade Boteler, Ivan Miller and Ray "Crash" Corrigan.

Country Gentlemen

Produced and Released by Republic Pictures Corp. on November 9, 1936. Copyright Republic Pictures Corp., November 9, 1936, LP6708. Running time, 60-68 minutes, 8 reels. *Directed by* Ralph Staub; *produced by* Nat Levine; *screen play,* Joseph Hoffman and Gertrude Orr; *associate producer,* Herman Schlom; *original story,* Milton Raison, Jack Harvey, and Jo Graham; *additional dialogue,* John P. Medbury; *supervising editor,* Murray Seldeen; *photography,* Ernest Miller; *film editor,* Ernest Nims; *musical supervision,* Harry Grey; *sound engineer,* Harry Jones; *costumes by* Eloise.

Cast:

Ole Olsen	J. D. Hamilton
Chic Johnson	Charlie Williams
Joyce Compton	Gertie
Lila Lee	Louise Heath
Pierre Watkin	Grayson
Donald Kirke	Martin
Ray Corrigan	Briggs
Sammy McKim	Billy Heath
Wade Boteler	First deputy
Ivan Miller	Second deputy
Olin Howland	Lawyer
Frank Sheridan	Chief of police
Harry Harvey	Shorty
Joe Cunningham	Chuck
Prince	Great Dane

Also featuring: Bruce Mitchell.

Synopsis:
This Olsen-Johnson mirth maker represents one of Republic's best efforts to date, and the crazy clowning of the pair, together with a double share of their sure-fire vaudeville gags, makes the picture a cinch for any spot, particularly where their stage unit has played. Lila Lee does well with her part, and good support is given by the others in the cast. Olsen and Johnson, a pair of wildcat promoters, hit a small town full of bonus money, and start selling phoney oil stock. Olsen falls for Lila and tries to keep the deal straight, but Johnson bungles his attempts and gets them both ridden out of town on a rail. A gusher comes in at the last minute to cinch the romance for Olsen.

Production Notes:
Filming began in late September 1936.

The Vigilantes Are Coming

Produced and Released by Republic Pictures Corp. Released on August 22, 1936. Copyright Republic Pictures Corp., Chapters 1-6, October 2, 1936 L6638, Chapters 7-12, November 9, 1936 L6713. Running time, 229 minutes, 25 chapters, 12 Reels. *Directed by* Mack V. Wright and Ray Taylor; *produced by* Nat Levine; *supervised by* J. Laurence Wickland; *screenplay by* John Rathmell, Maurice Geraghty, and Winston Miller; *original story*, Maurice Geraghty and Leslie Swabacker; *supervising editor*, Murray Seldeen; *photography*, William Nobles and Edgar Lyons; *film editors*, Dick Fantl and Helene Turner; *sound engineer*, Terry Kellum; *musical supervision*, Harry Grey.

Cast:

Robert Livingston	Don Loring/The Eagle
Kay Hughes	Doris Colton
Guinn (Big Boy) Williams	Salvation
Raymond Hatton	Whipsaw
Fred Kohler	Jason Burr
Robert Warwick	Ivan Raspinoff
William Farnum	Father Jose
Bob Kortman	Boris Petroff
John Merton	Rance Talbot
Lloyd Ingraham	John Colton
William Desmond	Anderson
Yakima Canutt	Barsam
Tracy Layne	Clem Peters
Bud Pope	Ivan
Steve Clemente	Pedro
Bud Osborne.	Harris

Also featuring: Phillip Armenta, Ray Corrigan, Stanley Blystone, Henry Hall, John O'Brien, Joe De La Cruz, Fred Burns, Tommy Coats, Ken Cooper, Frank Ellis, Sam Garrett, Herman Hack, Jack Ingram, Bob Jamison, Jack Kinney, Jack Kirk, Frankie Marvin, Pascale Perry, Vinegar Roan, Lloyd Saunders, John Slater, Al Taylor, Jerome Ward, Len Ward, Wes Warner, and Wally West.

Episode Titles:
1. The Eagle Strikes
2. Birth of the Vigilantes
3. Condemned by Cossacks
4. Unholy Gold
5. Treachery Unmasked
6. A Tyrant's Trickery
7. Wings of Doom
8. A Treaty with Treason
9. Arrow's Flight
10. Prison of Flame

11. A Race With Death
12. Fremont Takes Command

Synopsis:
A masked hero, "The Eagle", leads California ranchers in a struggle against Russian Cossacks who are plotting to take over California and turn it into a Russian colony.

Production Notes:
Filmed between May 28 and June 17, 1936, with location scenes at Kernville, San Luis Rey Mission, San Fernando Mission, and the Republic Studio backlot. Cost of the serial was $87,655. It was released to television in six 26½ minute chapters. Corrigan portrayed Captain Fremont.

Ghost-Town Gold

Produced and Released by Republic Picture Corp. on October 26, 1936. Copyright November 5, 1936, Republic Pictures Corp., LP6707. Running time, 55-57 minutes, 6 reels. *Directed by* Joseph Kane; *produced by* Nat Levine; *associate producer*, Sol C. Siegel; *supervised by* William Berke; *screen play*, John Rathmell and Oliver Drake; *original story*, Bernard McConville; *based on book by* William Colt MacDonald; *supervising editor*, Murray Seldeen; *photography*, Jack Marta; *film editor*, Lester Orlebeck; *musical supervisor*, Harry Grey; *sound engineer*, Harry Jones.

Cast:

Robert Livingston	Stony Brooke
Ray Corrigan	Tucson Smith
Max Terhune	Lullaby Joslin
Kay Hughes	Sabina Thornton
LeRoy Mason	Barrington
Burr Caruth	Mayor Thornton
Bud Kortman	Monk
Milburn Morante	Jake Rawlins
Frank Hagney	Wild Man Joe Kamatski
Don Roberts	Manager
F. Herrick Herrick	Catlett
Robert C. Thomas	Thunderbolt O'Brien
Yakima Canutt	Buck

Also featuring: Bob Burns, Horace B. Carpenter, Jess Cavin, Rube Dalroy, Art Dillard, Billy Franey, Herman Hack, Harry Harvey, Bill Hickey, Earle Hodgins, I. Stanford Jolley, Bert Lindley, Horace Murphy, Bud Osborne, Edward Peil Sr., Charles Sullivan, Harry Tenbrook, Wally West, and Hank Worden.

Synopsis:
The Three Mesquiteers drift into a Texas cowtown and sell a bunch of cattle for a nice sum, which is deposited in the local bank. When crooked fight promoters attempt to stage a fight in the town they are balked by the banker. To disgrace him the promoters rob his bank and hide the money in a little "ghost" mining town. It is up to The Three Mesquiteers to find the loot and rout the promoters.

Production Notes:
Filmed between August 29 and September 8, 1936. Exteriors were shot at the Brandeis Ranch and Iverson Movie Ranch in Chatsworth, and the Republic Studio backlot.

114

Roarin' Lead

Produced and Released by Republic Pictures Corp. on December 9, 1936. Copyright Republic Pictures Corp., December 9, 1936, LP6776. Running time, 53-61 minutes, 6 reels. *Directed by* Mack V. Wright and Sam Newfield; *produced by* Nat Levine; *associate producer,* Sol C. Siegel; *original screen play,* Oliver Drake and Jack Natteford; *based on book by* William Colt MacDonald; *photography,* William Nobles; *supervising editor,* Murray Seldeen; *film editor,* William Thompson; *musical supervisor,* Harry Grey; *songs by* Sam Stept and Ned Washington; *sound engineer,* Harry Jones.

Cast:

Robert Livingston	Stony Brook
Ray Corrigan	Tucson Smith
Max Terhune	Lullaby Joslin
Christine Maple	Doris Moore
Hooper Atchley	Hackett
Yakima Canutt	Canary
George Chesebro	Captain Gardner
Tommy Bupp	Bobby
Mary Russell	Blondie
Jane Keckley	Old lady at orphanage
Tamara Lynn Kauffman	Baby Mary
Beverly Luff	Prima donna
Theodore Frye	Apache dancer
Katherine Frye	Apache dancer
Frank Austin	Mr. Hiram Perkins
The Meglin Kiddies	Dancers

Also featuring: Bob Burns, Bobby Burns, Burr Caruth, Barney Furey, Grace Kern, Newt Kirby, Jack Kirk, Murdock MacQuarrie, Frank McCarroll, Forbes Murray, Pascale Perry, George Plues, Harry Tenbrook, Maston Williams, and Jay Silverheels.

Synopsis:
The Three Mesquiteers return from adventuring just in time to save the orphanage and the Cattlemen's Protective Association from bankruptcy. The work of cattle rustlers has so diminished the community's finances that the orphanage is being closed when the partners arrive and promise to get the money. In the meantime the pretty young matron of the home stages a benefit show which presents an opportunity for the cowboys to sing and dance.

Production Notes:
Filmed in November 1936, with location scenes taken at Walker Ranch, Iverson Movie Ranch, and the Republic backlot, with stock footage of Lake Sherwood and the Trem Carr Ranch.

THE 3 MESQUITEERS

ROBERT LIVINGSTON
RAY CORRIGAN
MAX TERHUNE

Roarin' Lead

A RE-RELEASE

Directed by MACK V. WRIGHT and SAM NEWFIELD
ORIGINAL SCREEN PLAY BY OLIVER DRAKE AND
JACK NATTEFORD
BASED ON STORIE BY WILLIAM COLT MacDONALD
Associate Producer SOL C. SIEGEL

A REPUBLIC PICTURE

117

118

The Riders of the Whistling Skull

Produced and Released by Republic Pictures Corp. on January 4, 1937. Copyright Republic Pictures Corp., January 4, 1937, LP6829. Running time, 55-56 minutes, 5,009 feet, 6 reels. *Directed by* Mack V. Wright; *produced by* Nat Levine; *associate producer*, Sol C. Siegel; *screen play by* Oliver Drake, John Rathmell; *original story by* Bernard McConville and Oliver Drake; *based on book by* William Colt MacDonald; *photography*, Jack Marta; *supervising editor*, Murray Seldeen; *film editor*, Tony Martinelli; *music supervision*, Harry Grey; *sound engineer*, Harry Jones.

Cast:

Robert Livingston	. . . . .	Stony Brooke
Ray Corrigan	. . . . .	Tucson Smith
Max Terhune	. . . . .	Lullaby Joslin
Mary Russell	. . . . .	Betty Marsh
Roger Williams	. . . . .	Rutledge
Fern Emmett	. . . . .	Henrietta McCoy
C. Montague Shaw	. . . . .	Faxon
Yakima Canutt	. . . . .	Otah
John Ward	. . . . .	Brewster
George Godfrey	. . . . .	Professor Fronc
Earle Ross	. . . . .	Professor Cleary
Frank Ellis	. . . . .	Coggins
Chief Thunder Cloud	. . . . .	High Priest
John Van Pelt	. . . . .	Professor Marsh

Also featuring: Edward Piel Sr., Jack Kirk, Iron Eyes Cody, Tracy Layne, Tom Steele, Wally West, Eddie Boland, Art Dillard, Tracy Layne, and Ken Cooper.

Synopsis:
The Three Mesquiteers head for the remote regions of the Painted Desert to join a searching party looking for a lost professor. The mystery of the professor's disappearance becomes greater as another is slain before their eyes with an arrow on which is carved strange cultist signs.

Production Notes:
Filmed from late October to mid November, 1936, at the Iverson Movie Ranch, the Republic Studio backlot, and the hills and desert near Mecca, California. The film was remade by Monogram Pictures in 1949 as *The Feathered Serpent*, a Charlie Chan mystery. Both screenplays were the work of Oliver Drake, whose name is misspelled as "Olive" in the onscreen credits.

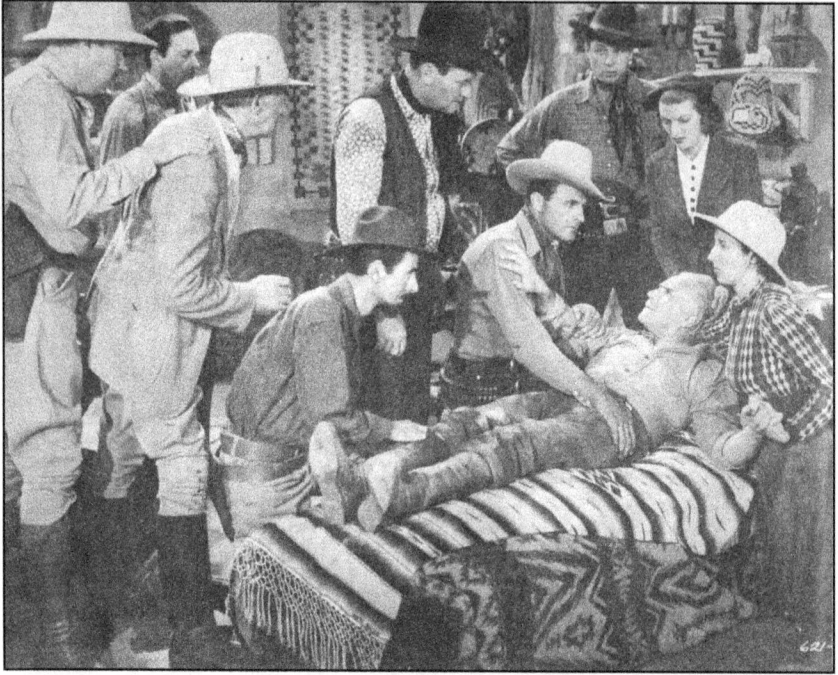

A REPUBLIC PRODUCTION
Join the MARINES
PRODUCED BY NAT LEVINE
Executive Producer
ALBERT E. LEVOY
Associate Producer
JOSEPH KRUMGOLD
Directed by
RALPH STAUB
Screen Play
JOSEPH KRUMGOLD
OLIVE COOPER
Original Story . . . KARL BROWN
Photography . . ERNEST MILLER
Costumes by . . . . . ELOISE

PAUL KELLY
JUNE TRAVIS
PURNELL PRATT
REGINALD DENNY
WARREN HYMER
And
IRVING PICHEL
STERLING HOLLOWAY
RAY CORRIGAN
JOHN HOLLAND
CARLETON YOUNG
JOHN SHEEHAN
ARTHUR HOYT
RICHARD BEACH
VAL DURAN
LANDERS STEVENS

Join the Marines

Produced and released by Republic Pictures Corp. on January 25, 1937. Copyright Republic Pictures Corp., January 25, 1937 L6922. Running time, 67 or 70 minutes, 8 reels. *Directed by* Ralph Staub; *produced by* Nat Levine; *executive producer*, Albert E. Levoy; *associate producer*, Joseph Krumgold; *screen play*, Joseph Krumgold and Olive Cooper; *original story*, Karl Brown; *photography*, Ernest Miller; *supervising editor*, Murray Seldeen; *film editors*, Ernest Nims and Lester Orlebeck; *sound engineer*, Terry Kellum; *musical supervision*, Harry Grey; costumes by Eloise.

Cast:

Paul Kelly	Philip H. Donlan
June Travis	Paula Denbrough
Purnell Pratt	Colonel J. B. Denbrough
Reginald Denny	Steve Lodge
Warren Hymer	Holman
Irving Pichel	Colonel Leonard
Sterling Holloway	Alfred, the steward
Ray Corrigan	Lieutenant Hodge
John Holland	Lieutenant
Carleton Young	Corporal
John Sheehan	O'Day
Arthur Hoyt	Captain James
Richard Beach	Marine
Howard Hickman	Pruitt
Val Duran	Joe
Landers Stevens	Dr. McCullough

Also featuring: Franklin Adreon, Edgar Allan, Roy Barcroft, Dean Benton, Gertrude Chorre, Frank Du Frane, Oscar Hendrian, William Hopper, Mailoa Kalili, Manual Kalili, Donald Kerr, Al Kikume, James C. Morton, and Mary Silva.

Synopsis:

Phil Donlan, star U.S. Olympic javelin-thrower, accidentally disrupts the intended elopement of Paula Denbrough and Steve Lodge in a hilarious series of entanglements aboard a Berlin-bound steamer. As a result of being caught with a champagne bottle, and later discovered on the bottom of a heap of Paula's drunken friends who attack him, Phil is dropped from the Olympic squad.

Paula and Phil make the sad trip back on the same boat and hatred dissolves into love. Paula promises to marry him as soon as he gets a job, and Phil, after a desperate search for work, enlists in the Marines only to learn that Paula detests discipline, having been brought up under a strict code of rules under her Marine-Colonel father.

Since only lieutenants or above can resign, Phil grimly works his way up to rank of first sergeant. He is transferred to dangerous Maragna Island, a possible base for clipper routes to China, where Paula's father is in charge. Bubonic plague strikes the island. Phil, with the aid of his pals, quells the native insurrection against disinfecting their village, and wins the natives' respect by a spear-throwing exhibition. As a result, he is made lieutenant. Immediately he resigns—only to learn that Paula now has grown to love the service.

Embittered, Phil sails to Arrango Island where he hears a radio report of a Maragna uprising against vaccination. The marine post and Paula are in peril. After convincing the owner and operator of the only plane on Arrango that there are Irishmen in danger, Phil flies with him to Maragna. Both land safely on one parachute and find themselves in the cross-fire of natives and marines. By accurately hurling dynamite-wrapped spears, Phil frightens the natives into surrender, takes back his resignation, and wins back his Paula.

Production Notes:
Filmed between November 18 and early December 1936. Exteriors were shot at Bronson Canyon and on the Republic Studio backlot.

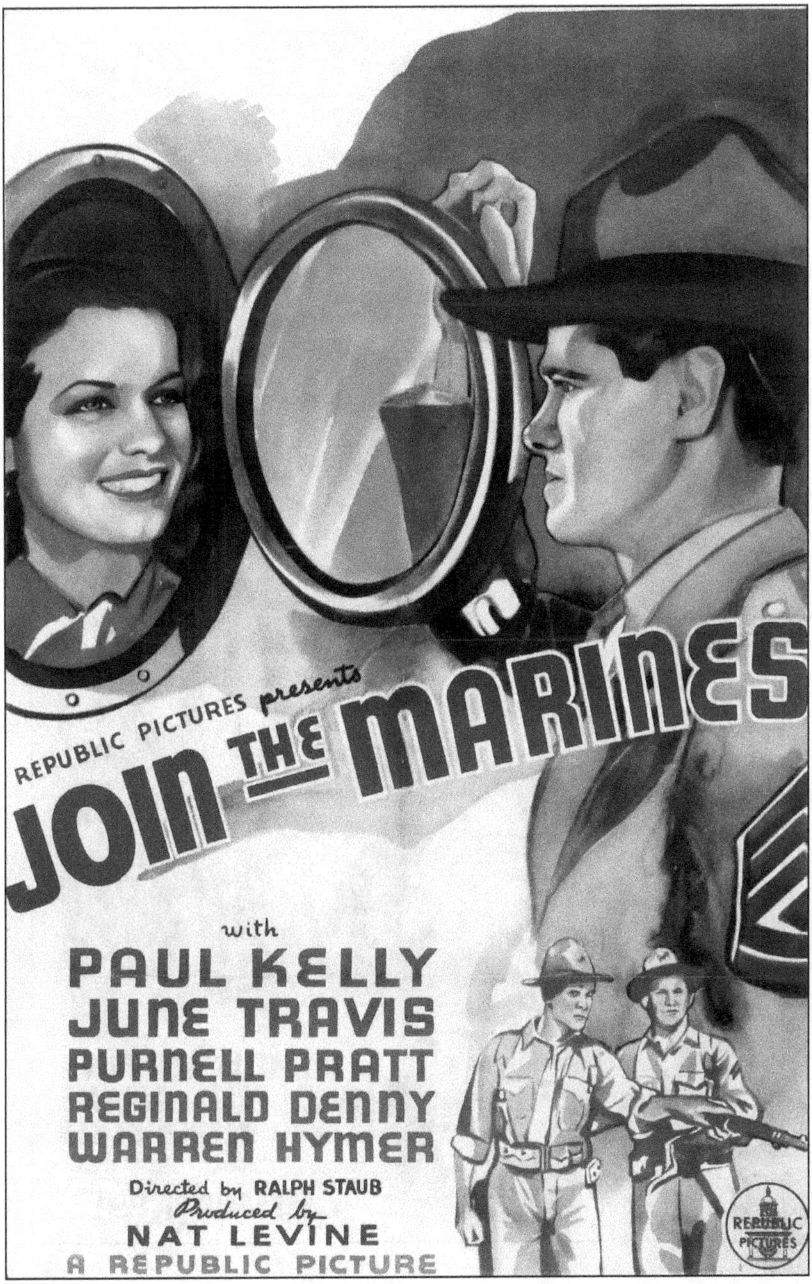
REPUBLIC PICTURES presents
JOIN THE MARINES
with
PAUL KELLY
JUNE TRAVIS
PURNELL PRATT
REGINALD DENNY
WARREN HYMER
Directed by RALPH STAUB
Produced by
NAT LEVINE
A REPUBLIC PICTURE
REPUBLIC PICTURES

THRILLS!!
WHEN THE DEVILDOGS
SWING INTO ACTION!

JOIN THE MARINES

A RE-RELEASE

with PAUL KELLY · JUNE TRAVIS
PURNELL PRATT · REGINALD
DENNY · WARREN HYMER

directed by RALPH STAUB · screen play by JOSEPH
KRUMGOLD, OLIVE COOPER · original story by KARL
BROWN · produced by NAT LEVINE

A REPUBLIC PICTURE

"Join The Marines" Top Leatherneck Action Thriller

Sock entertainment for everyone — be he or she a lover of hilarity, adventure, thrills or fighting romance — is offered in top form in "Join the Marines," Republic's exciting re-release saga of soldier life and love which brought June Travis, Paul Kelly, Purnell Pratt, Reginald Denny, Sterling Holloway and an excellent cast to the .... Theatre last night for a .... day run.

Exciting Story

Starting off as a rich satire on an Olympic Games personage and a champagne party, the exciting story quickly develops into tense melodrama, with Kelly carrying the top role in masterful fashion. A fighting romance begins with the dashing Miss Travis, and there are thrills, battles, and excitement a-plenty in a South Sea island overrun by both wild bushmen and feverish plagues.

Fine Actors

Republic has invested the picture with actors of the finest and most varied talents. Denny and Holloway furnish plenty of laughs, while Warren Hymer, Purnell Pratt, and Ray Corrigan give outstanding performances as the hard-boiled, fast talking buddies of Marine Sergeant Kelly.

Director Ralph Staub is responsible for much of the success of the film, with equal honors going to Producer Albert Levoy, who richly endowed it with vivid settings.

NATIVES BOMBED

Hurling hand grenades tied to the ends of spears is the startling and decidedly effective manner in which an attack of South Sea Island bushmen was stopped by Paul Kelly, Ray Corrigan, and other "Marines" in "Join the Marines," Republic's thrilling re-release saga of soldier life and love in the tropics. Co-starring Kelly and dashing June Travis, the picture now is holding audiences breathless at the .... Theatre.

"JOIN THE MARINES" (2A)

Paul Kelly — Warren Hymer

Laughs Galore in Marine Saga

The attempts of Paul Kelly to transform a mid-Pacific island and its savage occupants into the counterpart of a New York City borough results in several hilarious sequences in "Join the Marines," an action-crammed Republic re-release coming to the .... Theatre.

Kelly portrays a first sergeant who wins the natives over to submitting to the burning of their straw homes as a means of disinfecting the island. On the island is located a Marine Corps unit seeking to establish a possible Clipper ship base on the China route.

The island is rebuilt along the lines of a cosmopolite cross-section of Manhattan. Streets are called "42nd Street," "Tenth Avenue," and the like. Natives are re-named Finnegan, Schultz, O'Halloran, and in special cases "Big Shot," "Chief Barber," etc. Banana stalks take the place of policemen's night sticks.

Star Athletes in Marine Hit

Many athletes of world wide fame are among the hundreds of South Sea Island natives who play in awesome and barbarious war scenes of "Join the Marines," Republic's exciting re-release saga of soldier life and loves in the mystic Pacific, which now is co-starring Paul Kelly and June Travis with Purnell Pratt, Reginald Denny, Warren Hymer and Sterling Holloway at the .... Theatre.

"JOIN THE MARINES" (1A)

Paul Kelly

Hit the Saddle

Produced and Released by Republic Pictures Corp. on March 3, 1937. Copyright February 1, 1937, Republic Pictures Corp., LP6901. Running time, 57-62 minutes, 5,240 feet, 6 reels. *Directed by* Mack Wright; *produced by* Nat Levine; *associate producer,* Sol C. Siegel; *screen play,* Oliver Drake; *original story,* Oliver Drake and Maurice Geraghty; *based on book by* William Colt MacDonald; *photography,* Jack Marta; *supervising editor,* Murray Seldeen; *film editor,* Tony Martinelli; *musical supervision,* Harry Grey; *sound engineer,* Terry Kellum; *songs by* Oliver Drake and Sam H. Stept.

Cast:

Robert Livingston	Stony Brooke
Ray Corrigan	Tucson Smith
Max Terhune	Lullaby Joslin
Rita Cansino	Rita
J. P. McGowan	Rance McGowan
Edward Cassidy	Sheriff Miller
Sammy McKim	Tim Miller
Yakima Canutt	Buck
Harry Tenbrook	Joe Harvey
Robert Smith	Hank
Ed Boland	Pete
George Plues	Henchman
Jack Kirk	Henchman

Also featuring: Bob Burns, Budd Buster, Allan Cavan, Kernan Cripps, Oscar Gahan, Herman Hack, Robert Hoag, Tracy Layne, Harley Luse, George Morrell, Tex Palmer, Tex Phelps, Russ Powell, Rudy Sooter, Sheila Terry, Jack Tornek, and Wally West.

Synopsis:
A story of a wild pinto, the efforts of horse thieves to catch him, and the fight waged by The Three Mesquiteers to save and protect him.

Production Notes:
Filmed from December 8 to mid December 1936, with exterior locations at the Iverson Movie Ranch, Brandeis Ranch, Red Rock Canyon, and the Republic Studio backlot.

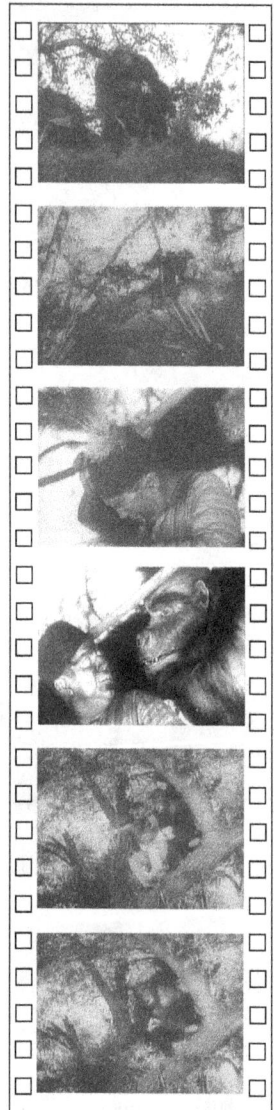

Round-Up Time In Texas

Produced and Released by Republic Pictures Corp. on February 28, 1937. Copyright Republic Pictures Corp., February 8, 1937, LP6904. Running time, 58-63 minutes, 5,372 feet, 7 reels. *Directed by* Joseph Kane; *produced by* Nat Levine; *associate producer,* Armand Schaefer; *original screen play,* Oliver Drake; *photography,* William Nobles; *supervising editor,* Murray Seldeen; *film editor,* Lester Orlebeck; *musical supervision,* Harry Grey; *sound engineer,* Harry Jones; *songs by* Gene Autry, Smiley Burnette, Sam H. Stept, Sidney Mitchell, Ned Washington, Sam Lewis, Joe Young, Harry Akst, Vincent and Howard, Andy Razof.

Cast:

Gene Autry	. . . .	Gene Autry
Smiley Burnette	. . . .	Frog Millhouse
Maxine Doyle	. . . .	Gwen Barclay
Cabin Kids	. . . .	Bosuto's children
Champion	. . . .	Champion
Le Roy Mason	. . . .	John Cardigan
Earle Hodgins	. . . .	Barkey McCuskey
Dick Wessel	. . . .	Craig Johnson
Buddy Williams	. . . .	Bosuto
Elmer Fain	. . . .	Bosuto's son
Cornie Anderson	. . . .	Namba
Frankie Marvin	. . . .	Second Cape policeman
Ken Cooper	. . . .	Tex Autry
Ray Corrigan	. . . .	Gorilla

Also featuring: Jim Corey, Charles Whitaker, Al Ferguson, Al Knight, Carleton Young, Jack C. Smith, Jack Kirk, George Morrell.

Synopsis:

Gene Autry and Frog Millhouse travel to Africa to avenge the honor of his brother and outwitting the crooks and saving a diamond mine. Frog teaches the natives to sing and pals around with an ape.

Production Notes:

Filmed from November 7 to mid November 1936 on the Republic Studio backlot. Stock footage of Corrigan as a gorilla swinging through the trees was lifted from "Darkest Africa". His interaction with Smiley Burnette was newly filmed.

Gunsmoke Ranch

Produced and Released by Republic Pictures Corp. on May 5, 1937. Copyright May 5, 1937, Republic Pictures Corp., LP7132. Running time, 56-59 minutes, 6 reels. *Directed by* Joseph Kane; *associate producer* Sol C. Siegel; *screen play,* Oliver Drake; *original story,* Oliver Drake and Jack Natteford; *based on idea by* William Colt MacDonald; *photography,* Gus Peterson; *supervising editor,* Murray Seldeen; *film editor,* Russell Schoengarth; *musical supervision,* Raoul Kraushaar; *song by* Oliver Drake; *sound engineer,* Terry Kellum.

Cast:

Robert Livingston	Stony Brooke
Ray Corrigan	Tucson Smith
Max Terhune	Lullaby Joslin
Kenneth Harlan	Phineas Flagg
Julia Thayer	Marion Warren
Sammy McKim	Jimmy
Oscar and Elmer	Oscar and Elmer
Burr Caruth	Warren
Allen Connor	Reggie
Yakima Canutt	Spider
Horace Carpenter	Larkin
Jane Keckley	Mathilda
Bob Walker	Williams
Jack Ingram	Jed
Jack Kirk	Sheriff
Loren Riebe	Hank
Vinegar Roan	Zeko
Wes Warner	Old man
Jack Padjan	Duke

Also featuring: Silver Tip Baker, Richard Beach, Bob Burns, Budd Buster, Bob Card, Lee Ford, June Johnson, William McCall, Bud McClure, Eva McKenzie, Peggy McKim, Jack O'Shea, Fred Parker, Duke Taylor, Fred "Snowflake" Toones, John Merton, Robert McKenzie, Edward Piel Sr., and Fred Burns.

Synopsis:
A great flood in the West destroys the ranchers' property to such an extent that they are willing to sell for any price. The Three Mesquiteers are avenging cowboys who are determined the ranchers shall not be exploited. Marion Warren and her brother Jimmy appeal to the Mesquiteers when their grandfather is kidnapped by a gang of bad men and held for ransom in the form of a cancelled deed.

Production Notes:
Filmed between March 12 and 23, 1937. Exteriors were shot at Lone Pine, Red Rock Canyon, and the Republic Studio backlot.

REPUBLIC PICTURES presents THE THREE MESQUITEERS, Bob Livingston, Ray Corrigan and
Max Terhune in "GUNSMOKE RANCH"   PRINTED IN U. S. A.

138

Come On, Cowboys

Produced and Released by Republic Pictures Corp. on May 24, 1937. Copyright Republic Pictures Corp., May 24, 1937, LP7195. Running time, 53-58 minutes, 5,282 feet, 6 reels. *Directed by* Joseph Kane; *associate producer* Sol C. Siegel; *original screen play,* Betty Burbridge; *based on characters created by* William Colt MacDonald; *photography,* Ernest Miller; *supervising editor,* Murray Seldeen; *film editor,* Lester Orlebeck; *musical supervision,* Raoul Kraushaar; *sound engineer,* Terry Kellum.

Cast:

Robert Livingston	. . . . .	Stony Brooke
Ray Corrigan	. . . . .	Tucson Smith/Gorilla
Max Terhune	. . . . .	Lullaby Joslin
Maxine Doyle	. . . . .	Ellen Reed
Willie Fung	. . . . .	Charlie
Edward Piel Sr.	. . . . .	Thomas Ridby
Horace Murphy	. . . . .	Jeff Harris
Anne Bennett	. . . . .	Nancy Harris
Edward Cassidy	. . . . .	Tom Rigby
Roger Williams	. . . . .	Lou
Fern Emmett	. . . .	Bus passenger mother
Yakima Canutt	. . . . .	Henchman
George Burton	. . . . .	Sheriff
Merrill McCormick	. . . . .	Dan
Loren Riebe	. . . . .	Red
Victor Allan	. . . . .	Jim
Al Taylor	. . . . .	Tim
George Plues	. . . . .	Mike

Also featuring: Ernie Adams, Lynton Brent, Bobby Burns, Jim Corey, Oscar Gahan, Henry Hall, Jack Kirk, Lillian Lawrence, Harley Luse, James A. Marcus, Milburn Morante, George Morrell, Jack O'Shea, Rose Plumer, Tom Smith, and Carleton Young.

Synopsis:
A small girl becomes the ward of the Three Mesquiteers and when malevolent forces seek to take her away from them, there is action a-plenty.

Production Notes:
Filmed from April 2 to mid April 1937. Exteriors were shot at the Brandeis Ranch, Iverson Movie Ranch, and the Republic Studio backlot.

142

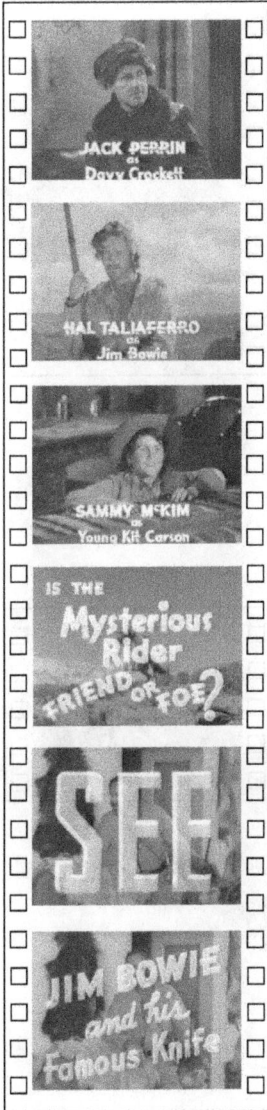

143

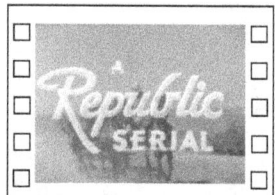

The Painted Stallion

Produced and Released by Republic Pictures Corp. on June 5, 1937. Copyright Republic Pictures Corp., Chapter 1-6, June 18, 1937 L7235, Chapter 7-12, August 6, 1937 L7385. Running time, 212 minutes, 12 Chapters, 25 Reels. *Directed by* William Witney, Alan James, and Ray Taylor; *associate producer:* J. Laurence Wickland; *screen play,* Barry Shipman and Winston Miller; *original story,* Morgan Cox and Ronald Davidson; *based on idea by* Hal G. Evarts; *photography,* William Nobles and Edgar Lyons; *supervising editor:* Murray Seldeen; *film editors,* Helene Turner and Edward Todd; *sound engineer:* Terry Kellum; *musical supervision:* Raoul Kraushaar

Cast:

Ray Corrigan	Clark Stuart
Hoot Gibson	Walter Jamison
LeRoy Mason	Alfredo Dupray
Duncan Renaldo	Zamorro
Sammy McKim	Kit Carson
Hal Taliaferro	Jim Bowie
Jack Perrin	Davy Crockett
Oscar and Elmer	Oscar and Elmer
Julia Thayer	The Rider
Yakima Canutt	Tom
Matson Williams	Macklin
Duke Taylor	Bill
Loren Riebe	Pedro
George De Normand	Oldham
Gordon De Main	Governor
Charles King	Bull Smith
Vinegar Roan	Pete

Also featuring: Lake McKee, Frank Leyva, Frankie Marvin, Curley Dresden, John Big Tree, Pascale Perry, Don Orlando, Henry Hale, Edward Peil Sr., Horace Carpenter, Lee White, Joe Yrigoyen, Paul Lopez, Monte Montague, Gregg Star Whitespear, Ralph Bucko, Roy Bucko, Leo Dupee, Babe DeFreest, Jose Dominguez, Jack Padjan, Al Haskell, James A. Marcus, Milburn Morante, George Morrell, Jack Padjan, Tex Palmer, Tom Smith, and Augie Gomez.

Chapter Titles:
1. Trail to Empire
2. The Rider of the Stallion
3. The Death Leap
4. Avalanche
5. Volley of Death
6. Thundering Wheels
7. Trail Treachery
8. The Whistling Arrow

145

9. The Fatal Message
10. Ambush
11. Tunnel of Terror
12. Human Targets

Synopsis:
An American agent, Clark Stuart, is dispatched to Santa Fe to negotiate a trade agreement with the Mexican governor, newly appointed when Mexico broke away from Spain. At the same time, the first American wagon train, led by Walter Jamison, started from Independence, Missouri for Santa Fe, bearing goods for trade. The train is accompanied by Jim Bowie, famed inventor of the knife, and by the youthful Kit Carson.

The former governor of Santa Fe, Alfredo Duprey, anxious to regain his lucrative control of the territory, plots to sabotage the treaty by substituting one of his own men for Stuart before the new governor arrives.

Duprey's confederate, Zamorro and his henchmen attempt to destroy the wagon train by stirring up an Indian attack, later by luring it into a mountain pass where they use dynamite to send a landslide down upon it. They also make several attempts to kill Stuart, but each time are foiled by a mysterious girl rider on a painted stallion who warns of danger to the Americans by shooting a whistling arrow.

Duprey's men steal the papers from Stuart that authorize him to deal with the new Mexican governor. Stuart trails them into Santa Fe where he meets Davey Crockett. After more adventures and the arrival of the governor, the Americans trap the Duprey forces in their hideout in the caves. After a climatic battle, again aided by the rider on the painted stallion, Zamorro and Duprey are killed and the rest of the gang routed.

The agreement establishing trade relations, is signed by the governor, guaranteeing welcome and safety to American travelers.

Production Notes:
Filmed between February 10 and March 3, 1937, at a cost of $109.164, with location filming at Snow Valley, near St. George, Utah, Iverson Movie Ranch, and the Republic Studio backlot. The film was dedicated "To the heroes of yesterday! Those pioneers who braved the perilous trek westward, defeated a hostile wilderness, and blazed a glorious trail acros the pages of American history!" A 67 minute feature version was released on February 11, 1938. It was released to television in six 26½ minute chapters. This serial marked the directorial debut of William Witney.

146

182

Range Defenders

Produced and Released by Republic Pictures Corp. on June 30, 1937. Copyright Republic Pictures Corp., June 30, 1937, LP7327. Running time, 56 minutes, 5,109 feet, 6 reels. *Directed by* Mack V. Wright; *associate producer* Sol C. Siegel; *original screen story,* Joseph Poland; *based on characters created by* William Colt MacDonald; *photography,* Jack Marta; *supervising editor,* Murray Seldeen; *film editor,* Lester Orlebeck; *musical supervision,* Raoul Kraushaar; *song by* Fleming Allan; *sound engineer,* Terry Kellum.

Cast:

Robert Livingston	. . . .	Stony Brooke
Ray Corrigan	. . . .	Tucson Smith
Max Terhune	. . . .	Lullaby Joslin
Eleanor Stewart	. . . .	Sylvia Ashton
Harry Woods	. . . .	John Harvey
Earle Hodgins	. . . .	Sheriff Dan Gray
Thomas Carr	. . . .	George Brooke
Yakima Canutt	. . . .	Hodge
John Merton	. . . .	Crag
Harrison Greene	. . . .	Auctioneer
Horace Carpenter	. . . .	Pete
Frank Ellis	. . . .	Henchman
Snowflake	. . . .	Cook

Also featuring: Ernie Adams, Curley Dresden, Milburn Morante, Jack O'Shea, Jack Rockwell, Merrill McCormack, Jack Kirk, George Morrell, Al Taylor, C. L. Sherwood, Clyde McClary, Jack Evans, Bob Reeves, Art Dillard, Fred Parker.

Synopsis:
Not one, but three stalwart cowboys ride the western plains in this fast-moving action picture with the result that the average fan's enjoyment will undoubtedly be tripled. Although the action is generously sprinkled with comedy, the suspense is maintained throughout. The Three Mesquiteers have that camaraderie which places them in an audience's favor from the start and their present adventure is built around the rivalry between cattle and sheep ranchers. Stoney Brooke's brother is falsely accused of murder to cover up the scheme of a group of sheep owners who are in power. The trio round up the cattle men, exonerate the youngster, have Tucson Smith elected Sheriff and straighten out Stoney's romance.

Production Notes:
Exteriors shot on location at Kernville and the Republic Studio backlot.

REPUBLIC PICTURES presents
THE THREE MESQUITEERS
BOB LIVINGSTON as "Stony Brooke"
RAY CORRIGAN as "Tucson Smith"
MAX TERHUNE as "Lullaby Joslin"
in
"Range Defenders"
Directed by MACK V. WRIGHT
Original Story by JOSEPH POLAND
Based on characters created by WILLIAM COLT MacDONALD
Associate Producer SOL C. SIEGEL
a REPUBLIC picture

Heart of the Rockies

Produced and Released by Republic Pictures Corp. on September 6, 1937. Copyright Republic Pictures Corp., September 6, 1937, LP7393. Running time, 56-58 minutes, 5,172 feet, 6 reels. *Directed by* Joseph Kane; *associate producer* Sol C. Siegel; *screenplay*, Jack Natteford and Oliver Drake; *original story*, Bernard McConville; *based on characters created by* William Colt MacDonald; *photography*, Jack Marta; *film editor*, Lester Orlebeck; *musical director*, Raoul Kraushaar.

Cast:

Robert Livingston	. . . . .	Stony Brooke
Ray Corrigan	. . . . .	Tucson Smith/Bear
Max Terhune	. . . . .	Lullaby Joslin
Lynn Roberts	. . . . .	Lorna
Sammy McKim	. . . . .	Davey
J. P. McGowan	. . . . .	Big Ed Dawson
Yakima Canutt	. . . . .	Charley Coe
Hal Taliaferro	. . . . .	Brady
Maston Williams	. . . . .	Enoch Dawson
Guy Wilkerson	. . . . .	Reese
Ranny Weeks	. . . . .	Clayton
Georgia Simmons	. . . . .	Ma Dawson
Herman's Mountaineers	. . . . .	Herman's Mountaineers

Also featuring: Frankie Marvin, Nelson McDowell, George C. Pearce, Glen Walters, Blackjack Ward, Slim Whitaker, and Blackie Whiteford.

Synopsis:
The Three Mesquiteers find themselves in a different predicament, with wild animals making way with their cattle, but the Rangers from the game preserve forbidden by the law their killing any of the marauders. The boys engage the aid of a clan of backwoods trappers, paying a bounty on each animal killed on their land in the act of destroying their cattle. Unbeknownst to the Mesquiteers, Ed Dawson and his clan are in reality the true cattle rustlers, cloaking their activity by forcing Davey, a small son of the clan, to stooge for them. Matters come to a head when one of the Rangers, who guard the game in the nearby national park, is killed, and Stony is named as the murderer.

Production Notes:
Filming began in early July 1937. Exteriors were shot in the Idyllwild area.

159

The Trigger Trio

Produced and Released by Republic Pictures Corp. on October 18, 1937. Copyright Republic Pictures Corp., October 18, 1937, LP7535. Running time, 55-56 minutes, 5,013 feet, 6 reels. *Directed by* William Witney; *associate producer*, Sol C. Siegel; *supervisor*, John T. Coyle; *screen play*, Joseph Poland and Oliver Drake; *original story*, Houston Branch and Joseph Poland; *based on characters created by* William Colt MacDonald; *photography*, Ernest Miller; *film editor*, Tony Martinelli; *musical director*, Raoul Kraushaar.

Cast:

Ray Corrigan	. . . . .	Tucson Smith
Max Terhune	. . . . .	Lullaby Joslin
Ralph Byrd	. . . . .	Larry Smith
Sandra Corday	. . . . .	Anne Evans
Robert Warwick	. . . . .	John Evans
Cornelius Keefe	. . . . .	Tom Brent
Sammy McKim	. . . . .	Mickey Evans
Hal Taliaferro	. . . . .	Luke
Willie Fung	. . . . .	Chong
Buck	. . . . .	Buck

Also featuring: Ted Billings, Bob Burns, Fred Burns, Art Davis, Jerry Frank, Henry Hall, Jack Ingram, and Harry Semels.

Synopsis:
Tucson Smith is appointed a deputy assistant to John Evans, inspector for the State Agricultural Service. His pals, Lullaby and Larry, disapprove of his fanatic vigilance in ordering the destroying of entire herds of cattle where one beast is found to be infected. But they are soon persuaded that forces even more sinister than the dread hoof-and-mouth disease are threatening the well-being of the community. Cattle rustlers, criminals who would deliberately contaminate entire herds, and even murderers, are abroad. The Mesquiteers clean them all up.

Production Notes:
Filming began on August 13, 1937, in Kernville. While the director and second unit were off filming background material, the three stars, Robert Livingston, Ray Corrigan, and Max Terhune, went to the Kern River to swim and bask in the sun. Livingston dove off the swinging bridge, which is seen in the film, but instead of diving downstream, he dove upstream, striking his head on the bottom of the river. At first it was feared that he had injured or broken his neck. He would be unavailable for filming for many weeks as he recuperated. Ralph Byrd was rapidly brought up to Kernville along with a rewritten script. Byrd received most of Livingston's role.

THE THREE MESQUITEERS

in

The
TRIGGER
TRIO

with
RAY CORRIGAN
MAX TERHUNE
and RALPH BYRD
Directed by WILLIAM WITNEY

A RE-RELEASE

Screen play by Joseph Poland
Oliver Drake · Original story by
Houston Branch, Joseph Poland
Based on characters created by
WILLIAM COLT MacDONALD
Associate producer Sol C. Siegel

A REPUBLIC PICTURE

THE THREE
MESQUITEERS
The
TRIGGER
TRIO
A RE-RELEASE
A REPUBLIC PICTURE

162

| A REPUBLIC PRODUCTION | ASSOCIATE PRODUCER SOL C. SIEGEL SUPERVISOR JOHN T. COYLE | |

A REPUBLIC PRODUCTION

THE THREE MESQUITEERS

ROBERT LIVINGSTON
Stony Brooke

RAY CORRIGAN
Tucson Smith

MAX TERHUNE
Lullaby Joslin

IN
WILD
HORSE
RODEO

ASSOCIATE PRODUCER
SOL C. SIEGEL
SUPERVISOR
JOHN T. COYLE

DIRECTED BY
GEORGE SHERMAN

Screen play
BETTY BURBRIDGE
Original story
GILBERT WRIGHT • OLIVER DRAKE
Based on Characters Created by
WILLIAM COLT MacDONALD
Photography Musical Director
WILLIAM NOBLES ALBERTO COLOMBO
Film Editor Song by
LESTER ORLEBECK FLEMING ALLAN

WITH
JUNE MARTEL
WALTER MILLER
EDMUND COBB
WILLIAM GOULD
JACK INGRAM
DICK WESTON
HENRY ISABELL
ART DILLARD
RALPH ROBINSON
SNOWFLAKE

Throughout the great southwest
large bands of wild horses
roam the arid wastelands.
The mighty leaders, unbroken
and untamed, are relentlessly
hunted down to supply the

The mighty leaders, unbroken
and untamed, are relentlessly
hunted down to supply the
wild west shows with their
greatest attractions....The
bucking broncos.

164

Wild Horse Rodeo

Produced and Released by Republic Pictures Corp. on December 6, 1937. Copyright Republic Pictures Corp., June 12, 1937 LP7734. Running time, 56 Minutes, 6 reels. *Directed by* George Sherman; *produced by* Sol C. Siegel; *supervisor*, John T. Coyle; *screen play*, Betty Burbridge; *original story*, Gilbert Wright and Oliver Drake; *based on characters created by* William Colt MacDonald; *photography*, William Nobles; *musical director*, Alberto Colombo; *film editor*, Lester Orlebeck; *song by* Fleming Allan.

Cast:

Robert Livingston	. . . . .	Stony Brooke
Ray Corrigan	. . . . .	Tucson Smith
Max Terhune	. . . . .	Lullaby Joslin
June Martel	. . . . .	Alice Harkley
Walter Miller	. . . . .	Colonel Nye
Edmund Cobb	. . . . .	Hank Bain
William Gould	. . . . .	Harkley
Jack Ingram	. . . . .	Jim
Dick Weston	. . . . .	Singer
Henry Isabell	. . . . .	Slim
Art Dillard	. . . . .	Henchman Bud
Ralph Robinson	. . . . .	Announcer
Snowflake	. . . . .	Snowflake

Also featuring: Bob Burns, Bob Card, Frank Ellis, Jerry Frank, June Gittelson, Duke Green, Jack Kirk, Kermit Maynard, Charles Murphy, and Harry Willingham.

Synopsis:

The Three Mesquiteers' already well-established knack for delivering what the western fans like is here expanded to include those audiences where robust adventure dramas, expertly handled, provide a welcome change from the usual fare. True to the tradition of the west, in that it reproduces a faithful picture of ranch life, the film is additionally interesting for a particularly sound and plausible plot, creditable performances, intelligent direction and an almost complete absence of typically absurd villainy. Against the magnificent settings of mountains and rocky plains, it tells a story of a wild horse and how opposing factions settle their differences so that the animal may be free of the rodeo life for which he was captured and again roam the open spaces.

Production Notes:

Filmed from October 13 to late October 1937. Exteriors were shot at Lone Pine and the Republic Studios backlot.

167

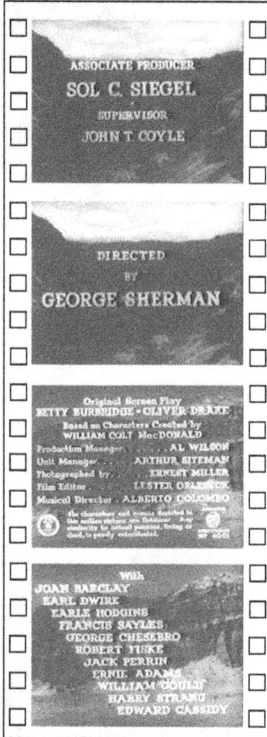

The Purple Vigilantes

Produced and Released by Republic Pictures Corp. on January 24, 1938. Copyright Republic Pictures Corp., January 24, 1938, LP7803. Running time, 58 minutes, 5,254 feet, 6 reels. *Directed by* George Sherman; *associate producer*, Sol C. Siegel; *supervisor*, John T. Coyle; *original screenplay by* Betty Burbridge and Oliver Drake; *based on characters created by* William Colt MacDonald; *production manager*, Al Wilson; *unit manager*, Arthur Siteman; *photographed by* Ernest Miller; *film editor*, Lester Orlebeck; *musical director*, Alberto Colombo.

Cast:

Robert Livingston	. . . . .	Stony Brooke
Ray Corrigan	. . . . .	Tucson Smith
Max Terhune	. . . . .	Lullaby Joslin
Joan Barclay	. . . . .	Jean McAllister
Earl Dwire	. . . . .	David Ross
Earl Hodgins	. . . . .	J. T. "Mack" McAllister
Frances Sayles	. . . . .	Detective William Jones
George Chesebro	. . . . .	Eggers
Robert Fiske	. . . . .	Drake
Jack Perrin	. . . . .	Duncan
Ernie Adams	. . . . .	Blake
William Gould	. . . . .	Jenkins
Harry Strang	. . . . .	Murphy
Edward Cassidy	. . . . .	Sheriff Dyer

Also featuring: Brandon Beach, Billy Bletcher, Bob Burns, Fred Burns, Allan Cavan, Jim Corey, Curley Dresden, Frank Ellis, Dot Farley, Herman Hack, Jack Kirk, Frankie Marvin, Merrill McCormick, George Montgomery, Frank O'Connor, Bill Patton, Edward Peil Sr., Jason Robards Sr., Lee Shumway, Tom Smith, and Wally West.

Synopsis:

The Three Mesquiteers clean up the town of Trails End, but not without a whirlwind series of lightning thrills. Excitement begins when a few law-abiding citizens in the notorious town decide to clean out lawlessness. Led by David Ross, the citizens enlist the aid of the Mesquiteers and form the "Purple Vigilantes" band, so-called because of the purple robes and masks they wear. In a short time, they have driven out the law-breakers, so the group disbands. A band of outlaws decide to steal the robes of the purple Vigilantes and begin outragous raids on the townspeople who believe the marauders are the original Vigilantes. The Three Mesquiteers roar into action to clear their names and avenge themselves.

Production Notes:

Filming began on December 13, 1937. Location work was done at the Iverson Movie Ranch and the Republic Studio backlot.

Tonight and Saturday
Air-Conditioned—Cool, Comfortable
REGENT
Tonight and Saturday
THREE BIG ATTRACTIONS! MATINEES 25c; EVENINGS 30c.
MYSTERY MOBSTERS TERRORIZE THE LAND!
THE 3 MESQUITEERS
THE PURPLE VIGILANTES
WITH
BOB LIVINGSTON
RAY CORRIGAN
MAX TERHUNE
3 STOOGES
in
"Three Missing Links"
Wow!
What a Comedy!
Extra! Special Extra!
THE OFFICIAL, EXCLUSIVE, THE THRILLING
FIGHT PICTURES
OF
JOE LOUIS--SCHMELING
The biggest upset in fight history! See the unparalleled attack by Joe Louis. See the Brown Bomber crowd 15 rounds into one round of the most vicious fighting ever filmed! It's a thrill you'll never forget!
WAS THE KIDNEY PUNCH A FOUL?
Schmeling Said Yes—the Referee Said No—What Do You Think?
SEE ALL IN SLOW MOTION!

REPUBLIC PICTURES
The 3 Mesquiteers
"The Purple Vigilantes"
BOB LIVINGSTON
RAY CORRIGAN
MAX TERHUNE
WILLIAM COLT MacDONALD
SOL C. SIEGEL
REPUBLIC PICTURES

Double Action Thrills In Two Sure Fire Adventure packed hits.
• TODAY •
KEN MAYNARD
In "Lawless Riders"
Also COMEDY and "Disaster At Sea"
Episode No. 1
SOS Coast Guard
WOOD
SUN Thru TUES. First Run
THRILLS!
Mystery Mobsters Terrorize the Land
Until your Mesquiteer Trio of Trouble Busters Blaze Into Action Against the Purple Horde!
A smile on their lips . . A six-gun in their hands —your fun-loving Trigger Trio defies death in ambush to rid the West of the Masked Menace!
"The THREE MESQUITEERS"
—In—
PURPLE VIGILANTES
Bob Livingston as Stony
Ray Corrigan as Tucson
Max Terhune & "Elmer"
Adults 15c
Swing Fever all star comedy
Knights For A Day cartoon
Child'n 10c
COMEDY!
ACTION!

A
REPUBLIC
PRODUCTION
THE THREE
MESQUITEERS
RAY CORRIGAN
Tucson Smith
The Three Mesquiteers
Lullaby Joslin
"CALL THE
MESQUITEERS"

WILLIAM BERKE
JOHN ENGLISH
Screen Play ... LUCI WARD
Photographed by ... WILLIAM NOBLES
Film Editor ... LESTER ORLEBECK
Musical Director ALBERTO COLOMBO
with
EDDIE HART
PAT GLEASON
WARREN JACKSON
HAL PRICE
FLASH

Call the Mesquiteers

Produced and Released by Republic Pictures Corp. on March 7, 1938. Copyright Republic Pictures Corp. July 3, 1938 LP7865. Running time, 55 Minutes, 6 reels. *Directed by* John English; *associate producer*, William Berke; *screen play*, Luci Ward; *original story*, Bernard McConville; *based on characters created by* William Colt MacDonald; *production manager*, Al Wilson; *unit manager*, Arthur Siteman; *photographed by* William Nobles; *film editor*, Lester Orlebeck; *musical director*, Alberto Colombo.

Cast:

Robert Livingston	. . . . .	Stony Brooke
Ray Corrigan	. . . . .	Tucson Smith
Max Terhune	. . . . .	Lullaby Joslin
Lynn Roberts	. . . . .	Madge Irving
Earle Hodgins	. . . . .	Dr. Algemon Irving
Sammy McKim	. . . . .	Timothy Irving
Eddy Waller	. . . . .	Hardy
Maston Williams	. . . . .	Phillips
Eddie Hart	. . . . .	Lefty
Pat Gleason	. . . . .	Joe
Roger Williams	. . . . .	Frank
Warren Jackson	. . . . .	Mac
Hal Price	. . . . .	Sheriff Jed Benton
Flash	. . . . .	Hawkshaw

Also featuring: Bob Burns, Bob Card, Jim Corey, Curley Dresden, Frank Ellis, Jerry Frank, Jack Ingram, Ethan Laidlaw, Bud McClure, Ralph Peters, Loren Riebe, Tom Steele, Al Taylor, and Francis Walker.

Synopsis:
A band of Eastern racketeers hijack a truck-load of silk on the plains and then attempt to pass the blame onto The Three Mesquiteers, a trio of harmless wandering rodeo riders.

Production Notes:
Filming began in mid-January 1938. Exteriors were shot at the Iverson Movie Ranch, Vasquez Rocks, and Republic Studios backlot.

THE THREE MESQUITEERS

BOB LIVINGSTON
RAY CORRIGAN
MAX TERHUNE

CALL the MESQUITEERS

Directed by John English · Screen Play by Luci Ward
Original Story by Bernard M°Conville · Based on
Characters Created by William Colt MacDonald·
Associate Producer·William Berke

A *Republic* PICTURE

Outlaws of Sonora

Produced and Released by Republic Pictures Corp. on April 14, 1938. Copyright Republic Pictures Corp. April 14, 1938 LP7967. Running time, 55-58 Minutes, 6 reels. *Directed by* George Sherman; *associate producer*, William Berke; *screen play*, Betty Burbridge and Edmund Kelson; *original story*, Betty Burbridge; *based on characters created by* William Colt MacDonald; *production manager*, Al Wilson; *unit manager*, Arthur Siteman; *photography*, William Nobles; *film editor*, Tony Martinelli; *musical director*, Alberto Colombo; *song by* Eduargo Durant, Harold Peterson, and Carlos Ruffino.

Cast:

Robert Livingston	Stony Brooke
Ray Corrigan	Tucson Smith
Max Terhune	Lullaby Joslin
Jack Mulhall	Dr. Martin
Otis Harlan	Newt
Jean Joyce	Miss Burke
Stelita Peluffo	Rosita
Tom London	Sheriff Trask
Gloria Rich	Jane
Edwin Mordant	Pierce
Ralph Peters	Gabby
George Chesebro	Slim
Frank La Rue	Coroner
Jack Ingram	Nick
Merrill McCormick	Pete

Also featuring: Ralph Bucko, Bob Burns, Fred Burns, Bob Card, Horace B. Carpenter, George Cleveland, Tommy Coats, Jim Corey, Art Dillard, Curley Dresden, Earl Dwire, Frank Ellis, Jack Kirk, George Montgomery, Dick Morehead, Jack O'Shea, Bob Reeves, Blackjack Ward, and Herman Willingham.

Synopsis:
A murderous outlaw leader, who closely resembles Stony Brooke, one of The Three Mesquiteers, takes advantage of his likeness by capturing Stony, holding him captive, and, dressed in Stony's clothes and riding Stony's horse, commits a series of daring robberies.

Production Notes:
Filmed from February 28 to early March 1938. Exteriors shot at the Iverson Movie Ranch and the Republic Studios backlot.

RAY "CRASH" CORRIGAN
in *Outlaws of Sonora*

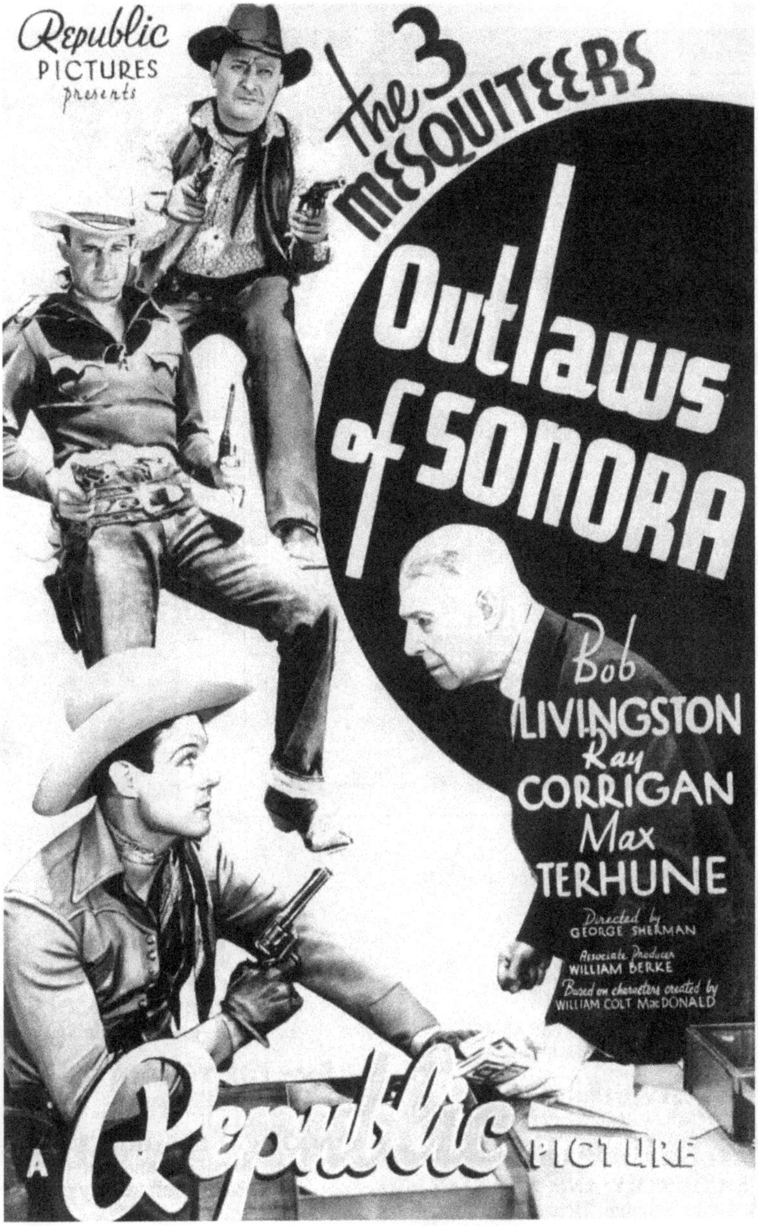
Republic
PICTURES
presents
The 3 MESQUITEERS
Outlaws of SONORA
Bob
LIVINGSTON
Ray
CORRIGAN
Max
TERHUNE
Directed by
GEORGE SHERMAN
Associate Producer
WILLIAM BERKE
Based on characters created by
WILLIAM COLT MacDONALD
A Republic PICTURE

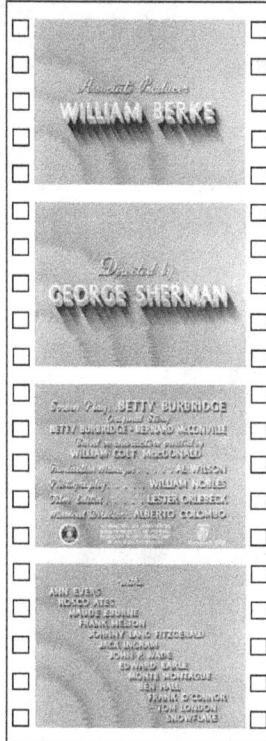

Riders of the Black Hills

Produced and Released by Republic Pictures Corp. on June 15, 1938. Copyright Republic Pictures Corp. June 15, 1938 LP8103. Running time, 55 Minutes, 6 reels. *Directed by* George Sherman; *associate producer*, William Berke; *screen play*, Betty Burbridge; *original story*, Betty Burbridge and Bernard McConville; *based on characters created by* William Colt MacDonald; *production manager*, Al Wilson; *photography*, William Nobles; *film editor*, Lester Orlebeck; *musical director*, Alberto Colombo.

Cast:

Robert Livingston	. . . .	Stony Brooke
Ray Corrigan	. . . .	Tucson Smith
Max Terhune	. . . .	Lullaby Joslin
Ann Evers	. . . .	Joyce Garth
Rosco Ates	. . . .	Sheriff Brown
Maude Eburne	. . . .	Mrs. Peg Garth
Frank Melton	. . . .	Doc Weston
Johnny Lang Fitzgerald	. . . .	Buck
Jack Ingram	. . . .	Lefty
John P. Wade	. . . .	Ed Harvey
Edward Earle	. . . .	Steward
Monte Montague	. . . .	Sam
Ben Hall	. . . .	Ethelbert
Frank O'Connor	. . . .	Doctor
Tom London	. . . .	Rod Stevens
Snowflake	. . . .	Snowflake

Also featuring: Art Dillard, Dick Elliott, George Magrill, John Merton, Milburn Morante, Jack O'Shea, Bud Osborne, Gloria Rich, David Sharpe, Lester Sharpe, Slim Whitaker, and Jette White.

Synopsis:
A famous racehorse is stolen by bandits while on the way to a western track. At the same time, The Three Mesquiteers capture a wild horse that is a perfect double for the stolen racer. Arrested as horsethieves, they prove their innocence and arrange to run the wild mustang in the race. Then the racketeers close in again, demanding the profits but the young cowhands have their own way of dealing with city crooks in thrilling fashion.

Production Notes:
Filmed between April 29 and May 11, 1938. Exteriors were shot at the Iverson Movie Ranch, Ray Corrigan Ranch, Vasquez Rocks, and Republic Studio backlot.

THE 3 MESQUITEERS

RIDERS OF THE BLACK HILLS

WITH
BOB LIVINGSTON · RAY CORRIGAN
MAX TERHUNE

Directed by GEORGE SHERMAN
Associate Producer · WILLIAM BERKE

A Republic PICTURE

Three Missing Links

Produced and Released by Columbia Pictures Corp. on July 29, 1938. Copyright Columbia Pictures Corp., June 21, 1938, L8097. Running time, 18 minutes, 2 Reels. *Directed by* Jules White; *associate producer,* Jules White; *story and screen play by* Searle Kramer; *photography,* Henry Freulich, a.s.c.; *film editor,* Charles Nelson.

Cast:

Curly	. . . . .	Curly
Larry	. . . . .	Larry
Moe	. . . . .	Moe
Monte Collins	. . . . .	Herbert
Jane Hamilton	. . . . .	Mirabel Mirabel
Naba	. . . . .	Gorilla

Synopsis:
The Three Stooges are janitors working in a movie studio. They are hired as actors in an African movie. Curly plays a gorilla while Moe and Larry are primitive natives. In Africa, Curly buys some "love candy" from a witch doctor in hopes of attracting the beautiful leading lady. When a real gorilla arrives, Curly eats some of the candy, falls in love, and chases after the gorilla.

Production Notes:
Corrigan, using his alias "Naba", played the gorilla. This Three Stooges short was filmed entirely on a sound stage in 4 days—April 7 to April 12, 1938.

Heroes of the Hills

Produced and Released by Republic Pictures Corp. on August 1, 1938. Copyright Republic Pictures Corp. August 1, 1938 LP8213. Running time, 55-56 Minutes, 6 reels. *Directed by* George Sherman; *associate producer*, William Berke; *screen play*, Betty Burbridge and Stanley Roberts; *original story*, Stanley Roberts and Jack Natteford; *based on characters created by* William Colt MacDonald; *production manager*, Al Wilson; *unit manager*, Arthur Siteman; *photography*, Reggie Lanning; *film editor*, Tony Martinelli; *song by* Eddie Cherkose and Alberto Colombo.

Cast:

Robert Livingston	Stony Brooke
Ray Corrigan	Tucson Smith
Max Terhune	Lullaby Joslin
Priscilla Lawson	Madeline Reynolds
Le Roy Mason	Red
James Eagles	The Kid
Roy Barcroft	Robert Beaton
Barry Hays	Regan
Carleton Young	Jim Connors
Forrest Taylor	Sheriff
John Wade	Board chairman
Maston Williams	Nick
John Beach	Crane
Jerry Frank	Slim
Roger Williams	Warden
Kit Guard	Mac

Also featuring: Chuck Baldra, Bob Card, Tommy Coats, Art Dillard, Curley Dresden, I. Stanford Jolley, Jack Kirk, Lew Meehan, Buck Morgan, and Gloria Rich.

Synopsis:

A genuine effort to inject something more than the customary A, B, C western formula has not been lost here. Excusing a minor flaw or two in production, the piece shows clearly as having been worked on diligently in the scenario department. It packs more than the average quota of suspense, and this more from plot construction than from the usual sneery, heavy and overloaded six-shooters. The dependable Three Mesquiteers give workmanlike performances, getting good support in direction and camera work. The trio befriends two escaped convicts, believing their story of prison oppression. They convince the board to try an outdoor prison camp experiment, which results in trouble with a construction company.

Production Notes:

Filming began on December 13, 1937. Location work was done at the Iverson Movie Ranch, Ray Corrigan Ranch, and the Republic Studio backlot. Corrigan was

187

to be replaced with Guinn "Big Boy" Williams, but complaints from exhibitors convinced Republic to retain Corrigan. After this film, Corrigan was hired on a film-by-film contract which lasted for 8 more entries in the series.

Pals of the Saddle

Produced and Released by Republic Pictures Corp. on August 28, 1938. Copyright Republic Pictures Corp., August 20, 1938, LP8300. Running time, 55 minutes, 4,933 feet, 6 reels. *Directed by* George Sherman; *associate producer* William Berke; *original screen play*, Stanley Roberts and Betty Burbridge; *based on characters created by* William Colt MacDonald; *production manager*, Al Wilson; *unit manager*, Arthur Siteman; *photography*, Reggie Lanning; *film editor*, Tony Martinelli; *musical direction*, Cy Feuer.

Cast:

John Wayne	Stony Burke
Ray Corrigan	Tucson Smith
Max Terhune	Lullaby Joslin
Doreen McKay	Ann aka Mirandy
Josef Forte	Judge Hastings
George Douglas	Paul Hartman
Frank Milan	Frank Paige
Ted Adams	Henry C. Gordon
Harry Depp	Hotel clerk
Dave Weber	Russian musician
Don Orlando	Italian musician
Charles Knight	English musician
Jack Kirk	Sheriff Johnson

Also featuring: John Beach, Bob Burns, Yakima Canutt, Art Dillard, Curley Dresden, Olin Francis, Otto Hoffman, Kenner G. Kemp, Philip Kieffer, Monte Montague, George Letz, Herman Nowlin, Tex Palmer, George Plues, Bill Yrigoyen, Joe Yrigoyen, Tommy Coats, and Nellie Walker.

Synopsis:
The Mesquiteers become involved with a munitions gang who are engaged in smuggling a valuable chemical used for poisonous gases over the border. Ann, a government agent, is the reason the boys get mixed up in the affair. Her cohort is killed by one of the gang and Stoney is forced to step in and do his duty. When the gang attempts to cross the line, the Mesquiteers in concerted action prevent it until the army takes over.

Production Notes:
Filming began on July 14, 1938. Location scenes were shot at Red Rock Canyon, the Ray Corrigan Ranch, and the Republic Studios backlot. The "Acme Salt Refinery" was located at Saltdale, near Red Rock Canyon. This is the first film for Corrigan at Republic Studios since his two-year contract expired. He now was on a per picture deal of $2,000 per.

REPUBLIC PICTURES presents THE THREE MESQUITEERS featuring JOHN WAYNE, and RAY CORRIGAN, MAX TERHUNE in "PALS OF THE SADDLE"   PRINTED IN U.S.A.

THE THREE MESQUITEERS and featuring JOHN WAYNE RAY CORRIGAN MAX TERHUNE

"PALS OF THE SADDLE"

A Republic PICTURE

192

THE THREE MESQUITEERS

"PALS of the SADDLE"

A Republic PICTURE

A REPUBLIC PRODUCTION

REPUBLIC PICTURES presents

The Three Mesquiteers

Overland Stage Raiders
featuring JOHN WAYNE and
RAY CORRIGAN · MAX TERHUNE

WILLIAM BERKE

GEORGE SHERMAN

Production Manager ... AL WILSON
Unit Manager ... ARTHUR SITEMAN
Photography ... WILLIAM NOBLES
Film Editor ... TONY MARTINELLI

JOHN WAYNE

RAY CORRIGAN

MAX TERHUNE

ROY JAMES
OLIN FRANCIS
FERN EMMETT
HENRY OTHO
GEORGE SHERWOOD
ARCHIE HALL
FRANK LA RUE

Overland Stage Raiders

Produced and Released by Republic Pictures Corp. on September 20, 1938. Copyright by Republic Pictures Corp. on September 20, 1938, LP8299. Running Time 55 Minutes, 6 reels. *Directed by* George Sherman; *associate producer,* William Berke; *screenplay by* Luci Ward; *original story,* Bernard McConville and Edmond Kelso; *based on characters created by* William Colt MacDonald; *production manager,* Al Wilson; *unit manager,* Arthur Siteman; *photography,* William Nobles; *film editor,* Tony Martinelli.

Cast:

John Wayne	. . . . .	Stony Brooke
Ray Corrigan	. . . . .	Tucson Smith
Max Terhune	. . . . .	Lullaby Joslin
Louise Brooks	. . . . .	Beth Hoyt
Anthony Marsh	. . . . .	Ned Hoyt
Ralph Bowman	. . . . .	Bob Whitney
Gordon Hart	. . . . .	Mullins
Roy James	. . . . .	Frank Harmon
Olin Francis	. . . . .	Jake
Fern Emmett	. . . . .	Ma Hawkins
Henry Otho	. . . . .	Sheriff Mason
George Sherwood	. . . . .	Clanton
Archie Hall	. . . . .	Joe Waddell
Frank La Rue	. . . . .	Milton

Also featuring: Yakima Canutt, Milton Kibbee, Jack Kirk, Slim Whitaker, Bud Osborne, Dirk Thane, Bud McClure, John Beach, Curley Dresden, George Plues, Edwin Gaffney, Fred Burns, George Morrell, Bill Wolfe, and Tommy Coats.

Synopsis:

The Three Mesquiteers are ranchers in Oro Grande County. They also have interests in some mines nearby. The Oro Grande Stage Line has been robbed several times of gold and cattle shipments, and so, to avoid any more losses, the Mesquiteers join with Ned Hoyt and his sister Beth in an attempt to establish an airline out of Oro Grande. The idea is to make the gold shipments by air. The airline is established and operates successfully until some Eastern gangsters come west, and stage a mid-air robbery. These bandits learn that Ned Hoyt has a past. He had been a pilot on an Eastern airline and had been involved in a crash, and had served time in jail for it. The Mesquiteers are held responsible for the robbery, due to their connection with Hoyt. It is up to them to not only clear him, but to capture the bandits and prove their innocence.

Production Notes:

Filmed in early August 1938. The Iverson Movie Ranch, Conejo Valley Airport, Santa Clara River and railroad along Highway 126 near Castaic, and the Republic Studios backlot were used in the production.

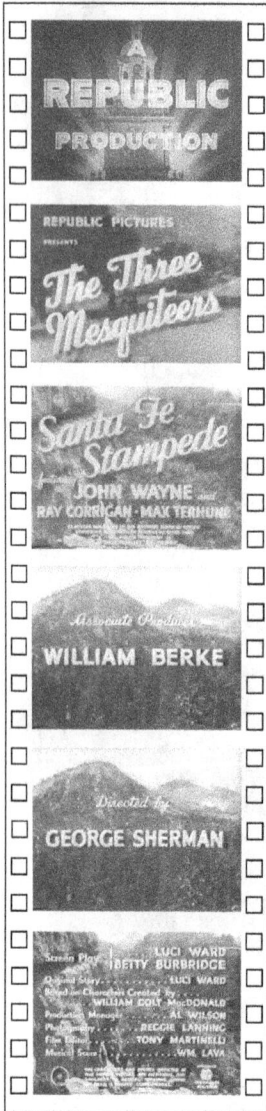

Santa Fe Stampede

Produced and Released by Republic Pictures Corp. on November 18, 1938. Copyright by Republic Pictures Corp on November 18, 1938, LP8442. Running Time 56 Minutes, 6 reels. *Directed by* George Sherman; *associate producer,* William Berke; *screenplay by* Luci Ward and Betty Burbridge; *original story,* Luci Ward; *based on characters created by* William Colt MacDonald; *production manager,* Al Wilson; *photography,* Reggie Lanning; *film editor,* Tony Martinelli; *musical score,* William Lava.

Cast:

John Wayne	. . . . . Stony Brooke
Ray Corrigan	. . . . . Tucson Smith
Max Terhune	. . . . . Lullaby Joslin
June Martel	. . . . . Nancy Carson
William Farnum	. . . . . Dave Carson
Le Roy Mason	. . . . . Mayor Gilbert Byron
Martin Spellman	. . . . . Billy Carson
Genee Hall	. . . . . Julie Jane Carson
Walter Wills	. . . . . Harris
Ferris Taylor	. . . . . Judge Henry J. Hixon
Tom London	. . . . . Marshall
Dick Rush	. . . . . Sheriff
John F. Cassidy	. . . . . Newton

Also featuring: George Chesebro, Yakima Canutt, Bud Osborne, Richard Alexander, Nelson McDowell, Curley Dresden, Bill Wolfe, Charles King, Jerry Frank, Cliff Parkinson, Bob Woodward, Blackjack Ward, Robert Milasch, Jim Corey, Frank O'Connor, Marin Sais, Russ Powell, George Morrell, Horace B. Carpenter, Bud McClure, Charles Murphy, Griff Barnette, and John Elliott.

Synopsis:
The Three Mesquiteers ride herd on a lawless western community and a group of crooked politicians who have murdered a friend of theirs in an attempt to secure the rights to a gold mine in which the Mesquiteers have an interest.

Production Notes:
Production began in early October 1938. Location work was performed at the Brandeis Ranch, Ray Corrigan Ranch, and the Republic Studios backlot.

"SANTA FE STAMPEDE"

With THE THREE MESQUITEERS

A Republic PICTURE

"SANTA FE STAMPEDE"

With THE THREE MESQUITEERS

A Republic PICTURE

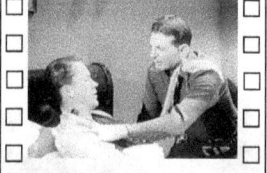

Red River Range

Produced and Released by Republic Pictures Corp. on December 22, 1938. Copyright December 22, 1938, Republic Pictures Corp., LP8559. Running time, 55-56 Minutes, 5018 feet, 6 reels. *Directed by* George Sherman; *associate producer*, William Berke; *screenplay by* Stanley Roberts, Betty Burbridge, and Luci Ward; *original story*, Luci Ward; *based on characters created by* William Colt MacDonald; *production manager*, Al Wilson; *photography*, Jack Marta; *film editor*, Tony Martinelli; *musical score*, William Lava; *assistant director*, Bill Strohbach.

Cast:

John Wayne	Stony Brooke
Ray Corrigan	Tucson Smith
Max Terhune	Lullaby Joslin
Polly Moran	Mrs. Maxwell
Lorna Gray	Jane Mason
Kirby Grant	Tex Reilly
Sammy McKim	Tommy Jones
William Royle	Payne
Perry Ivins	Hartley
Stanley Blystone	Randall
Lenore Bushman	Evelyn Maxwell
Burr Caruth	Pop Mason
Roger Williams	Sheriff Wood
Earl Askam	Morton
Olin Francis	Kenton

Also featuring: Fred Toones, Bob McKenzie, Theodore Lorch, Al Taylor, Jack Montgomery, and Edward Cassidy.

Synopsis:

The Three Mesquiteers are appointed Red River County special deputies by the Governor in order to rid the county of cattle rustlers. They arrive in time to discover that they have been preceded by an old pal, Tex Reilly, on a similar mission. Because Tex's identity is known to the rustlers, a scheme is cooked up whereby Stony Brooke vanishes and Tex assumes his identity as the third Mesquiteer.

Production Notes:

Kirby Grant made his film debut in this entry of The Three Mesquiteer series. Production began in late October 1938 and lasted through November 7, 1938. Location work was performed at the Iverson Movie Ranch, Ray Corrigan Ranch, Red Rock Canyon, and the Republic Studios backlot.

THE THREE MESQUITEERS "RED RIVER RANGE" A *Republic* PICTURE

THE THREE MESQUITEERS "RED RIVER RANGE" A *Republic* PICTURE

"RED RIVER RANGE" A Re-release Starring JOHN WAYNE, RAY CORRIGAN
A Republic Picture

Printed in U.S.A.

R53/177

The Night Riders

Produced and Released by Republic Pictures Corp. on April 12, 1939. Copyrighted by Republic Pictures Corp. on April 12, 1939, LP8797. Running Time 58 Minutes, 6 reels. *Directed by* George Sherman; *associate producer*, William Berke; *original screen play by* Betty Burbridge and Stanley Roberts; *based on characters created by* William Colt MacDonald; *production manager*, Al Wilson; *photography*, Jack Marta; *film editor*, Lester Orlebeck; *musical score*, William Lava.

Cast:

John Wayne	. . . . .	Stony Brooke
Ray Corrigan	. . . . .	Tucson Smith
Max Terhune	. . . . .	Lullaby Joslin
Doreen McKay	. . . . .	Soledad
Ruth Rogers	. . . . .	Susan Randall
George Douglas	. . . . .	Talbot
Tom Tyler	. . . . .	Jackson
Kermit Maynard	. . . . .	Sheriff
Sammy McKim	. . . . .	Tim
Walter Wills	. . . . .	Hazleton
Ethan Laidlaw	. . . . .	Andrews
Edward Peil, Sr	. . . . .	Harper
Tom London	. . . . .	Wilson
Jack Ingram	. . . . .	Wilkins
William Nestell	. . . . .	Allen

Also featuring: Cactus Mack, Lee Shumway, Hal Price, Hank Worden, Roger Williams, Olin Francis, Francis Walker, Hugh Prosser, Jack Kirk, Yakima Canutt, Glenn Strange, David Sharpe, Bud Osborne, and Georgia Summer.

Synopsis:
A ruthless gambler who poses as a Spanish nobleman, and with a phony land grant, supposedly issued by King Phillip of Spain, establishes himself as a virtual dictator over a large territory in the western United States. He immediately imposes outlandish taxes on ranchers residing in his territory and if one of them refuses to pay or cannot meet his payments, he is promptly ejected by the "dictator's" gunmen. The Mesquiteers are among these ranch owners who refuse to pay and they are forced to vacate their property. They try to organize a vigilante band but the terrified ranchers are unwilling to take the law into their own hands. The Mesquiteers then decide to strike alone. Bcause they are greatly outnumbered, they ride at night, heavily masked, and strike quickly and quietly. Thus they become known as the mysterious "Night Riders" and the way in which they complete their deadly work brings the story to its climax.

Production Notes:
Production wrapped up on February 25, 1939. Location work was performed at the west Morrison Agoura Ranch and the Republic Studios backlot.

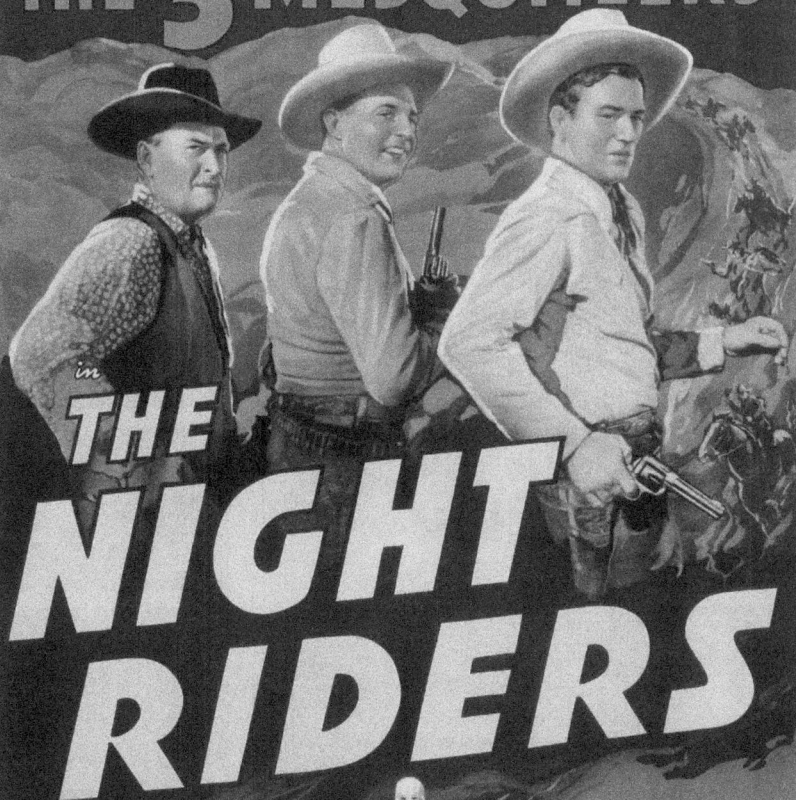

209

Three Texas Steers

Produced and Released by Republic Pictures Corp. on May 12, 1939. Copyright by Republic Pictures Corp. on May 12, 1939, LP8880. Running Time 56-57 Minutes, 6 reels. *Directed by* George Sherman; *associate producer* William Berke; *original screen play by* Betty Burbridge and Stanley Roberts; *based on characters created by* William Colt MacDonald; *production manager*, Al Wilson; *photography*, Ernest Miller; *film editor*, Tony Martinelli; *musical score*, William Lava.

Cast:

John Wayne	Stony Brooke
Ray Corrigan	Tucson Smith
Max Terhune	Lullaby Joslin
Carole Landis	Nancy Evans
Ralph Graves	George Ward
Rosco Ates	Sheriff
Collette Lyons	Lillian
Billy Curtis	Hercules
Ted Adams	Steve
Stanley Blystone	Rankin
David Sharpe	Tony
Ethan Laidlaw	Morgan
Lew Kelly	Postman
Naba	Willie the Gorilla

Also featuring: John Merton, Dave Willock, and Ted Mapes.

Synopsis:
Returning from their travels, the Mesquiteers discover that a lovely, blonde stranger, Nancy, has moved in on their ranch, bringing an entire circus with her. Through an error she has mistaken the boys' ranch for hers, newly inherited from her grandfather along with the circus. She is quartering the circus personnel on the ranch, trying to put the show which is near bankruptcy, on a paying basis. The Mesquiteers, learning of Nancy's difficulty, haven't the heart to inform her that she is on their property, and that her own ranch is decrepit and run down. So they undertake to help her rehabilitate the circus, taking her ranch as security for the funds they advance her. When it develops that Nancy's ranch is extremely valuable due to its desirability for a government dam site, Nancy thinks the boys are out to cheat her. The manner in which they prove otherwise brings the story to its climax.

Production Notes:
Filming commenced on March 17, 1939 and lasted through late March 1939. The start of the film was held up due to Wayne's participation in John Ford's *Stagecoach*. Locations used were the Brandeis Ranch, Ray Corrigan Ranch, Devonshire Downs, and the Republic Studio backlot. Corrigan performed two parts in the film: Tucson Smith and Willie the Gorilla (Naba was a stage name for Corrigan's ape).

The Three Mesquiteers
JOHN WAYNE
Ray Corrigan - Raymond Hatton
—in—
"WYOMING OUTLAW"

Wyoming Outlaw

Produced and Released by Republic Pictures Corp. on June 27, 1939. Copyrighted by Republic Pictures Corp. on June 7, 1939, LP8943. Running Time 56-58 Minutes, 6 reels. *Directed by* George Sherman; *associate producer*, William Berke; *screen play*, Betty Burbridge and Jack Natteford; *original story*, Jack Natteford; *based on characters created by* William Colt MacDonald; *production manager*, Al Wilson; *photography*, Reggie Lanning; *film editor*, Tony Martinelli; *musical score*, William Lava.

Cast:

John Wayne	. . . . .	Stony Brooke
Ray Corrigan	. . . . .	Tucson Smith
Raymond Hatton	. . . . .	Rusty Joslin
Donald Barry	. . . . .	Will Parker
Adele Pearce	. . . . .	Irene Parker
Leroy Mason	. . . . .	Balsinger
Charles Middleton	. . . . .	Luke Parker
Katherine Kenworthy	. . . . .	Mrs. Parker
Elmo Lincoln	. . . . .	U.S. marshal
Jack Ingram	. . . . .	Sheriff
David Sharpe	. . . . .	Newt
Jack Kenney	. . . . .	Amos
Yakima Canutt	. . . . .	Ed Sims

Also featuring: Dave O'Brien, Curley Dresden, Tommy Coates, Ralph Peters, Jack Kirk, Al Taylor, Bud McTaggart, Bud Buster, and Ed Payson.

Synopsis:
The Three Mesquiteers befriend an old man thrown out of his job by a ruthless politician. They are thrown in jail, later hide the old fellow's son in a cave. The final battle takes place on a cliff edge.

Production Notes:
Filming lasted from May 11 to May 20, 1939. Locations used were the Iverson Movie Ranch, Ray Corrigan Ranch, the Lancaster area, and the Republic Studios backlot.

New Frontier

Produced and Released by Republic Pictures Corp. on August 10, 1939.
Copyrighted by Republic Pictures Corp. on August 10, 1939, LP9054. Running
Time 56-57 Minutes, 6 reels. *Directed by* George Sherman; *associate producer,*
William Berke; *original screen play,* Betty Burbridge and Luci Ward; *based on
characters created by* William Colt MacDonald; *production manager,* Al Wilson;
photography, Reggie Lanning; *film editor,* Tony Martinelli; *musical score,* William
Lava.

Cast:

John Wayne	. . . .	Stony Brooke
Ray Corrigan	. . . .	Tucson Smith
Raymond Hatton	. . . .	Rusty Joslin
Phylis Isley	. . . .	Celia
Eddy Waller	. . . .	Major Steven Braddock
Sammy McKim	. . . .	Stevie
Leroy Mason	. . . .	M. C. Gilbert
Harrison Greene	. . . .	William Proctor
Reginald Barlow	. . . .	Judge Lawson
Burr Caruth	. . . .	Doc William Hall
Dave O'Brien	. . . .	Jason
Hal Price	. . . .	Sheriff
Jack Ingram	. . . .	Harmon
Bud Osborne	. . . .	Dickson
Charles Whitaker	. . . .	Turner

Also featuring: Curley Dresden, Jody Gilbert, Cactus Mack, George Chesebro,
Robert Burns, Bob Reeves, Frank Ellis, Walt LaRue, Oscar Gahan, Charles
Murphy, Herman Hack, George Plues, Wilbur Mack, and Bill Wolfe.

Synopsis:

The story deals with the efforts of an enormous utility company to evict an entire
town so that a dam may be built to supply water for a nearby city. The typical
promises of the demagogue are made to the hapless ranchers. They will be moved
from their pleasant homes which have sheltered them for generations, onto
equally pleasant farm sites in regions that will be as fertile as their own. The
simple folk are persuaded to accept new ranch sites on a nearby desert, with the
promise that a pipe line will provide irrigation and reclaim the entire region. The
dam is completed and the ranchers prepare to move to their new houses when
they discover that they have been double-crossed and the pipe line has not been
completed. The Three Mesquiteers put up a tremendous fight in the interest of
justice and, through a series of highly thrilling events, they see that the rights of
the ranchers are upheld and bring the story to a roaring climax.

Production Notes:

Filmed between June 26 and early July 1939. Location work was performed at the
Brandeis Ranch and the backlot of Republic Studios.

COLUMBIA PICTURES CORPORATION
Walter Catlett
YOU'RE NEXT!
COLLINS & DICKERSON
DEL LORD - HUGH McCOLLUM
DEL LORD
ELWOOD ULLMAN
HARRY EDWARDS
JOHN GREY
GEORGE MEEHAN
ARTHUR SEID

I MADE SUCH A FUNNY
PICTURE, THIS APE THOUGHT HE COULD
FRAME ME, THE BIG BABOON!
WALTER
CATLETT
MONTY COLLINS - DUDLEY DICKERSON

You're Next

Produced and Released by Columbia Pictures Corp. on May 3, 1940. Copyright Columbia Pictures Corp. May 21, 1940, L9683. Running Time 2 reels. *Directed by* Del Lord; *produced by* Del Lord and Hugh McCollum; *screen play by* Elwood Ullman and Harry Edwards; *story by* John Grey; *director of photography*, George Meehan, a.s.c.; *film editor*, Arthur Seid.

Cast:

Walter Catlett	. . . .	Slocum
Monty Collins	. . . .	Pruitt
Dudley Dickerson	. . . .	Sam
Roscoe Ates	. . . .	Mr. Tillson
John T. Murray	. . . .	Baby-Face Wessel
Chester Conklin	. . . .	Janitor
Dudley Dickerson	. . . .	Servant
Ray Corrigan	. . . .	Gorilla

Synopsis:
Two goofball private detectives are hired to find a millionaire who has been kidnapped by a mad scientist. They encounter a gorilla and underground tunnels.

Production Notes:
Filmed at the Short Subjects sound stages at Columbia Studios.

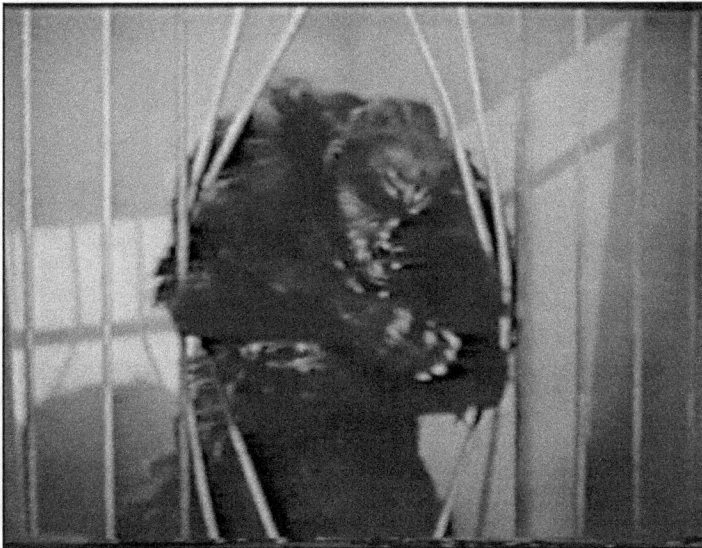

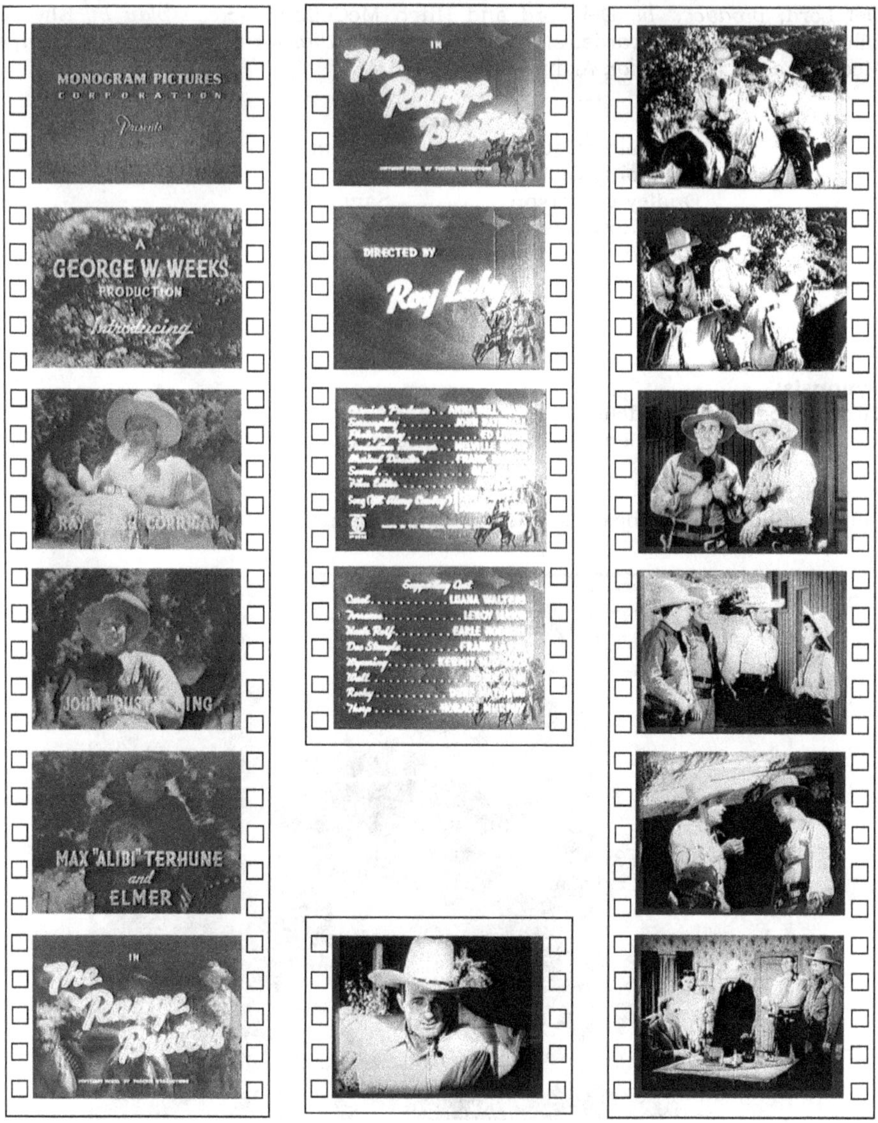

The Range Busters

Produced by George W. Weeks and Released by Monogram Pictures Corporation on August 22, 1940. Copyright Phoenix Productions Inc. on August 22, 1940, LP9955. Running Time 54-56 Minutes. *Directed by* Roy Luby; *a George W. Weeks production*; *associate producer*, Anna Bell Ward; *screenplay*, John Rathmell; *photography*, Ed Linden; *production manager*, Melville Shyer; *musical director*, Frank Sanucci; *sound*, Glen Glenn; *film editor*, Roy Claire; *Song "Get Along Cowboy"*, Lew Porter and Johnny Lange..

Cast:

Ray "Crash" Corrigan	Ray "Crash" Corrigan
John "Dusty" King	John "Dusty" King
Max "Alibi" Terhune	Max "Alibi" Terhune
Luana Walters	Carol
Leroy Mason	Torrence
Earle Hodgins	Uncle Rolf
Frank LaRue	Doc Stengle
Kermit Maynard	Wyoming
Bruce King	Wall
Duke Mathews	Rocky
Horace Murphy	Thorpe

Also featuring: Karl Hackett.

Synopsis:
A mysterious phantom is murdering the hands at the Circle T Ranch and the owner sends for the Range Busters just before he too is killed. The Range Busters quickly run into trouble with Torrence and his gang. Torrence is after the Circle T, in order to keep his cave hideout a secret. The phantom has found a rich vein in the cave and is trying to get everyone to leave the ranch.

Production Notes:
Production began in early July 1940. Filmed on location at the Ray Corrigan Ranch, Iverson Movie Ranch, and Placeritos (Monogram) Ranch.

Range Busters
Roy "Crash" Corrigan   John "Dusty" King   Max "Alibi" Terhune
A Geo. W. Weeks Production

228

The Ape

Produced and Released by Monogram Pictures Corporation on September 30, 1940. Copyright Monogram Pictures Corp., on September 24, 1940, LP9964. Running Time, 61-62 minutes, 7 reels. *Directed by* William Nigh; *in charge of production,* Scott R. Dunlap; *associate producer,* William Lackey; *suggested from the play by* Adam Hull Shirk; *adaptation by* Kurt Siodmak; *screenplay by* Kurt Siodmak and Richard Carroll; *director of photography,* Harry Neumann, a.s.c.; *assistant director,* Allen Wood; *recording engineer,* Karl Zint; *technical director,* E. R. Hickson; *film editor,* R. Schoengarth; *production manager,* C. J. Bigelow; *musical director,* Edward Kay.

Cast:

Boris Karloff	Dr. Bernard Adrian
Maris Wrixon	Frances Clifford
Gene O'Donnell	Danny
Dorothy Vaughan	Mrs. Clifford
Gertrude W. Hoffman	Housekeeper
Henry Hall	Sheriff
Selmer Jackson	Dr. McNulty
Ray Corrigan	Gorilla

Also featuring: Jack Kennedy, Jessie Arnold, Philo McCullough, and George Cleveland.

Synopsis:
Doctor Bernard Adrian is a reticent, somewhat mysterious doctor, who is not too well liked in the village where he lives, principally because he holds himself aloof. All his energies are centered on experiments looking toward making a paralyzed young neighbor girl walk. For this he must have a spinal serum, and when that which he legitimately obtains gives out, and he manages to kill a run-away ape, he dons the animal's skin and prowls around looking for victims from whom to get serum. Desperately he at last tries to kill a man to get the spinal fluid, but is shot. His patient, finally able to walk, runs to him as he is dying.

Production Notes:
Filming began on July 29, 1940. Placeritos (Monogram) Ranch was used for exterior location work.

MONOGRAM PICTURES
CORPORATION
Presents
A
GEORGE W. WEEKS
PRODUCTION
Introducing
MAX "ALIBI" TERHUNE
and
ELMER
IN
The Range Busters

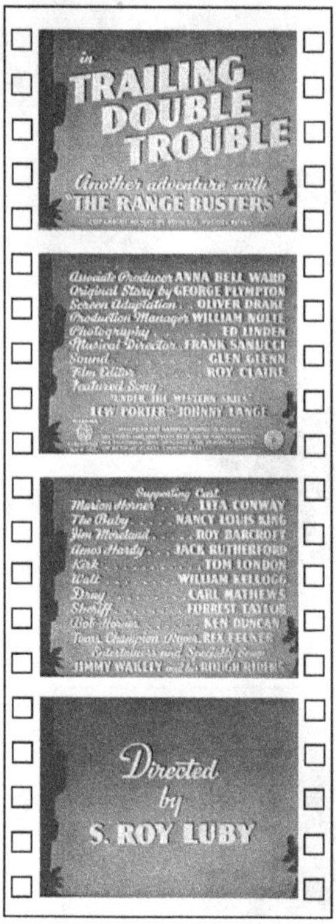
in
TRAILING DOUBLE TROUBLE
Another adventure with
"THE RANGE BUSTERS"
Associate Producer ANNA BELL WARD
Original Story by GEORGE PLYMPTON
Screen Adaptation OLIVER DRAKE
Production Manager WILLIAM NOLTE
Photography ED LINDEN
Musical Director FRANK SANUCCI
Sound GLEN GLENN
Film Editor ROY CLAIRE
Featured Song
"UNDER THE WESTERN SKIES"
LEW PORTER - JOHNNY LANGE
Supporting Cast
Marion Horner LITA CONWAY
The Baby NANCY LOUIS KING
Jim Moreland ROY BARCROFT
Amos Hardy JACK RUTHERFORD
Kirk TOM LONDON
Watt WILLIAM KELLOGG
Dray CARL MATHEWS
Sheriff FORREST TAYLOR
Bob Horner KEN DUNCAN
Texas Champion Roper REX FECKER
Entertainers and Specialty Song
JIMMY WAKELY and his ROUGH RIDERS
Directed
by
S. ROY LUBY

Trailing Double Trouble

Produced by George W. Weeks. Released by Monogram Pictures Corporation on October 10, 1940. Copyright Phoenix Productions, Inc., on September 25, 1940, LP10029. Running Time 56-58 Minutes. *Directed by* S. Roy Luby; *a George W. Weeks production*; *associate producer*, Anna Bell Ward; *original story by* George Plympton; *screen adaptation*, Oliver Drake; *production manager*, William Nolte; *photography*, Ed Linden; *musical director*, Frank Sanucci; *sound*, Glen Glenn; *film editor*, Roy Claire; *featured song "Under the Western Skies"*, Lew Porter and Johnny Lange.

Cast:

Ray "Crash" Corrigan	Ray "Crash" Corrigan
John "Dusty" King	John "Dusty" King
Max "Alibi" Terhune	Max "Alibi" Terhune
Lita Conway	Marion Horner
Nancy Louis King	The Baby
Roy Barcroft	Jim Moreland
Jack Rutherford	Amos Hardy
Tom London	Kirk
William Kellogg	Walt
Carl Mathews	Drag
Forrest Taylor	Sheriff
Ken Duncan	Bob Horner
Rex Felker	Texas Champion Roper
Jimmy Wakely and his Rough Riders	Entertainers and Specialty Songs

Synopsis:
Bob Horner is murdered. He and his sister, Marian, run the Bar H ranch. The three Range Busters witness the shooting of Horner in a wagon, drive off his assailants, and find a baby in the wagon. They take charge of the infant, and later trail down, and capture the gunmen scheming to obtain control of the ranch.

Production Notes:
Filmed at the Iverson Movie Ranch, Brandeis Ranch, and Placeritos (Monogram) Ranch.

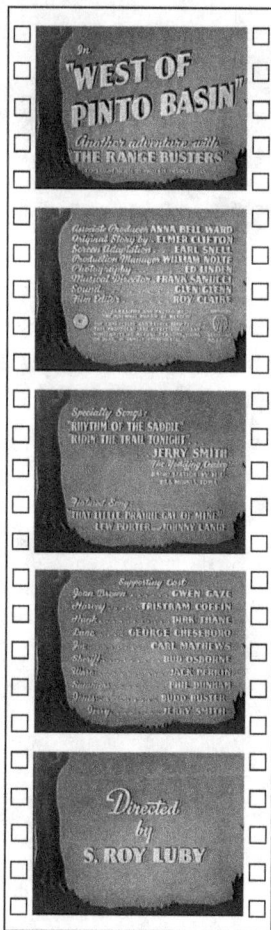

West of Pinto Basin

Produced by George W. Weeks. Released by Monogram Pictures Corporation on November 25, 1940. Copyright by Phoenix Productions Inc., on October 1, 1940, LP10158. Running Time, 60 Minutes, 6 reels. *Directed by* S. Roy Luby; *associate producer*, Anna Bell Ward; original story by Elmer Clifton; *screen adaptation*, Earl Snell; *production manager*, William Nolte; *photography*, Ed Linden; *musical director*, Frank Sanucci; *sound*, Glen Glenn; *film editor*, Roy Claire; *specialty songs*: "Rhythm of the Saddle" and "Ridin' the Trail Tonight", Jerry Smith; *featured song*: "That Little Prairie Gal of Mine", Lew Porter and Johnny Lange.

Cast:

Ray "Crash" Corrigan	Ray "Crash" Corrigan
John "Dusty" King	John "Dusty" King
Max "Alibi" Terhune	Max "Alibi" Terhune
Gwen Gaze	Joan Brown
Tristram Coffin	Harvey
Dirk Thane	Hank
George Cheseboro	Lane
Carl Mathews	Joe
Bud Osborne	Sheriff
Jack Perrin	Ware
Phil Dunham	Summers
Budd Buster	Jones
Jerry Smith	Jerry

Also featuring: Dick Cramer.

Synopsis:
When the ranchers of Pinto Basin are in danger of losing their drought-stricken land because of stagecoach robbers endangering an irrigation project, The Range Busters come to investigate. Harvey, the saloon owner, is behind the wrongdoing and hopes to force the ranchers out so he can purchase the land cheaply.

Production Notes:
Filmed on location at the Ray Corrigan Ranch and Placeritos (Monogram) Ranch. The working title of this film was "Triple Threat". Jerry Smith was billed as the yodeling cowboy of station WHO in Des Moines, Iowa.

Trail of the Silver Spurs

Produced by George W. Weeks. Released by Monogram Pictures Corporation on January 4, 1941. Copyright by Range Busters Inc., on January 5, 1941, LP10341. Running Time, 58 Minutes, 6 reels. *Directed by* S. Roy Luby; a George W. Weeks production; *associate producer,* Anna Bell Ward; *original story by* Elmer Clifton; *screen adaptation by* Earl Snell; *production manager,* William Nolte; *photography,* Robert Cline; *musical direction,* Frank Sanucci; *sound,* Glen Glenn; *film editor,* Roy Claire; *featured songs: "A Rainbow is Riding the Range" by* Lew Porter and Johnny Lange; *"Goodbye Old Paint"; photographed on the* Ray Corrigan Ranch.

Cast:

Ray "Crash" Corrigan	. . . . .	Ray "Crash" Corrigan
John "Dusty" King	. . . . .	John "Dusty" King
Max "Alibi" Terhune	. . . . .	Max "Alibi" Terhune
I. Stanford Jolley	. . . . .	Jingler
Dorothy Short	. . . . .	Nancy
Milt Morante	. . . . .	Nordick
George Chesebro	. . . . .	Wilson
Eddie Dean	. . . . .	Stoner

Also featuring: Kermit Maynard, Frank Ellis, Carl Mathews, and Steve Clark.

Synopsis:
The Range Busters help old man Nordick to get back not only his gold and mine, but his self-respect as well, defeating the Jingler, one of the sultriest villians ever. If there wasn't gold in them thar hills, so that the threesome had to salt the mine, at least there was gold in that thar cellar, with more in the adjoining ground.

Production Notes:
Filming was from middle November to late November 1941. Locations utilized were the Brandeis Ranch and the Ray Corrigan Ranch.

242

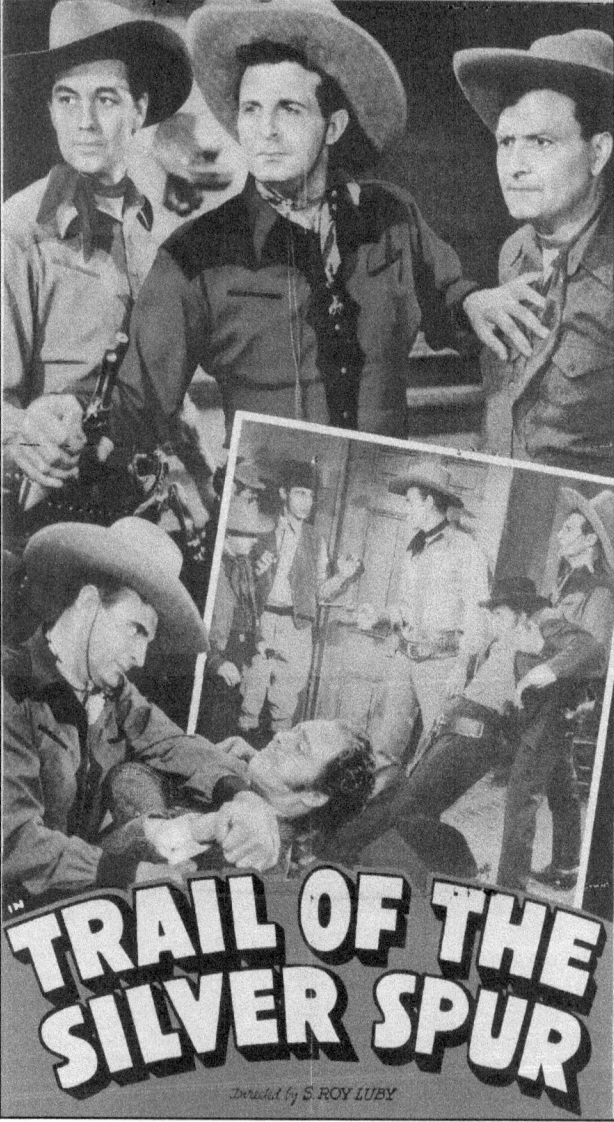

MONOGRAM PICTURES CORP presents A GEO. W. WEEKS Production

The Range Busters

RAY (Crash)   JOHN (Dusty)   MAX (Alibi)

CORRIGAN · KING · TERHUNE

IN

TRAIL OF THE SILVER SPUR

Directed by S. ROY LUBY

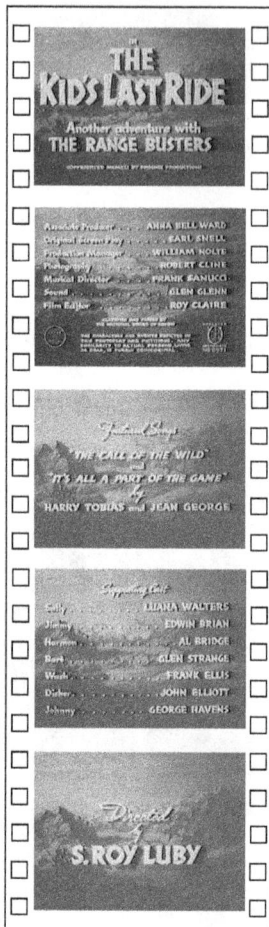

246

The Kid's Last Ride

Produced by Phoenix Productions, Inc. Released by Monogram Pictures Corp. on February 10, 1941. Copyright February 10, 1941, Range Busters Inc., LP10342. Running time, 55 minutes, 6 reels. Directed by S. Roy Luby; produced by George W. Weeks; original screenplay by Earl Snell; associate producer, Anna Bell Ward; production manager, William Notle; photography, Robert Cline; musical director, Frank Sanucci; sound, Glen Glenn; film editor, Roy Claire; featured songs, "The Call Of The Wild" by Harry Tobias and Jean George, and and "It's All A Part Of The Game" by Harry Tobias and Roy Ingraham.

Cast:

Ray "Crash" Corrigan	"Crash" Corrigan
John "Dusty" King	"Dusty" King
Max "Alibi" Terhune	"Alibi" Terhune
Elmer	Elmer
Luana Walters	Sally Rowell
Edwin Brian	Jimmy Rowell
Al Bridge	Bob Harmon, aka Jim Breeden
Glen Strange	Bart Gill, aka Ike Breeden
Frank Ellis	Henchman Wash
John Elliott	Disher
George Havens	School boy
Jack Baxley	Jack
Roy Bucko	Gambler
Jack Evans	Gambler
Herman Hack	Barfly
Al Haskell	Dealer Blackie
Walter James	Bartender
Ray Jones	Gambler
Carl Mathews	Henchman
Jack Montgomery	Barfly
George Morrell	Rancher Fleming
Tex Palmer	Henchman Tex

Synopsis:

On their way to Gopher City where they are to become peace officers, the Rangebusters are ambushed and lose their horses. Involved in a poker game at this time is Jimmy, a likeable but weak kid. Words between the boy and one of Harmon's men leads to a near shooting. The Range Busters interfere, and march Harmon's man to jail. The Range Busters are just establishing themselves when a schoolboy rushes in and tells them they are needed at the schoolhouse. Due to the fact that a skunk is underneath the schoolhouse. The two boys stay after school to question the teacher, Sally, about the set-up in the town. They learn that Jimmy is Sally's brother and a source of worry to her. Later they learn that Sally's and Jimmy's father was a prominent judge in Nebraska before moving out west.

At about the same time, through Harmon and Bart, we learn that they are in reality brothers and that their names are Breedon. The remaining two of the

Breedon brothers had previously been notorious outlaws, also in Nebraska. It was Jimmy's father who had sentenced their younger brother to the gallows and partly because of this and partly to keep Jimmy from inheriting a homestead once belonging to the Breedons. Bart and Harmon are now trying to get him involved in their outlaw activities. This plot culminates in an attempted robbery of a ranch house. While the crime is being perpetrated, the Range Busters come onto the scene. The rancher and Bart are killed and Jimmy, who was with the outlaws is wounded, but succeeds in making his escape. Sally, to shield her brother, is tricked by Harmon into going to him at the outlaw hideout. Harmon's idea is that Crash will follow. Crash does follow as Harmon expected and arrives at the hideout shortly after Sally. Crash is about to take Jimmy away with him when Sally gets the gun, covers Crash and demands that he let the boy go. Jimmy is about to ride away from the hideout when he sees Harmon and his men coming. He realizes that they are after Crash. He hurries back into the hideout, gets Crash's hat and rides away on Crash's horse. The outlaws see, think Jimmy is Crash, and give pursuit. Jimmy is shot and killed in this effort to save Crash. A gun battle between Crash and the outlaws then ensues with Dusty and Alibi arriving just in time to turn the tide of battle. The outlaws are beaten and captured and Jimmy, in death, has found himself.

Production Notes:
Filming began in mid December and ended in late December 1940. Exterior locations used were the Placeritos (Monogram) Ranch, Andy Jauregui Ranch, and Walker Ranch.

MONOGRAM PICTURES CORP presents A GEO. W. WEEKS Production
The Range Busters

RAY (Crash)
CORRIGAN · KING · TERHUNE
JOHN (Dusty)
MAX (Alibi)

IN
The KID'S LAST RIDE

Luana WALTERS · WITH · Edwin BRIAN
Directed by S. ROY LUBY

Tumbledown Ranch in Arizona

Produced by Range Busters, Inc. Released by Monogram Pictures Corp. on April 20, 1941. Copyright April 20, 1941, Range Busters, Inc., LP10514. Running tine, 60-61 minutes, 5,700 feet. *Directed by* S. Roy Luby; *produced by* George W. Weeks; *original story by* Milton Raison; *featured songs,* "Tumbledown Ranch in Arizona" and "Wake Up With the Dawn" by Bill Watters and Howard Stelner, "All Hail, Arizona" by E. C. Monroe and Dorothy H. Monroe; *production manager,* William L. Nolte; *associate producer,* Anna Bell Ward; *photography,* Robert Cline; *musical direction,* Frank Sanucci; *sound,* Glen Glenn; *film editor,* Roy Claire.

Cast:

Ray "Crash" Corrigan	Crash Corrigan
John "Dusty" King	Dusty King
Max "Alibi" Terhune	Alibi Terhune
Elmer	Elmer
Sheila Darcy	Dorothy Jones
Marian Kerby	Mother Rogers
Quen Ramsey	Gallop
James Craven	Slocum
John Elliott	Judge Uriah Jones
Jack Holmes	Sheriff Nye
Steve Clark	Shorty
Sam Bernard	Nick

Also featuring: Rex Felker, Carl Mathews, Tex Palmer, Tex Cooper, Frank Ellis, Frank McCarroll, Chick Hannon.

Synopsis:
John King, a student at Western University, is much confused, but impressed, by Professor Cooper's explanation of the Fourth Dimension.

Johnny is selected by the student body to represent the University as a contestant in the annual rodeo. Here Johnny meets a rodeo rider by the name of Ray Corrigan. Dialogue between them develops that their fathers were cronies. "Dusty" King and "Crash" Corrigan, who, with "Alibi" Terhune, constituted an old time trio, known as the Range Busters. The exploits of this trio still live in the memory of the West.

Johnny, while attempting to ride a bucking horse, is pitched onto his head and suffers a concussion, not particularly serious, but enough to relieve him of consciousness, and to allow him to escape into the Fourth Dimension. Instead of Johnny King, the student, he becomes "Dusty" King, the Range Buster, again riding with his two cronies.

Gallop, a political-boxx, is trying to force Mother Rogers to sell him a right of way across her land at his own low price. To further his campaign, he has lured away her ranch-hands. While "Crash" and "Alibi" go to town to get the ranchers back, the sheriff, in cahoots with Gallop, refuses to accept the Judge's credentials. In a phony trial, the sheriff acquits the attackers of the Judge but in the fight that follows, the Rangebusters succeed in forcing Mother Rogers' helpers back to work.

Dissatisfied with Gallop, Slocum the higher-up now attempts to defraud Mother Rogers. Telling her he wants to buy cattle, he gets her to sign a bill of sale in triplicate, the two copies of which turn out to be releases giving the railroad the right-of-way.

When Mother Rogers and the Rangebusters disrupt the railroads efforts to lay their track, Mother Rogers is arrested but by now the Judge has definite proof of his office and holding trial, he admits her to bail. The Rangebusters decide to burglarize Gallop's possessions to gain the original bill of sale.

But meanwhile Gallop tries to blackmail Slocum over this paper and in a fight Slocum is killed. Gallop escapes in time to elude "Crash" and "Dusty" but the sheriff finds them with the body and arrests them. As Gallop reappears and is about to burn the bill of sale, he is caught by "Alibi" with enough evidence to hang him.

A dissolve discovers "Dusty", again the college student, on a hospital cot. He is just arousing from his unconsciousness. Beside the cot is the counterpart of the Judge's daughter, but now she is clothed in modern nurse's garb.

"Dusty" thinks he recognizes her as Dorothy Jones. The girl tells him that Dorothy Jones was the maiden name of her mother. "Dusty" concludes that he has been riding in the Fourth Dimension.

Production Notes:
Filmed between February 23 and early March 1941 at the Ray Corrigan Movie Ranch in Simi Valley, California, and at the University of Arizona's annual Rodeo.

252

Range Gangsters Scattered Like Rats On The Run When Rangebuster Law Came To Town!!

MONOGRAM PICTURES CORP presents *The Range Busters*

a GEO. W WEEKS Production

RAY (Crash) · JOHN (Dusty) · MAX (Alibi)
CORRIGAN · KING · TERHUNE

TUMBLEDOWN RANCH in ARIZONA

Directed by S. ROY LUBY

Featured Song "TUMBLEDOWN RANCH IN ARIZONA"

HERE THEY ARE! "THE RANGE BUSTERS"

John (*Dusty*) King   Ray (*Crash*) Corrigan   Max (*Alibi*) Terhune

1 Col. Star Cut or Mat No. 3   1 Col. Star Cut or Mat No. 4   1 Col. Star Cut or Mat No. 5

255

P O S T E R S

MONOGRAM PICTURES CORP. presents A GEO. W. WEEKS Production
THE RANGE BUSTERS
RAY (Crash)   JOHN (Dusty)   MAX (Alibi)
CORRIGAN — KING — TERHUNE
"TUMBLEDOWN RANCH IN ARIZONA"
Directed by S. ROY LUBY

SIX SHEET

22 x 28

1 SHEET

2 TO A SET

3 SHEET

NEWEST "RANGEBUSTERS" PICTURE PROMISES SOMETHING DIFFERENT

"TUMBLEDOWN RANCH IN ARIZONA" PRESAGES NEW TYPE OF WESTERN

(Advance)

Not content with stealing the thunder of the old guard Western movie-makers, "Crash" Corrigan, "Dusty" King and "Alibi" Terhune, the celebrated "Rangebusters" trio come to the Theatre next .... in their latest, and as reports have it, their greatest triumph, "Tumbledown Ranch In Arizona."

Echoes from the Hollywood battlefield have it that not only does the picture have a mouthful of name but it has a mouthful of action, melody and story for it seems that with the making of "Tumbledown Ranch" the producer, George W. Weeks and the Rangebusters have succeeded in dismantling completely the old type of bang-bang epic in favor of a streamlined, smooth and brilliant production heretofore never attempted in Hollywood.

1 Col. Scene Cut or Mat No. 8

Photographed on "Crash" Corrigan's ranch in Arizona, the picture uses an entirely new technique in story telling and fans and critics have agreed that this latest effort of the boss is going to change a lot of picture making habits.

Not the least of the innovations is the melody part of the production. "Tumbledown Ranch In Arizona" and "Wake Up With The Dawn" have been top flight radio and recording smashes since their introduction and the boys give what the trade calls "terrific" renditions of them.

New Western Hit Filmed On Corrigan's Acres

(Current)

If "Crash" Corrigan appears to be more at ease than usual during the activity of "Tumbledown Ranch In Arizona" now playing at the .... Theatre, it's probably because he felt perfectly at home during the making of the picture.

This latest smash-hit starring the Rangebusters was filmed at the University of Arizona during that institution's celebrated Rodeo and later at "Crash's" ranch in Arizona. So why shouldn't the popular leader of this dashing trio feel "right in the groove"?

Featured in this new Monogram release are two smash tunes composed especially for the Rangebusters and sung by them with such great success that they have recently climbed high on the nation's hit-parade.

Hit Tunes Featured In New Film

(Advance)

Film fans who demand the best in action, romance, laughter and melody are in for the time of their lives beginning next .... when "Tumbledown Ranch In Arizona" starring that slam-bang musical trio, "The Rangebusters" comes to the .... Theatre for a .... day engagement.

Not only is this, their latest film, loaded with dynamite and romantic fervor but it enjoys more than its share of top-notch musical appeal. Two song hits which already have reached the "Hit-Parade" rating are important parts of the festivities.

Taking its title from the name of the picture "Tumbledown Ranch In Arizona" is a smooth ditty that has proved popular with all dance bands; juke-box fiends, radio broadcasters and songsters from coast to coast.

Right on its heels comes a lively little tune called "Wake Up With The Dawn" and it is proving to be a mighty fine running mate to "Tumbledown Ranch" in its quest for national recognition.

Both of these melodies are the brain-children of a pair of talented west-coast musicians Bill Watters and Howard Steiner. The songs were not wildcats picked up to fill in but were written especially for the production which was under the supervision of George W. Weeks for Monogram distribution.

"Tumbledown Ranch In Arizona" is a thrilling tale of a railroad and land boom in the old west wherein the Rangebusters fall into a neatly laid plot to divest an aged widow of her land and money.

2 Col. Scene Cut or Mat No. 19

Plug "Tumbledown Ranch In Arizona" Through These Hit Tunes and Add To Your Receipts

"Tumbledown Ranch In Arizona" is not only a bang-up show as far as action is concerned but it offers movie fans a chance to hear two of the nation's biggest song smashes.

"Tumbledown Ranch In Arizona" and "Wake Up With The Dawn" both by Bill Watters and Howard Steiner are the smooth melodies that are selling in sheet and record form from coast to coast. Every music store will be happy to help you plug the picture by cooperating with displays, etc.

Displayed here is the cover-sheet of the music, available everywhere. Below you'll find where you can procure a good supply of displays like the one illustrated. Order a load now—tie up with your local merchants and see the results at your Box-Office.

"Tumbledown Ranch In Arizona" has been recorded by the following companies and artists: see that you take advantage of this opportunity to plug the picture.

DECCA: Dick Powell assisted by the Foursome & Victor Young and His Orchestra. Record: 3389-A.

BLUEBIRD: Freddie Martin and His Orchestra. Vocal by Clyde Rogers. Record: B-10830-B.

VOCALION: Frankie Masters and His Orchestra. Vocal by Frankie Masters and His Swing Masters. Record: 5603.

For further information and orchestrations get in touch with
BROADWAY MUSIC CORPORATION
1619 BROADWAY, NEW YORK CITY

258

Wrangler's Roost

Produced by Range Busters, Inc. Released by Monogram Pictures Corp. on June 4, 1941. Copyright April 6, 1941, Range Busters, Inc., LP10701. Running time 57-58 minutes, 5,130 feet, 6 reels. *Directed by* S. Roy Luby; *produced by* George W. Weeks; *production* manager, William L. Nolte; *associate producer*, Anna Bell Ward; original story by Earle Snell; *screen adaption*, John Vlahos and Robert Finkel; *photography*, Robert Cline; *musical direction*, Frank Sanucci; *sound*, Glen Glenn; *film editor*, Roy Claire; *featured songs*, "Wrangler's Roost" by Roger Lohrman and Ekko Whelan and "Joggin" by Romero, Ekko Whelan and Roger Lohrman; *assistant director*, Bobbie Ray; *photographed on the* Ray Corrigan Ranch.

Cast:

Ray "Crash" Corrigan	Crash Corrigan
John "Dusty" King	Dusty King
Max "Alibi" Terhune	Alibi Terhune
Elmer	Elmer
Forrest Taylor	The Deacon
Gwen Gaze	Molly Collins
George Chesebro	Miller
Frank Ellis	Brady
Jack Holmes	Joe Collins
Walter Shumway	Grover

Also featuring: Frank McCarroll, Carl Mathews, Hank Bell, Tex Palmer, Jim Corey, Al Haskell, Ray Jones, Horace B. Carpenter, Tex Cooper, Herman Hack, Chick Hannon.

Synopsis:

On the trail of Black Bart, notorious stage coach bandit, the Rangebusters learn he is extremely courteous, always carries an unloaded gun and has a habit of playing the number "3" in all gambling enterprises. They enter Apache Butte separately and discover the town wide-open. A man known as "The Deacon" is trying to bring order via religion while Miller and Brady, owners of the leading saloon and gambling den are running the town's Barbary Coast from the El Dorado. They also discover Molly Collins, the prettiest gal in town.

Crash arouses Miller's suspicions by playing the number "3" at roulette and winning heavily. At a church social, Brady and his men start a fracas when The Deacon pulls a gun and scares the brawlers. When The Rangebusters learn the gun was unloaded, they begin to suspect the suave Deacon. Then when he later enters Brady's saloon and starts winning heavily at poker by playing treys exclusively, the Rangebusters are almost certain he is their man. They decide to follow The Deacon on his next trip. Crash rides the stage but Dusty and Alibi are trapped by Brady, set on their trail by Miller.

Miller, disguised as Black Bart attempts a hold-up of the stage, but Crash drives him off with a shot. Confronted then by The Deacon, Miller shoots him. Crash returning, finds The Deacon but finds two hats, Miller's with a bullet hole in it and realizes The Deacon was not the bandit. Taking The Deacon's horse,

Crash follows Miller's trail to the hide-out where Brady has Alibi and Dusty as prisoners.

Miller spots Crash approaching the hut through the window and prepares to shoot him as he gets into range but the prisoners pull a surprise trick and start a free-for-all. In the ensuing mix-up, Miller accidentally kills Brady and as he tries a getaway, Crash rides up to shoot him down. The Deacon is absolved, Apache Butte is cleaned of its unsavory element and nobody is the wiser—except perhaps The Rangebusters, who ride off, waving good-bye to The Deacon and Molly.

Production Notes:

Filmed from mid April to early May, 1941, at the Ray Corrigan Movie Ranch in Simi Valley, California. There is a written opening forward after the credits: "In the annals of Western outlaws, there was no more colorful, more elusive figure than Black Bart, who committed all his robberies with an unloaded rifle. With scores of stagecoach robberies to his credit, he successfully baffled a frantic express company by keeping his identity unknown, until a carelessly dropped hand-kerchief with a laundry mark led to his capture. Then, after a long term in prison he was paroled. He then disappeared and how he eventually finished his days is a mystery."

262

RANGEBUSTERS GAINING
RAPIDLY IN LATEST FILM POLL

MONOGRAM'S TRIO RANKS THIRD
ON RECENT BALLOT

(Advance)

Film fans who like statistics will be interested if not downright amazed when the latest Trade Paper Poll of Box-Office ratings are released because for the first time in the history of the movie industry a brand-new group of stars has succeeded in crashing the "Big Three" of Western money-makers before their first group of pictures has been completed.

Monogram Pictures has this record-breaking trio under contract; "Crash" Corrigan, "Dusty" King and "Alibi" Terhune, "The Rangebusters" are the boys and at the moment they are worth their weight in gold for in less than twelve months they have come from nowhere to rank third in the national poll.

"Wrangler's Roost," their latest streamlined smash which comes to the .... Theatre for a .... day

1 Col. Scene Cut or Mat No. 8

run beginning .... is in the true Rangebuster tradition for in it the boys show enough stuff, songs and trip-hammer action to please the most avid western fan.

"Wrangler's Roost" is a wild and thrilling tale of old Arizona which has brought cheers from critics and fans for its smashing daring action and smooth melody. S. Roy Luby directed for George W. Weeks, the producer.

Here is entertainment for the entire family. Don't fail to see it.

'Wrangler's Roost' Features Melodies

(Current)

"Wrangler's Roost," the newest Rangebuster hit currently playing at the .... Theatre follows the pattern of previous Rangebuster pictures as far as music is concerned. "Wrangler's Roost" boasts two popular ditties which are rapidly taking the nation by storm, "Wrangler's Roost" which takes its name from the picture and a novelty ditty, "Joggin'" help make this latest picture from the Rangebuster camp just a bit better than its predecessors, and that, sir, makes "Wrangler's Roost" almost "out of this world," as any Rangebuster fan will attest. These boys, "Crash" Corrigan, "Alibi" Terhune and "Dusty" King have the happy knack of turning out just about the best in western action films.

S. Roy Luby directed from a script by Earl Snell.

Jilted By A Girl—
Starts Famous Trio

(Advance)

"Crash" Corrigan, "Dusty" King and "Alibi" Terhune, whose latest hit "Wrangler's Roost" comes to the .... Theatre, for a .... day run beginning .... were brought together by, of all strange things, three blighted romances.

A very pretty young lady in Hollywood appealed to three unknown extras at the same time. For a while the young lady was showered with affection by three swains who kept falling over each other's feet trying to beat each other's time; then when the lady in question upped and eloped with a ribbon salesman, three broken cowboy hearts resulted.

Misery loves company and Corrigan, King and Terhune found themselves, three strangers to that moment, offering each other solace. When notes had been compared and stock taken, they decided that in union there was strength. Taking the bit in their mouths, they decided that instead of being extras, they'd turn themselves into stars.

Calling themselves "The Rangebusters," they approached Monogram's George Weeks who is celebrated for "taking chances." They demanded (and got) a screen test, they demanded (and got) star billing and Mr. Weeks got himself a smash-bang trio of box-office wallopers. Since their first picture less than a year ago, "The Rangebusters" have climbed to the number 3 position in the box-office ratings of the western movie stars.

"Wrangler's Roost" is a slambang epic of old Arizona and adds further to the trio's laurels.

2 Col. Scene Cut or Mat No. 20

264

Australian Lassie In New Film

(Current)

Although Gwen Gaze, appearing with The Rangebusters in their latest hit "Wrangler's Roost" currently playing at the .... Theatre, was born way "down under" in Melbourne, Australia, she received her schooling in New York City. No, she didn't go home for lunch!

Gwen, who is Melbourne's gift to the movie colony, later studied in London and appeared in numerous stage hits in the British capital. Then she returned to America and Hollywood where movie-makers have seen that she hasn't had many idle moments. Miss Gaze is currently one of the most sought-after leading ladies in the film center.

"Crash" Corrigan, "Dusty" King and "Alibi" Terhune provide the excitement in "Wrangler's Roost" when they shoot the works to clean up a mushroom town. They fall in love in true Rangebuster style, fight their way into plenty of trouble and then turn about and fight their way out.

Hit tunes "Wrangler's Roost" and "Joggin'" help make this latest Rangebuster production a true companion to their previous efforts.

In addition to The Rangebusters and Miss Gaze, the cast includes an all-star list of talent. Forrest Taylor, George Chesebro, Jack Holmes and Frank Ellis head the supporting players. Produced by George W. Weeks for Monogram Pictures, "Wrangler's Roost" was directed by S. Roy Luby from a story by Earl Snell.

Last Showing Of Rangebuster Film

(Current)

It's last call for Rangebuster fans to see their favorites for with tonight's performance at the .... Theatre, "Wrangler's Roost" closes up shop and moves along to other pastures. And since this latest Rangebuster show is the best of the series so far, it's a mighty foolish fan who turns down this last opportunity to enjoy swell screen entertainment.

In "Wranglers Roost," The Rangebusters blow the top off an Arizona mushroom town while pretty Gwen Gaze, Australian lass blows, the top off their collective hearts and with plenty of swell tunes, a merry time is had by all.

An all star cast aids in keeping the pace at breakneck speed. Produced by George W. Weeks for Monogram, the picture was directed by S. Roy Luby.

"WRANGLER'S ROOST" PROVIDES 'BUSTERS WITH PERFECT SCRIPT

LATEST PICTURE RANKS WITH BEST WESTERNS OF THE YEAR

(Review)

It's about time that somebody in Hollywood began to think of a special award — one for the outfit that has succeeded in completely refurbishing the old time bang-bang western to a new streamlined, smooth entertaining bit of entertainment; because Monogram's Mr. George Weeks and his three Rangebusters certainly should be cited — especially after turning out their latest smasheroo, "Wrangler's Roost" which came yesterday to the .... Theatre for a .... day engagement.

1 Col. Scene Cut or Mat No. 9

"Wrangler's Roost" is just about as classy a screenplay as you'll ever care to see. Around Corrigan, King and Terhune, three young men who know their way around, Producer Weeks has taken an excellent dramatic tale of old-time Arizona, some delightful music and a competent cast of supporting players to turn out sixty odd minutes of top-notch entertainment.

The Rangebusters try to clean up a mushroom town and discover both their friends and enemies to be desperados; they try their luck at roulette and win a fortune; they try their hands at romance and quickly lose their hearts; and finally when they get into a wild gun-fight they nearly succeed in losing their lives. But they slam their way out of danger, straighten out the tangle as to the identity of the true crooks and ride away to further adventure.

Under S. Roy Luby's smart direction, "Wrangler's Roost" pursues a trip-hammer pace.

2 Col. Scene Cut or Mat No. 19

266

Fugitive Valley

Produced by Range Busters, Inc. Released by Monogram Pictures Corp. on July 30, 1941. Copyright July 30, 1941, Range Busters, Inc., LP10711. Running time, 62 minutes, 5,459 feet. *Directed by* S. Roy Luby; *produced by* George W. Weeks; *associate producer*, Anna Bell Ward; *director of photography*, Robert Cline; *sound*, Glen Glenn; *original story*, Oliver Drake; *dialogue and continuity*, John Vlahos and Robert Finkel; *musical direction*, Frank Sanucci; *film editor*, Roy Claire; *production manager*, William L. Nolte; *assistant director*, Bob Ray; *featured songs*, "Riding Along" and "My Little Prairie Annie", *music by* Jean George, *lyrics by* Harry Tobias, and "The Chisholm Trail", *sung by* Doye O'Dell.

Cast:

Ray "Crash" Corrigan	Crash Corrigan
John "Dusty" King	Dusty King
Max "Alibi" Terhune	Alibi Terhune
Elmer	Elmer
Julie Duncan	Ann
Glenn Strange	Gray
Bob Kortman	Red Langdon
Ed Brady	Doctor
Tom London	Warren
Reed Howes	Brandon
Carl Mathews	Slick
Edward Peil, Sr.	Jailer
Doye O'Dell	Jim

Also featuring: Frank McCarroll.

Synopsis:
Ann is a leader of a band of avenging and revengeful homesteaders who are willing to fight for their property with their lives in the balance. And as a leader, Ann scorns directing operations from her desk to lead the band in actual battle. When Ann and the Range Busters meet in head-on battle and when romance throws everybody's plans out of joint, plenty of novel and exciting developments take place. In the end, Corrigan, King, and Terhune discover themselves involved in not one but two gang wars and only by some mighty headwork and mighty fast shooting are they able to extricate themselves.

Production Notes:
Filmed from early June to mid June 1941 with location scenes done at the Ray Corrigan Ranch.

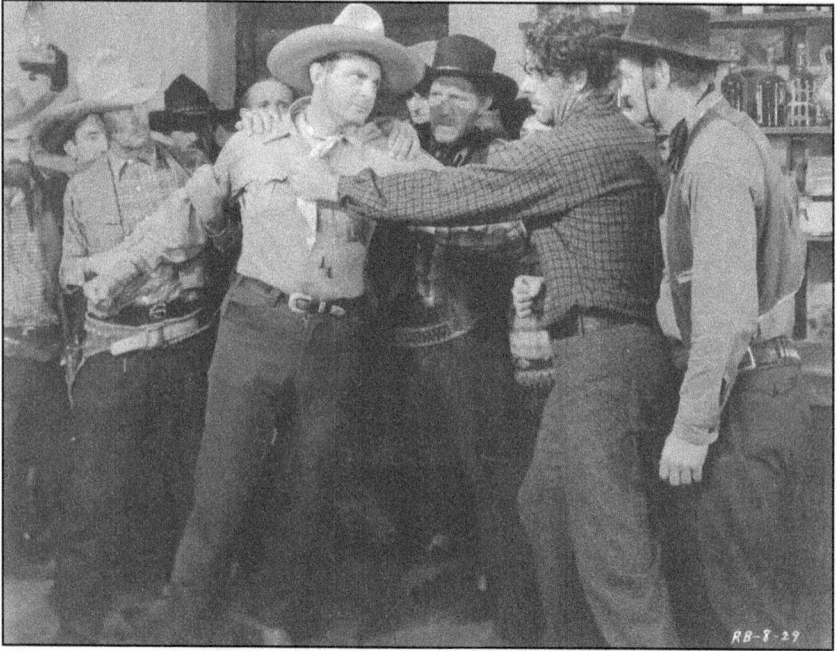

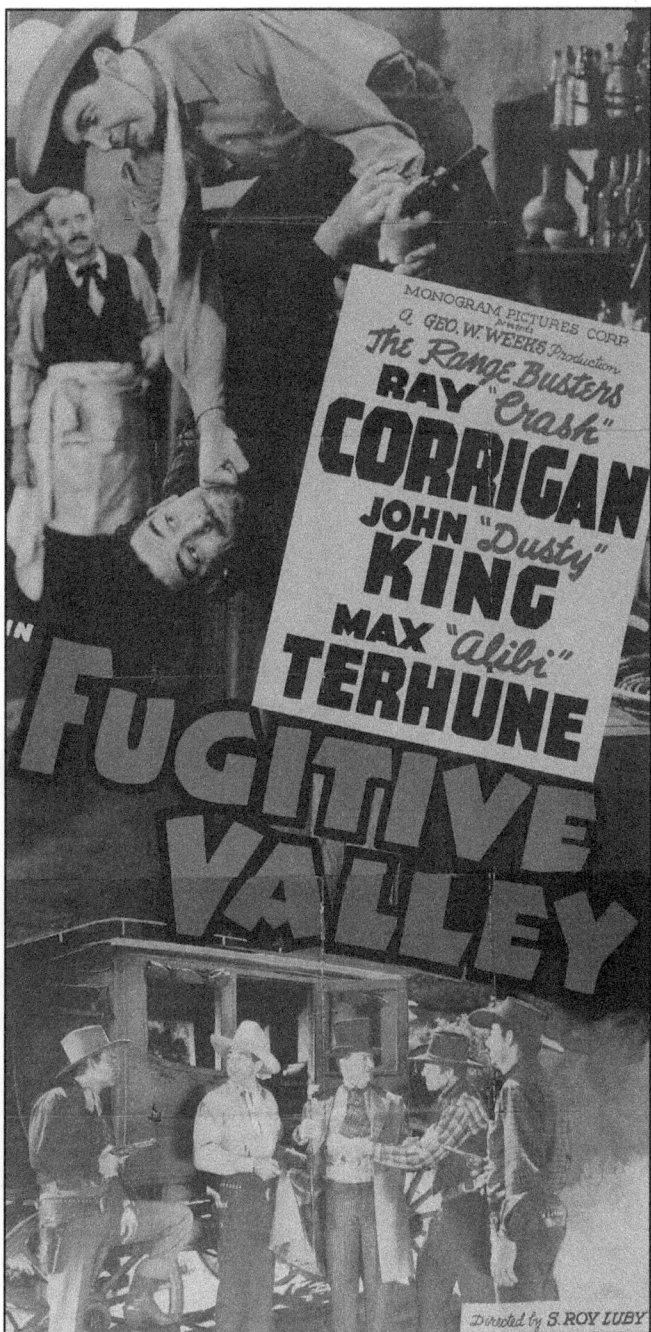

MONOGRAM PICTURES CORP
presents
a GEO. W. WEEKS Production
THE Range Busters
RAY "Crash"
CORRIGAN
JOHN "Dusty"
KING
MAX "Alibi"
TERHUNE

FUGITIVE VALLEY

Directed by S. ROY LUBY

272

Saddle Mountain Roundup

Produced by George W. Weeks. Released by Monogram Pictures Corporation on August 29, 1941. Copyright Range Busters Inc. August 31, 1941, LP10702. Running Time, 60 Minutes. *Directed by* S. Roy Luby; *a George W. Weeks production; production manager,* William L. Nolte; *associate producer,* Anna Bell Ward; *original story,* William L. Nolte; *dialogue and continuity,* John Vlahos and Earle Snell; *director of photography,* Robert Cline; *musical director,* Frank Sanucci; *sound,* Glen Glenn; *film editor,* Roy Claire; *featured songs: "The Doggone Dogie Got Away" and "That Little Green Valley of Mine",* music by Jean George, *lyrics by* John Dusty King; *"The Little Brown Jug"; photographed on the Ray Corrigan Ranch.*

Cast:

Ray "Crash" Corrigan	Ray "Crash" Corrigan
John "Dusty" King	John "Dusty" King
Max "Alibi" Terhune	Max "Alibi" Terhune
Lita Conway	Nancy
Jack Mulhall	Freeman
Willie Fung	Fang Way
John Elliott	Magpie Harper
George Chesebro	Blackie
Jack Holmes	Sheriff
Steve Clark	Henderson
Carl Mathews	Bill
Himself	Cousin Herald Goodman

Also featuring: Al Ferguson, Slim Whitaker, and Tex Palmer.

Synopsis:
An old man, Magpie Harper, and his Chinese servant, Fang Way, are in danager of becoming victims of the ruthless killer, "The Raven." Harper sends for The Range Busters. Crash and Dusty arrive to find Harper murdered. Then Alibi, who was bringing the Range Busters' cattle drive money, fails to show up. Dusty accidently finds a secret mine tunnel that leads to Alibi whom he sets free. Returning they see the murderer fleeing, but Crash is nearby to chase after him.

Production Notes:
Filmed from mid to late July 1941. Exteriors were filmed at the Ray Corrigan Ranch and the Andy Jauregui Ranch. Cousin Herald Goodman was a radio star on KVOO in Tulsa, Oklahoma, and WHO in Des Moines, Iowa. The magazine "Cowboy Movie Thrillers" for December 1941 (Frank A. Munsey Company), contained the story "Saddle Mountain Roundup" (see next page for a sample). It also appeared in a Big Little Book in 1942: "The Range Busters in Saddle Mountain Roundup", Retold from the MONOGRAM MOTION PICTURE (A George

W. Weeks Production) by Eleanor Packer, Illustrated by Henry E. Vallely[1], Whitman Publishing Company.

---

[1] A Big, Little Book measured about 3.5 x 4.5 x 1.5 inches. This one was 424 pages in length. Text was on the left hand page and the illustration on the right hand page. There was also a miniature illustration in the upper right corner of each odd number page, and if you flipped through the book, that illustration would appear to be animated. The books originally sold for a dime.

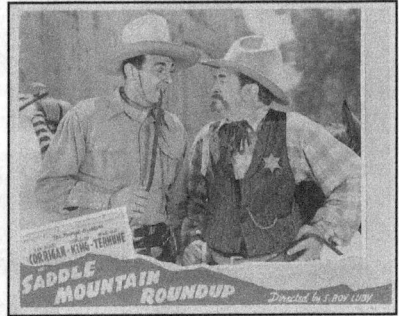

275

MONOGRAM
PICTURES INC
A
GEORGE W. WEEKS
PRODUCTION
STARRING

'TONTO BASIN
OUTLAWS'
RANGE BUSTERS
'CABIN OF MY DREAMS'
Music by Jean George
Lyrics by . . . John King
Frank Sanucci
WILLIAM L. NOLTE
ANNA BELL WARD
EARLE SNELL
JOHN VLAHOS
ROBERT CLINE
GLEN GLENN
ROY CLAIRE
Supporting Cast
JAN WILEY
TRISTRAM COFFIN
EDMUND COBB
TED MAPES
ART "DUSTBOWL" FOWLER
CARL MATHEWS
REED HOWES
REX LEASE
EDWARD PEIL, Sr.
BUDD BUSTER
DIRECTED BY
S. ROY LUBY

HOTEL

Tonto Basin Outlaws

Produced by George W. Weeks. Released by Monogram Pictures Corporation on October 10, 1941. Copyright Range Busters Inc., October 10, 1941, LP10918. Running Time, 60 Minutes. *Directed by* S. Roy Luby; *a George W. Weeks production; production manager,* William L. Nolte; *associate producer,* Anna Bell Ward; *original story,* Earle Snell; *dialogue and continuity,* John Vlahos; *director of photography,* Robert Cline; *sound,* Glen Glenn; *film editor,* Roy Claire; *featured song,* "Cabin of My Dreams", *music by* Jean George, *lyrics by* John King; *musical direction,* Frank Sanucci; *photographed on the Ray Corrigan Ranch.*

Cast:

Ray "Crash" Corrigan	. . . . .	Ray "Crash" Corrigan
John "Dusty" King	. . . . .	John "Dusty" King
Max "Alibi" Terhune	. . . . .	Max "Alibi" Terhune
Jan Wiley	. . . . .	Jane
Thristram Coffin	. . . . .	Miller
Edmund Cobb	. . . . .	Stark
Ted Mapes	. . . . .	Ricks
Art "Dustbowl" Fowler	. . . . .	Brown
Carl Mathews	. . . . .	Ed
Reed Howes	. . . . .	Captain
Rex Lease	. . . . .	Newspaper editor
Edward Peil, Sr.	. . . . .	Photographer
Budd Buster	. . . . .	Stage Driver

Also featuring: Tex Palmer, Hank Bell, Denver Dixon, and Jim Corey.

Synopsis:
The Range Busters, a well-established threesome with the action clientelle, saddle up again in this sloppily scripted shoot-'em-up saga and come out with disappointing fare for the western exhibitor. Plot rambles all over the place, and throughout the fan is aware of a constant struggle by the cast to overcome the screenplay. Time is 1898 and the first reel shows the Range Busters enlisting as Rough Riders. They're scarcely uniformed when they're ordered to report back to Wyoming as undercover agents to combat a gang of cattle rustlers. There's the ordinary disguise as cowhands out of jobs. Jane, a reporter from the Denver Daily, also arrives in town in search of a story, and is posing as a waitress. The Range Busters learn that Miller is behind the rustlers, but Miller also discovers that they are the Range Busters and on his trail. He and his gang engage the out-numbered Crash and Alibi in a fight, but Dusty stampedes a large herd of Miller's stolen cattle into the midst of the fight.

Production Notes:
Filming began on September 17, 1941. Exteriors were shot at the Ray Corrigan Ranch.

MONOGRAM PICTURES CORP presents A GEO. W. WEEKS Production
The Range Busters
RAY (Crash) CORRIGAN · JOHN (Dusty) KING · MAX (Alibi) TERHUNE
and ELMER
IN TONTO BASIN OUTLAWS
Directed by S. ROY LUBY

MONOGRAM PICTURES CORP presents A GEO. W. WEEKS Production
The Range Busters
RAY (Crash) CORRIGAN · JOHN (Dusty) KING · MAX (Alibi) TERHUNE
and ELMER
IN
TONTO BASIN OUTLAWS
Directed by
S. ROY LUBY

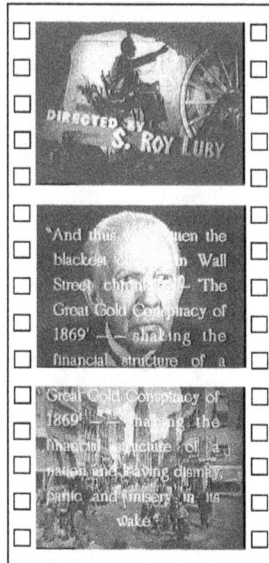

Underground Rustlers

Produced by George W. Weeks. Released by Monogram Pictures Corporation on November 21, 1941. Copyright Range Busters Inc., November 21, 1941, LP10926. Running Time, 56 Minutes. *Directed by* S. Roy Luby; *a George W. Weeks production; production manager,* William L. Nolte; *associate producer,* Anna Bell Ward; *original story,* John Rathnell; *screen play,* Bud Tuttle and Elizabeth Beecher; *adaptation and dialogue,* John Vlahos; *director of photography,* Robert Cline; *musical director,* Frank Sanucci; *sound,* Glen Glenn; *film editor,* Roy Claire; *featured songs:* "Followin' the Trail", *words and music by* Jean George, "Sweetheart of the Range" *by* Harry Tobias, Roy Ingraham, and Mickey Ford.

Cast:

Ray "Crash" Corrigan	. . . .	Ray "Crash" Corrigan
John "Dusty" King	. . . .	John "Dusty" King
Max "Alibi" Terhune	. . . .	Max "Alibi" Terhune
Gwen Gaze	. . . .	Irene
Robert Blair	. . . .	Ford
Forrest Taylor	. . . .	Bently
Tom London	. . . .	Tom
Steve Clark	. . . .	Jake
Bud Osborne	. . . .	Sheriff

Also featuring: Dick Cramer, John Elliott, Tex Palmer, Edward Peil, Sr., Carl Mathews, Tex Cooper, and Frank McCarroll.

Synopsis:
Gold stages are being held up in the far west at a time when the U.S. government needs bullion. The government sends the Range Busters to Gold Butte, an important bullion dispensing center, to put an end to the stage robberies.

Production Notes:
Filming began in late September and continued into early October 1941. Location scenes were shot at the Ray Corrigan Ranch and Iverson Movie Ranch. The magazine "Cowboy Movie Thrillers" for March 1942 (Frank A. Munsey Company), contained the story "Underground Rustlers" (see next page for a sample).

Underground Rustlers

Crash and Dusty start work tracking some bad hombres

Crash had a job to do with his two pals—in troubled spots of the West

MUD FLAT. Wolf's Hollow. Sulphur Springs. The names had appeared as black dots on the map in Ward's office. That was where the Range Busters first had been persuaded to leave their native San Joaquin to face this new menace to law and justice—these buzzards responsible for crimson headlines reading *Gold Stage Robbed*, and *High Graders Loot Yellow Jacket Mine*, and *Bandits Take $40,000 In Gold!*

Now, in this mountain country centering on Gold Butte, the dots on the map were becoming places, Shanty towns where wealth was dug from the earth and shipped to the Gold Butte smelter.

Crash Corrigan and Dusty King loped their ponies into the stage line's outpost relay station on toward one noon. Not far, now, to Gold Butte itself—where Ward had instructed them to report to his mining agent, Martin Ford. But it was at the outpost they figured on crossing trails with Alibi Terhune and his wooden dummy, Elmer.

Sure enough, there Alibi was. A small crowd had gathered around him, and he had a peddler's pack open. His sales talk, innocent as honey, reached the new arrivals before they dismounted.

"The marvelous articles I am about to display to you, folks, will open new vistas—"

You wouldn't think viciousness and death could lurk behind the peaceful

29

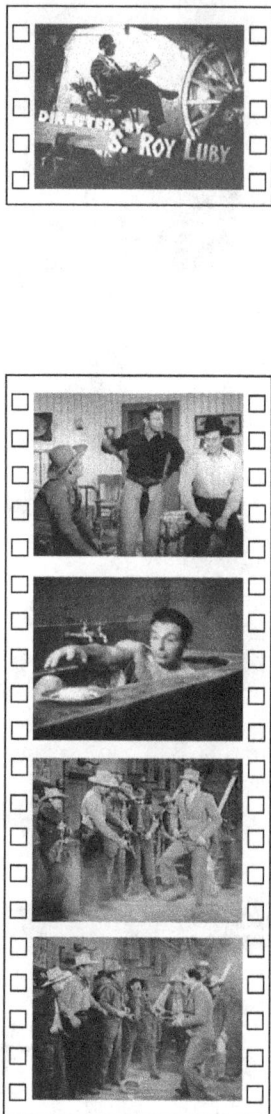

284

Thunder River Feud

Produced by George W. Weeks. Released by Monogram Pictures Corporation on January 9, 1942. Copyright Range Busters Inc., January 10, 1942, LP11150. Running Time, 51-58 Minutes. *Directed by* S. Roy Luby; *a George W. Weeks production*; *production manager*, William L. Nolte; *associate producer*, Anna Bell Ward; *original story*, Earle Snell; *screen play*, John Vlahos and Earle Snell; *director of photography*, Robert Cline; *musical direction*, Frank Sanucci; *sound engineer*, Glen Glenn; *film editor*, Roy Claire; *featured song, "What a Wonderful Day", words and music by* Jean George.

Cast:

Ray "Crash" Corrigan	Ray "Crash" Corrigan
John "Dusty" King	John "Dusty" King
Max "Alibi" Terhune	Max "Alibi" Terhune
Jan Wiley	Maybelle
Jack M. Holmes	Pembroke
Rick Anderson	Colonel
Carleton Young	Grover
George Chesebro	Taggart
Carl Mathews	Tex
Budd Buster	Sheriff
Ted Mapes	Buck
Steve Clark	Shorty

Synopsis:
Corrigan and King are rivals in the Tucson Rodeo. Corrigan wins the championship belt, but King impersonates him for a photographer. The photo appears in the newspaper. Later, attracted by a picture of Maybelle, the Range Busters, head for the Pembroke ranch separately. Corrigan arrives posing as a dude while King arrives posing as Corrigan. Later Alibi arrives and the three go to work when outlaws trick the Pembroke ranch and it's neighbor into a gunfight with each other.

Production Notes:
Filming began on November 24, 1941. Exteriors were shot at the Iverson Movie Ranch and Brandeis Ranch.

UNIVERSAL presents

THE STRANGE CASE OF DOCTOR RX

With
PATRIC KNOWLES
LIONEL ATWILL
ANNE GWYNNE
SAMUEL S. HINDS
MONA BARRIE
SHEMP HOWARD
PAUL CAVANAGH
EDMUND MacDONALD

Original Screenplay
CLARENCE UPSON YOUNG

Director of Photography
WOODY BREDELL, A.S.C.
Art Director . . . . . JACK OTTERSON
Associate . . . . . MARTIN OBZINA
Film Editor   Musical Director
BERNARD W. BURTON   H.J. SALTER
Sound Director . . BERNARD B. BROWN
Technician . CHARLES CARROLL
Gowns   Set Decorations
VERA WEST   R.A. GAUSMAN

Associate Producer
JACK BERNHARD

Directed by
WILLIAM NIGH

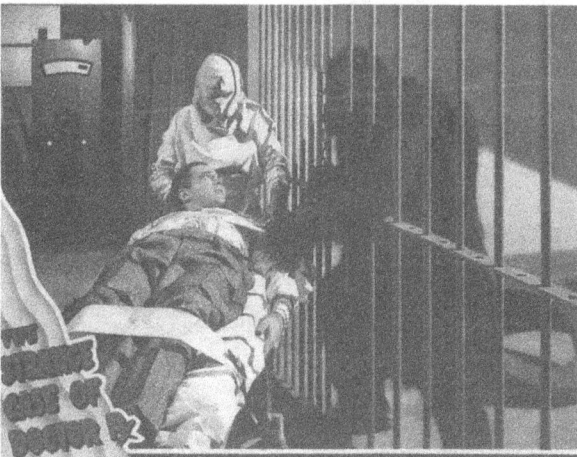

The Strange Case of Doctor RX

Produced and Released by Universal Pictures Co., Inc. on April 17, 1942. Copyright Universal Pictures Co., Inc. on February 24, 1942, LP11093. Running Time, 64-66 minutes. *Directed by* William Nigh; *associate producer*, Jack Bernhard; *original screenplay*, Clarence Upson Young; *director of photography*, Woody Bredell, a.s.c.; *art director*, Jack Otterson; *associate*, Martin Obzine; *film editor*, Bernard W. Burton; *musical director*, H. J. Salter; *sound director*, Bernard B. Brown; *technician*, Charles Carroll; *gowns*, Vera West; *set decorations*, R. A. Gausman.

Cast:

Patric Knowles	. . . . Jerry Church
Lionel Atwill	. . . . Dr. Fish
Anne Gwynne	. . . . Kit
Samuel S. Hinds	. . . . Dudley Crispin
Mona Barrie	. . . . Mrs. Dudley Crispin
Shemp Howard	. . . . Sweeney
Paul Cavanagh	. . . . John Crispin
Edmund MacDonald	. . . . Inspector Hurd
Ray Corrigan	. . . . Gorilla

Also featuring: Mantan Moreland, John Gallaudet, William Gould, Leyland Hodgson, Boyd Davis, Selmer Jackson, Mary Gordon, Jan Wiley, Gary Breckner, Matty Fain, Victor Zimmerman, Harry Harvey, Paul Bryar, Joe Recht, Leonard Sues, Drew Demorest, Jack Kennedy, Eddy Chandler, and Jack C. Smith.

Synopsis:
Six men are marked as murder victims when they are acquitted of murder charges. The story traces the mysterious career of a shadowy avenger who has strangled six men previously acquitted in court. Only clue the creepy killer leaves with his victim is a small piece of paper, on which is inscribed "Rx" and a numeral to indicate the murdered man's place in the strange series of garrotings.

Production Notes:
Filmed on the sound stages at Universal Studios.

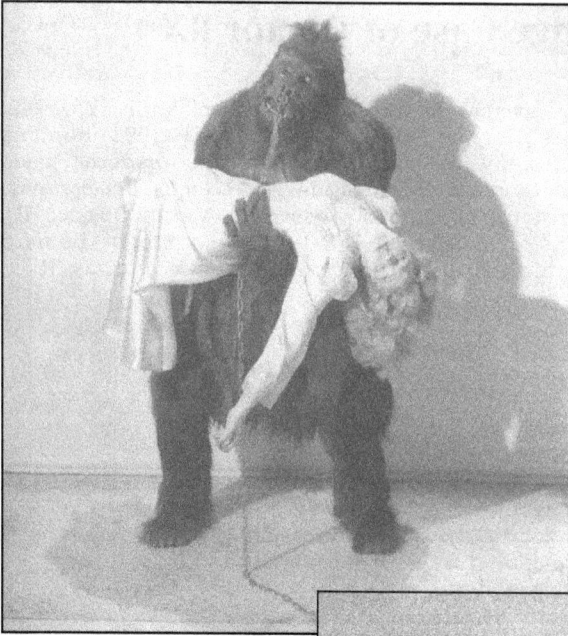

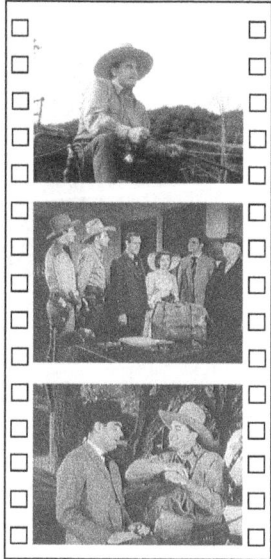

Rock River Renegades

Produced by George W. Weeks. Released by Monogram Pictures Corporation on February 27, 1942. Copyright Range Busters Inc., March 3, 1942, LP11218. Running Time, 56 Minutes, 6 reels. *Directed by* S. Roy Luby; *a George W. Weeks production; production manager,* William L. Nolte; *associate producer,* Anna Bell Ward; *original story by* Faith Thomas; *screen play by* John Vlahos and Earle Snell; *director of photography,* Robert Cline; *musical direction,* Frank Sanucci; *sound engineer,* Corson Jowett; *film editor,* Roy Claire; *featured song, "Prairie Serenade", words and music by* Jean George.

Cast:

Ray "Crash" Corrigan	Ray "Crash" Corrigan
John "Dusty" King	John "Dusty" King
Max "Alibi" Terhune	Max "Alibi" Terhune
Christine McIntyre	Grace Ross
John Elliott	Dick Ross
Weldon Heyburn	Jim Dawson
Kermit Maynard	Luke Graham
Frank Ellis	Chuck
Carl Mathews	Joe
Dick Cramer	Bartender
Tex Palmer	Tex

Also featuring: Hank Bell, Budd Buster, and Steve Clark.

Synopsis:
Dick Ross, editor and owner of the *Rock River Advocate*, is having trouble with outlaws who are taking over the Rock River territory. Marshal Graham sends for his friends, the Range Busters. Ross, dissatisfied with Graham, forms a vigilante committee and puts Jim Dawson in charge not knowing he is the leader of the outlaw gang. Dawson then has his men frame Crash and Dusty for robbery and murder and then has his men set out to lynch the two.

Production Notes:
Filming began on January 13, 1942. Exteriors were shot at the Andy Jauregui Ranch and Walker Ranch.

296

Boot Hill Bandits

Produced by George W. Weeks. Released by Monogram Pictures Corporation on April 24, 1942. Copyright Range Busters Inc., April 24, 1942, LP11593. Running Time, 58 Minutes, 6 reels. *Directed by* S. Roy Luby; *a George W. Weeks production*; *production manager*, William L. Nolte; *original story and screen play*, Arthur Durlam; *director of photography*, Robert Cline; *musical direction*, Frank Sanucci; *sound engineer*, Corson Jowett; *film editor*, Roy Claire.

Cast:

Ray "Crash" Corrigan	. . . . .	Ray "Crash" Corrigan
John "Dusty" King	. . . . .	John "Dusty" King
Max "Alibi" Terhune	. . . . .	Max "Alibi" Terhune
Jean Brooks	. . . . .	May Meadows
John Merton	. . . . .	Brand Bolton
Glenn Strange	. . . . .	The Maverick
Standford Jolley	. . . . .	The Mesquite Kid
Steve Clark	. . . . .	Sheriff
George Chesebro	. . . . .	Stoner
Dick Cramer	. . . . .	Hawkins
Budd Buster	. . . . .	Mayor
Milt Morante	. . . . .	Cameron
James Aubrey	. . . . .	The Drunk

Also featuring: Carl Mathews, Tex Palmer, Merrill McCormack, Hank Bell, Horace B. Carpenter, and Charles King.

Synopsis:
In this one the Range Busters focus their bustin'—carried through in their standard routine—upon cleaning up a frontier town in which the heavy is hiding behind his office of mayor. The adventure includes sufficient quantities of fisticuffs, gun-fighting, chaes and other action ingredients to satisfy the purchasers of westerns. Crash Corrigan is imported to round up the bad one, while the dishonest mayor, who imported him, secretly arranges to have him liquidated. Right prevails to the name of action, expected in this type of offering, and the baddies get their dose of justice as Crash and his buddies put in an appearance in the nick of time.

Production Notes:
Filming commenced on March 6, 1942. Exteriors were shot at Placeritos (Monogram) Ranch and Walker Ranch.

300

Texas Trouble Shooters

Produced by George W. Weeks. Released by Monogram Pictures Corporation on June 12, 1942. Copyright Range Busters Inc., June 12, 1942, LP11417. Running Time, 56 Minutes, 6 reels. *Directed by* S. Roy Luby; *a George W. Weeks production; production manager*, William L. Nolte; *associate producer*, Richard Ross; *story by* Elizabeth Beecher; *screen adaptation*, Arthur Hoerl; *photography*, Robert Cline; *sound engineer*, Corson Jowett; *musical direction*, Frank Sanucci; *film editor*, Roy Claire; *featured songs: "Deep in the Heart of Texas" by* June Hershey and Don Swonder, *"Light of Western Skies" by* Harry Tobias and Roy Ingraham; *photographed on the Ray Corrigan Ranch.*

Cast:

Ray "Crash" Corrigan	Ray "Crash" Corrigan
John "Dusty" King	John "Dusty" King
Max "Alibi" Terhune	Max "Alibi" Terhune
Julie Duncan	Judy
Glen Strange	Denby
Roy Harris	Bret
Eddie Phillips	Wade
Frank Ellis	Duke
Ted Mapes	Slim
Kermit Maynard	Pete
Gertrude W. Hoffman	Grannie
Steve Clark	Ames
Jack Holmes	Perry

Synopsis:
On his way to claim half interest in a ranch, left him by his late uncle, Roy Harris is chased by hired killers of a crooked lawyer (Glenn Strange) and left for dead. The lawyer thinking Harris is disposed of and knowing oil is on the property, tries to take possession by moving in with ahenchman to impersonate Harris. The Range Busters, however, get the low-down on Strange even though Julie Duncan, co-heir of the ranch, believes him her cousin. Strange attempts escape, but is foiled by the Range Busters and after several rough riding sequences, Harris, the real owner, and Julie are left in possession of their property.

Production Notes:
Filmed from April 22 to mid-May 1942. Exteriors shot at the Ray Corrigan Ranch.

MONOGRAM PICTURES CORP.
A GEO. W. WEEKS
production

The Range Busters

RAY "Crash" CORRIGAN
JOHN "Dusty" KING
MAX "Alibi" TERHUNE

IN

TEXAS TROUBLE SHOOTERS

Directed by S. ROY LUBY

Arizona Stage Coach

Produced by George W. Weeks. Released by Monogram Pictures Corporation on September 4, 1942. Copyright not registered. Running Time, 57-58 Minutes. *Directed by* S. Roy Luby; *a George W. Weeks production; production manager,* William L. Nolte; *associate producer,* Richard Ross; *story by* Oliver Drake; *screen adaptation,* Arthur Hoerl; *photography,* Robert Cline; *sound engineer,* Lyle Willey; *musical director,* Frank Sanucci; *film editor,* Roy Claire; *featured songs: "Where the Grass Grows" and "High in the Mountains" by* Rudy Sooter, *"Red River Valley"; photographed on Ray Corrigan Ranch.*

Cast:

Ray "Crash" Corrigan	. . . .	Ray "Crash" Corrigan
John "Dusty" King	. . . .	John "Dusty" King
Max "Alibi" Terhune	. . . .	Max "Alibi" Terhune
Nell O'Day	. . . .	Dorrie
Charles King	. . . .	Douglas
Roy Harris	. . . .	Ernie
Kermit Maynard	. . . .	Strike
Carl Mathews	. . . .	Ace
Slim Whitaker	. . . .	Red
Slim Harkey	. . . .	Panhandle
Steve Clark	. . . .	Jake
Frank Ellis	. . . .	Dan
Jack Ingram	. . . .	Sheriff
Stanley Price	. . . .	Tex
Forest Taylor	. . . .	Meadows

Also featuring: Dick Cramer and Eddie Dean.

Synopsis:

Dorrie and her uncle Meadows, visit the ranch of the Range Busters. Meadows seeks their aid against a gang of outlaws terrorizing his town. Ernie, Dorrie's brother, has been taken in by Tex who is using their ranch as an cover for his real occupation as a member of a gang of outlaws led by Douglas, a supposed friend of the Willards.

Production Notes:

Filming began on June 11, 1942. Exteriors were shot at the Ray Corrigan Ranch.

Dr. Renault's Secret

Produced and Released by Twentieth Century-Fox on December 11, 1942. Copyright by Twentieth Century-Fox Film Corp., on December 11, 1942, LP11846. Running Time, 58 minutes, 6 reels. *Directed by* Harry Lachman; *executive producer*, Sol M. Wurtzel; *screen play by* William Bruckner and Robert F. Metzler; *director of photography*, Virgil Miller, a.s.c.; *art direction*, Richard Day and Nathan Juran; *set decorations*, Thomas Little and Paul S. Fox; *film editor*, Fred Allen; *costumes*, Herschel; *sound*, Eugene Grossman and Harry M. Leonard; *music*, David Raksin and Emil Newman.

Cast:

J. Carrol Naish	. . . . .	Mr. Noel
John Shepperd	. . . .	Dr. Larry Forbes
Lynne Roberts	. . . .	Madeline Renault
George Zucco	. . . .	Dr. Renault
Ray Corrigan	. . . .	Gorilla

Also featuring: Bert Roach, Eugene Borden, Jack Norton, Arthur Shields, Mike Mazurki, Jean Del Val, Charles Wagenheim, Max Willenz, Charles La Torre, George Davis, Louis Mercier, Carmen Biretta, and Ann Codee.

Synopsis:
Dr. Renault has converted Mr. Noel from ape to man. Dr. Larry Forbes comes to the Renault chateau in France to marry Madeline Renault. Noel loves Miss Renault. She's kind to him. But he goes slowly haywire. This process speeds up during a Bastille Day celebration. He slays two of his tormentors. Then Dr. Renault gets it. Miss Renault is kidnapped. Dr. Forbes learns of the experiment. Noel trails Miss Renault and her kidnaper to an old mill. He is mortally wounded but, possessing great strength, kills the kidnaper and dies.

Production Notes:
Filming was completed on July 30, 1942. No location filming.

Dizzy Detectives

Produced and Released by Columbia Pictures Corp. on February 5, 1943. Copyright Columbia Pictures Corp., February 5, 1943, L11960. Running Time, 18-19 minutes. *Directed by* Jules White; *produced by* Jules White; *story and screen play by* Felix Adler; *director of photography*, Benjamin Kline, a.s.c.; *film editor*, Jerome Thoms; *art direction*, Carl Anderson.

Cast:

Curly	. . . .	Curly
Larry	. . . .	Larry
Moe	. . . . .	Moe
Ray Corrigan	. . . . .	Gorilla

Also featuring: Lynton Brent, Bud Jamison, Dick Jensen, and John Tyrrell.

Synopsis:
The Three Stooges are carpenters who become policemen. A mysterious burglar disguised as a gorilla has the cops baffled and Mr. Dill, the head of the citizens league, threatens the police chief's job. The boys go on the case and pose as night watchmen at an antiques store. They confront the crook, who turns out to be a real gorilla owned by Dill. After defeating Dill and his gang in a wild fight, the gorilla drinks some nitroglycerin and blows up.

Production Notes:
Filmed from June 29 to July 2, 1942. No exterior filming.

Land of Hunted Men

Produced by George W. Weeks. Released by Monogram Pictures Corp. on March 26, 1943. Copyright by Range Busters, Inc., February 5, 1943, LP11866. Running Time, 57 Minutes. *Directed by* S. Roy Luby; *a George W. Weeks production; in charge of production*, William L. Nolte; *original story*, William L. Nolte; *continuity*, Elizabeth Beecher; *photography*, James Brown; *sound*, Lyle Willey; *assistant production manager*, Clark L. Paylow; *musical director*, Frank Sanucci; *film editor*, Roy Claire; *featured song, "The Trail to Mexico" sung by* Phyllis Adair; *photographed on Ray Corrigan's Ranch.*

Cast:

Ray "Crash" Corrigan	"Crash" Corrigan
Denny Moore	Denny Moore
Max "Alibi" Terhune	"Alibi" Terhune
Phyllis Adair	Dorrie
Charles King	Faro
John Morton	Pelham
Ted Mapes	Piebald
Frank McCarrol	Tobasco
Forrest Taylor	Dad
Steve Clark	Wallace
Fred Toones	Snowflake

Also featuring: Carl Sepulveda, Tex Palmer, Augie Gomez, Al Haskell, and Ray Jones.

Synopsis:
The Range Busters are living outside a town prior to cleaning it up of a gang of mail robbers. Their cook is sent into town and they follow him to see the sheriff. When the boys win a lot of money at Charles King's gambling tables, King picks a fight with them. They escape and the cook finds the money. He also overhears that King plans to rob the mail coach again, and that John Merton, respected citizen, is behind the robberies. The Range Busters give this information to the sheriff, and a posse is formed to surround the territory where the robbery is to take place. As they overcome the holdup men, the crooks headed by King, ride to the gang's aid, but the Range Busters round them up. The gang and Merton are imprisoned and the mail coach can now go through unmolested.

Production Notes:
Filmed mid to late December 1942. Exteriors were shot at the Ray Corrigan Ranch.

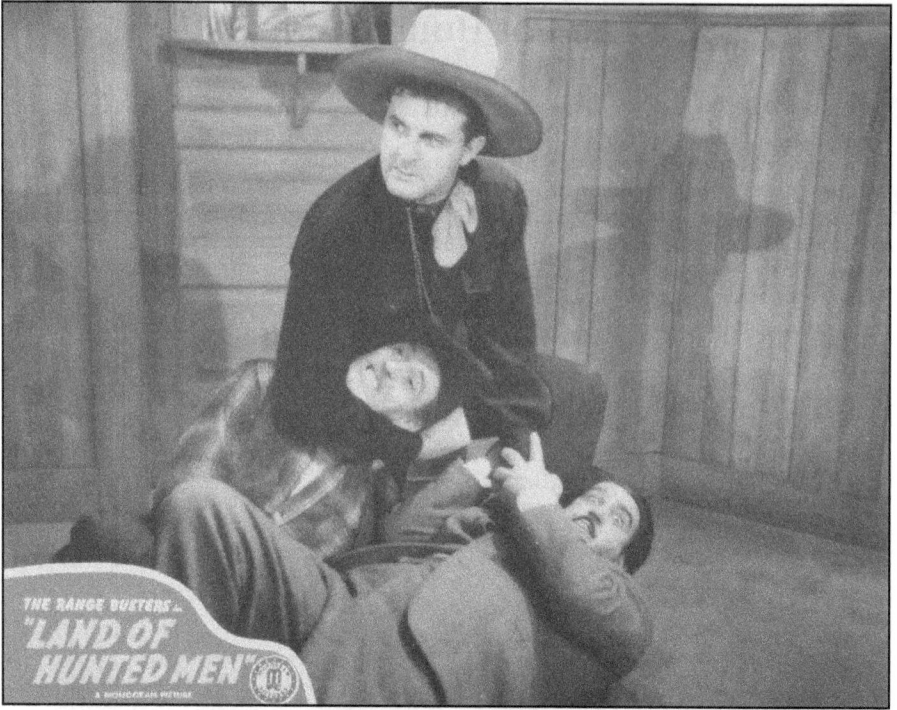

314

UNIVERSAL presents

CAPTIVE WILD WOMAN

COPYRIGHT MCMXLIII BY UNIVERSAL PICTURES COMPANY, INC.

With
JOHN CARRADINE
EVELYN ANKERS
MILBURN STONE
LLOYD CORRIGAN

And
Introducing
ACQUANETTA

Screenplay
GRIFFIN JAY
HENRY SUCHER

Original Story TED FITHIAN
NEIL P. VARNICK

Director of Photography....
........GEORGE ROBINSON ASC
Art Direction
JOHN B. GOODMAN • RALPH DeLACY
Film Editor............MILTON CARRUTH
Sound Director.......BERNARD B. BROWN
Technician..........WILLIAM HEDGCOCK
Musical Director..........H.J. SALTER
Gowns.............VERA WEST
Set Decorations
R.A. GAUSMAN • IRA S. WEBB

WE HEREBY MAKE GRATEFUL
ACKNOWLEDGMENT TO MR. CLYDE
BEATTY FOR HIS COOPERATION
AND INIMITABLE TALENT IN
STAGING THE THRILLING ANIMAL
SEQUENCES IN THIS PICTURE

Associate
Producer
BEN PIVAR

Directed By
EDWARD DMYTRYK

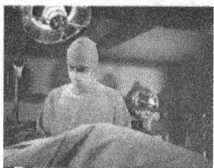

Captive Wild Woman

Produced and Released by Universal Pictures Co., Inc. on June 11, 1943. Copyright Universal Pictures Co., Inc. November 11, 1943, LP12179. Running Time, 60-61 minutes. *Directed by* Edward Dmytryk; *associate producer*, Ben Pivar; *screenplay*, Griffin Jay and Henry Sucher; *original story*, Ted Fithian and Neil P. Varnick; *director of photography*, George Robinson, a.s.c.; *art direction*, John B. Goodman and Ralph DeLacy; *film editor*, Milton Carruth; *sound director*, Bernard B. Brown; *technician*, William Hedgcock; *musical director*, H. J. Salter; *gowns*, Vera West; *set decorations*, R. A. Gausman and Ira S. Webb.

Cast:

John Carradine	. . . .	Dr. Sigmund Walters
Evelyn Ankers	. . . .	Beth Colman
Milburn Stone	. . . .	Fred Mason
Lloyd Corrigan	. . . .	John Whipple
Acquanetta	. . . .	Paula Dupree/Cheela
Ray Corrigan	. . . .	Gorilla

Also featuring: Fay Helm, Martha MacVicar, Vince Barnett, Paul Fix, Ed Peil Sr., Ray Walker, Gus Glassmire; Fern Emmett; William Gould; Grant Withers; Joey Ray; Frank Mitchell; Anthony Warde; Harry Holman; Alexander Gill; Charles McAvoy; Virginia Engels; and Joel Goodkind.

Synopsis:

Fred Mason, animal trainer, is greeted by his fiancee, Beth Colman, upon his return from Africa. Among other wild animals, he brings back a female gorilla named Chella. Dr. Sigmund Walters, an expert in glandular research, becomes convinced that his experiments involving lower animal species cannot succeed, so he arranges to have a very intelligent female gorilla kidnapped from the circus and brought to his lab. Using the glands of a patient and the brain of his faithful nurse, he performs transplant surgery on the intelligent simian. When the ape transforms into exotic and sexy Paula Dupree, the experiment seems to be a success.

Production Notes:

Filmed from December 10 to late December 1942. Opening credits state: "We hereby make grateful acknowledgment to Mr. Clyde Beatty for his cooperation and inimitable talent in staging the thrilling animal sequences in this picture."

318

CAPTIVE WILD WOMAN

with

EVELYN ANKERS   JOHN CARRADINE   MILBURN STONE
LLOYD CORRIGAN   MARTHA MacVICAR   VINCE BARNETT

and Introducing

ACQUANETTA

as the GORILLA GIRL

Directed by EDWARD DMYTRYK   Associate Producer, BEN PIVAR   A UNIVERSAL PICTURE   Screen Play, Henry Sucher   Griffin Jay   Original Story, Ted Fithian, Neil & Vernon

Cowboy Commandos

Produced by George W. Weeks. Released by Monogram Pictures Corp. on June 4, 1943. Copyright Monogram Pictures Corp., April 20, 1943, LP12015. Running Time, 53 Minutes, 6 reels. *Directed by* S. Roy Luby; *a George W. Weeks production; original story,* Clark L. Paylow; *screenplay,* Elizabeth Beecher; *photography,* Edward A. Kull; *sound,* Lyle Willey; *musical director,* Frank Sanucci; *asst. director,* Clark L. Paylow; *film editor,* Roy Claire; *in charge of production,* William L. Nolte; *featured song: "I'll Get the Fuehrer Sure as Shootin' "* sung by Johnny Bond.

Cast:

Ray "Crash" Corrigan	. . . . . "Crash" Corrigan
Denny Moore	. . . . . Denny Moore
Max "Alibi" Terhune	. . . . . "Alibi" Terhune
Evelyn Finley	. . . . . Joan
Johnny Bond	. . . . . Slim
Budd Buster	. . . . . Werner
John Merton	. . . . . Fraser
Frank Ellis	. . . . . Mario
Steve Clark	. . . . . Bartlett
Edna Bennett	. . . . . Katie
Bud Osborne	. . . . . Hans
George Chesebro	. . . . . Fred

Synopsis:
Trick rider Joan and the Range Busters are set to begin a war bond sales tour when Joan receives word that her brother, Sheriff Dave, has been killed. Joan's father has been mining magnacite, a valuable resource for the war effort. A group of Nazis are trying to sabotage the ore production.

Production Notes:
Filmed from March 13 to late March 1943. Exteriors shoot at the Ray Corrigan Ranch. When asked who was the best horseperson on the film, Corrigan replied "Evelyn Finley".

"COWBOY COMMANDOS"

with RAY (CRASH) CORRIGAN DENNIS MOORE MAX (ALIBI) TERHUNE

EVELYN FINLEY

Produced by
GEORGE W. WEEKS
Directed by
S. ROY LUBY
Story Continuity by
ELIZABETH BEECHER
Original Story by
CLARK PAYLOW
A MONOGRAM PICTURE

THE RANGE BUSTERS in

"COWBOY COMMANDOS"

with **RAY** (CRASH) **CORRIGAN**

DENNIS MOORE

MAX (ALIBI) **TERHUNE**

A MONOGRAM PICTURE
Produced by GEORGE W. WEEKS
Directed by S. ROY LUBY
Story Continuity by ELIZABETH BEECHER
Original Story by WILLIAM L. NOLTE

Black Market Rustlers

Produced by George W. Weeks. Released by Monogram Pictures Corp. on August 27, 1943. Copyright Monogram Pictures Corp. July 2, 1943, LP12160. Running Time, 54-59 Minutes, 6 reels. *Directed by* S. Roy Luby; *a George W. Weeks production*; *original screenplay* by Patricia Harper; *photography*, Edward Kull; *sound*, Lyle E. Willey; *musical director*, Frank Sanucci; *asst. director*, Clark L. Paylow; *film editor*, Roy Claire; *in charge of production*, William L. Nolte; *featured song*, "You Wink at Me and I'll Wink at You"; *specialty numbers*, Jim Austin, "Little" Jean Austin, Ingrid Austin, and Art Fowler.

Cast:

Ray "Crash" Corrigan	. . . .	"Crash" Corrigan
Denny Moore	. . . .	Denny Moore
Max "Alibi" Terhune	. . . .	"Alibi" Terhune
Evelyn Finley	. . . .	Linda
Steve Clark	. . . .	Prescott
Glen Strange	. . . .	Corbin
Carl Sepulveda	. . . .	Sheriff
George Chesebro	. . . .	Slade
Hank Worden	. . . .	Slim
Frank Ellis	. . . .	Kyper
John Merton	. . . .	Parry
Frosty Royce	. . . .	Ed

Also featuring: Stanley Price, Wally West, Carl Mathews, Tex Cooper, and Claire McDowell.

Synopsis:
The Cattlemen's Association invites government agents, the Range Busters, to help investigate rustlers around Winston who are stealing cattle for black market purposes. The gang are using trailer trucks. Crash comes across the body of the federal agent who had sent for him and is accused by gang-member Slade of the murder. He is turned over to the Sheriff. Denny takes a job on the ranch owned by Prescott, and immediately falls in love with Prescott's daughter, Linda. Alibi finally convinces the sheriff that Crash is a federal agent and the sheriff agrees to let Crash work, using the jail cell as his cover. Alibi learns that Corbin, respected citizen, is actually the gang leader, as well as discovering the truck used to convey the cattle to the slaughter house.

Production Notes:
Filming began on May 10, 1943. Exteriors were shot at the Placeritos (Monogram) Ranch, Andy Jauregui Ranch, and Walker Ranch. The opening includes a foreword urging American citizens not to buy black market beef during the war.

"Bullets And Saddles"

Opening with action and packed with menace by hoodlum westerners firing homes of ranchers and rustling cattle, "Bullets and Saddles" provides wide play for action by "Crash" Corrigan and his pals, Dennis Moore and "Alibi" Terhune.

They ride to rescue Mother Craig, who raised Corrigan, when she and her son stand firm against efforts to drive them from the valley by land-hungry outlaws. Efforts to pin a murder on Craig are thwarted by Corrigan and his pals, who in turn prove a stranger's guilt and round up his gang in a blazing climax.

Bullets and Saddles

Produced by George W. Weeks. Released by Monogram Pictures Corp. on October 29, 1943. Copyright Monogram Pictures Corp. September 17, 1943, LP12288. Running Time, 52-56 Minutes, 6 reels. *Directed by* Anthony Marshall; *a George W. Weeks production; based on an original story by* Arthur Hoerl; *screenplay by* Elizabeth Beecher; *photography,* Edward A. Kull; *sound engineer,* Lyle E. Willey; *musical director,* Frank Sanucci; *assistant director,* Clark L. Paylow; *film editor,* Roy Claire; *in charge of production,* William L. Nolte.

Cast:

Ray "Crash" Corrigan	"Crash" Corrigan
Denny Moore	Denny Moore
Max "Alibi" Terhune	"Alibi" Terhune
Julie Duncan	Laura Craig
Budd Buster	Charley Craig
Rose Plumer	Mother Craig
Forrest Taylor	Marshal Claiburn
Glen Strange	Hammond
Steve Clark	Blair
John Merton	Mike
Ed Cassidy	Weber
Joe Garcia	Butch
Silver Harr	Landers

Synopsis:
A gang of marauders is terrorizing ranchers and driving them off their land. Hammond is after the Craig ranch and has framed Charlie Craig for murder. Mother Craig brings in the Range Busters. They capture one of Hammond's men and Alibi plans to trick him into a confession as to who the real murderer is. Meanwhile, Denny has overheard Hammond's plans for his next move and he and Crash set out to round up the gang.

Production Notes:
Filming began on June 18 and lased through late June 1943. Exteriors were shot at the Ray Corrigan Ranch.

Range Busters
Ray "Crash" Corrigan • Dennis Moore • Max "Alibi" Terhune
A Geo. W. Weeks Production

UNIVERSAL presents
She's For Me
with
GRACE McDONALD
DAVID BRUCE
LOIS COLLIER
GEORGE DOLENZ
CHARLES DINGLE
ROGERS TRIO
EDDIE LeBARON
and His Orchestra
Original Screenplay by
HENRY BLANKFORT
Associate Producer
FRANK GROSS

Directed by
REGINALD LeBORG
THE END
A UNIVERSAL PICTURE
The Players
GRACE McDONALD
DAVID BRUCE
LOIS COLLIER
GEORGE DOLENZ
CHARLES DINGLE
HELEN BROWN

She's For Me

Produced and Released by Universal Pictures Co., Inc. on December 10, 1943. Copyright Universal Pictures Co., Inc. November 12, 1943, LP12364. Running Time, 60 minutes, 6 reels. *Directed by* Reginald LeBorg; *produced by* Milton Schwarzwald; *original screenplay by* Henry Blankfort; *director of photography*, Paul Ivano; *art direction*, John B. Goodman and Ralph DeLacy; *film editor*, Fred R. Feitshans Jr., and Paul Landres; *set decorations*, R. A. Gausman and L. R. Smith; *gowns*, Vera West; *music director*, Charles Previn; *director of sound*, Bernard B. Brown; *dances staged by* Louis Da Pron..

Cast:

Grace McDonald	. . . . . Jan Lawton
David Bruce	. . . . . Michael Reed
Lois Collier	. . . . . Eileen Crane
George Dolenz	. . . . . Phil Norwin
Charles Dingle	. . . . . Crane
Helen Brown	. . . . . Miss Carpenter
Rogers Trio	. . . . . Themselves
Eddie LeBaron and His Orchestra	. . . . . Themselves

Also featuring: Mantan Moreland, Louis DaPron, Douglas Wood, Leon Belasco, Charles Coleman, Frank Faylen, Charles Trowbridge, Grace Hayle, Carol Hughes, Eddie Bruce, Frank Penny, Gerald Pierce, Teddy Infuhr, and Ray Corrigan.

Synopsis:
This is a musical comedy farce with popular song hits sung by Grace McDonald who also exhibits a flair for dancing. The plot revolves around the niece of a conservative attorney, her resentment at Bruce's handling of her estate and how she preceeds to set out to win his playboy chum, whom Bruce persuaded her uncle to hire. In breaking it up, Bruce falls for her himself.

Production Notes:
Filmed from July 21 to early August 1943. Corrigan's role is listed as "Gorilla Man".

333

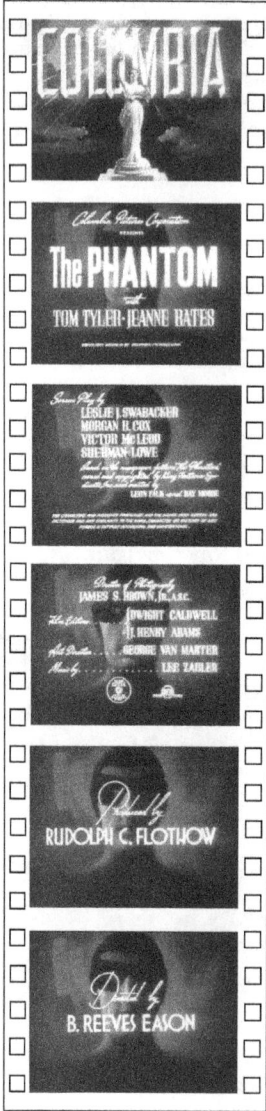

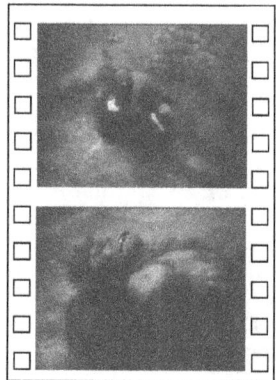

The Phantom

Produced and Released by Columbia Pictures Corp. on December 24, 1943. Copyright Columbia Pictures Corp. . Running Time, 15 Chapters. *Directed by* B. Reeves Eason; *produced by* Rudolph C. Flothow; *screen play by* Leslie J. Swabacker, Morgan B. Cox, Victor McLeod, and Sherman Lowe; *director of photography*, James S. Brown, Jr. a.s.c.; *film editors*, Dwight Caldwell and J. Henry Adams; *art director*, George Van Marter; *music by* Lee Zahler; *based on the newspaper feature "The Phantom", owned and copyrighted by King Features Syndicate, Inc. and created by* Leon Falk and Ray Moore.

Cast:

Tom Tyler	. . . . .	The Phantom/Godfrey Prescott
Jeanne Bates	. . . . .	Diana Palmer
Kenneth MacDonald	. . . . .	Dr. Max Bremmer
Frank Shannon	. . . . .	Prof. Davidson
Guy Kingsford	. . . . .	Byron Anderson
Joe Devlin	. . . . .	Singapore Smith
Ernie Adams	. . . . .	Rusty Fenton
John S. Bagni	. . . . .	Moku
Ace the Wonder Dog	. . . . .	Devil
Ray Corrigan	. . . . .	Gorilla

Also featuring: Robert Barron, Early Cantrell, Anthony Caruso, George Chesebro, Edmund Cobb, Iron Eyes Cody, Wade Crosby, Angel Cruz, Dick Curtis, Al Ferguson, Sam Flint, Sol Gorss, Alex Havier, Al Hill, Reed Howes, John Indrisano, I. Stanford Jolley, Pierce Lyden, Knox Manning, Paul Marion, John Maxwell, Kermit Maynard, Lal Chand Mehra, Ernesto Morelli, Paul Newlan, Pat O'Malley, Eddie Parker, Stanley Price, Jay Silverheels, Anthony Warde, and Dan White.

Episode Titles:

1. The Sign of the Skull — copyright 12-24-43 L12529
2. The Man Who Never Dies — copyright 12-31-43 L12537
3. A Traitor's Code — copyright 1-7-44 L12560
4. The Seat of Judgment — copyright 1-15-44 L12567
5. The Ghost Who Walks — copyright 1-22-44 L12583
6. Jungle Whispers — copyright 1-29-44 L12608
7. The Mystery Well — copyright 2-5-44 L12779
8. In Quest of the Keys — copyright 2-12-44 L12617
9. The Fire Princess — copyright 2-19-44 L12632
10. The Chamber of Death — copyright 2-26-44 L12641
11. The Emerald Key — copyright 3-5-44 L12648
12. The Fangs of the Beast — copyright 3-12-44 L12780
13. The Road to Zoloz — copyright 3-17-44 L12684
14. The Lost City — copyright 3-24-44 L12691
15. Peace in the Jungle — copyright 3-31-44 L12714

Synopsis:

Professor Davidson plans an expedition to find the Lost City of Zoloz. The location of the city is contained on seven pieces of ivory, three of which Davidson already possesses. Doctor Bremmer, however, intends to find the lost city and use it as a secret airbase for his unnamed country. He kills The Phantom in order to remove him as an obstacle. The Phantom's son returns in time to learn of the secret of The Phantom's and to take over as The Phantom. Three of the remaining ivory pieces are owned by Singapore Smith, who initially steals Davidson's pieces. The seventh, and most important, piece is missing at first but turns up in the possession of Tartar (which The Phantom acquires by wrestling Tartar's pet gorilla).

Production Notes:
Exteriors shot at the Iverson Movie Ranch, Beale's Cut, and Lake Sherwood/Sherwood Forest.

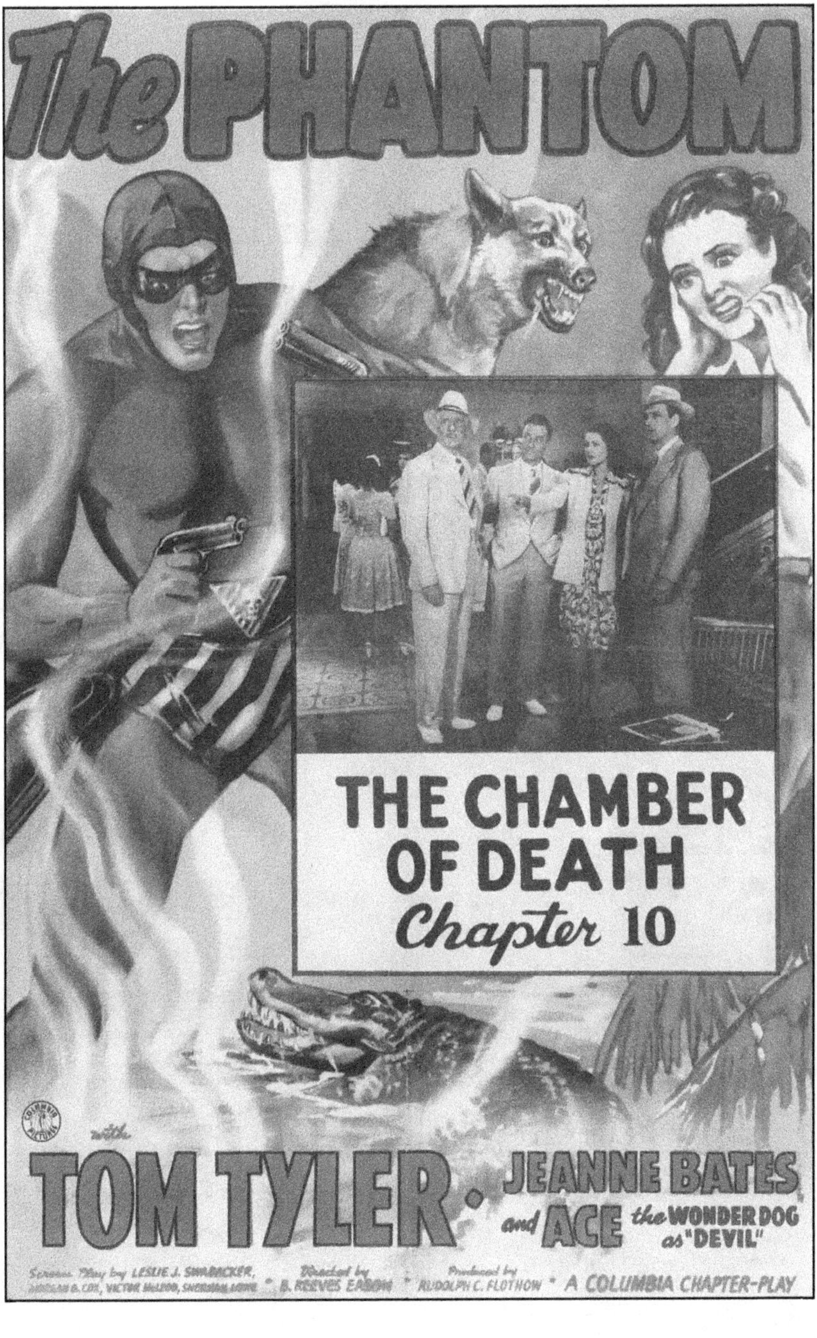
The PHANTOM
THE CHAMBER OF DEATH
Chapter 10
with
TOM TYLER
JEANNE BATES
and ACE the WONDER DOG as "DEVIL"
Directed by B. REEVES EASON
Produced by RUDOLPH C. FLOTHOW
A COLUMBIA CHAPTER-PLAY

PRC PICTURES

PRC
NABONGA
GORILLA
Copyright MCMXLIV
by PRC PICTURES, Inc.

Starring
BUSTER CRABBE
BARTON MacLANE
FIFI D'ORSAY
and
JULIE LONDON

Produced by
SIGMUND
NEUFELD

Original Story & Screenplay by FRED MYTON
Director of Photography ROBERT CLINE
Sound Engineer CORSON JOWETT
Art Director PAUL PALMENTOLA
Film Editor HOLBROOK N. TODD
Special Effects GENE STONE
Assistant Director MELVILLE DeLAY
Production Manager BERT STERNBACH
Music Score WILLY STAHL
Musical Supervision DAVID CHUDNOW

Directed by
SAM NEWFIELD

THE END
A Producers Releasing Corporation Picture

The Cast:
The Gorilla Man .... BUSTER CRABBE
Marie .... FIFI D'ORSAY
Carl Hurst .... BARTON MacLANE
Doreen Stockwell .... JULIE LONDON
Hunter .... BRYANT WASHBURN
Stockwell .... HERBERT RAWLINSON
Tobo .... PRINCE MODUPE
The Gorilla as a child .... JACKIE NEWFIELD
Gorilla .... NBONGO

CALLING
80,000,000
AMERICAN MOVIEGOERS!
BUY
WAR SAVING STAMPS
and BONDS
On Sale in this Theatre!

338

Nabonga Gorilla

Produced by Sigmund Neufeld Productions, Inc. Released by Producers Releasing Corp. on January 25, 1944. Copyright January 30, 1944, PRC Pictures, Inc., LP12467. Running time, 70-73 minutes, 6,387 feet. *Directed by* Sam Newfield; *produced by* Sigmund Neufeld; *original story and screenplay by* Fred Myton; *director of photography*, Robert Cline; *sound engineer*, Corson Jowett; *set designer*, Paul Palmentola; *film editor*, Holbrook N. Todd; *special effects*, Gene Stone; *assistant director*, Melville DeLay; *production manager*, Bert Sternbach; *music score*, Willy Stahl; *musical supervision*, David Chudnow.

Cast:

Buster Crabbe	Raymond Gorman
Barton MacLane	Carl Hurst
Fifi D'Orsay	Marie
Julie London	Doreen Stockwell
Bryant Washburn	Hunter
Herbert Rawlinson	T. F. Stockwell
Prince Modupe	Tobo
Jackie Newfield	Doreen, as a child
N'bonga (Ray Corrigan)	Sampson, the gorilla
I. Stanford Jolley	Policeman

Synopsis:
In an effort to clear the name of his deceased father, Ray Gorman travels to Africa to try to track down the money embezzled from his father's bank years earlier. After a long trek through the jungle, Gorman finds the money in the care of beautiful "white witch" Doreen, daughter of the now long-dead embezzler. Gorman finds his goal difficult to accomplish as not only does Doreen, guarded by a huge, ferocious gorilla, not want to give up the money, but greedy guide Carl Hurst has followed Gorman's trail, intent on getting the money himself by any means necessary.

Production Notes:
Filmed from late October to early November 1943.

The Monster Maker

Produced and Released by PRC Pictures Inc. n April 15, 1944. Copyright PRC Pictures Inc. April 15, 1944, LP13611. Running Time, 62-64 minutes. *Directed by* Sam Newfield; produced by Sigmund Neufeld; original story, Lawrence Williams; *screenplay by* Pierre Gendron and Martin Mooney; *sound engineer*, Ferol Redd; *set designer*, Paul Palmentola; *set dressings*, Elias H. Reif; *film editor*, Holbrook N. Todd; *assistant director*, Melville DeLay; *music score*, Albert Glasser; *musical supervision*, David Chudnow; *make-up*, Maurice Seiderman; *production manager*, Bert Sternbach.

Cast:

J. Carrol Naish	. . . . .	Markoff
Ralph Morgan	. . . . .	Lawrence
Tala Birell	. . . . .	Maxine
Wanda McKay	. . . . .	Patricia
Terry Frost	. . . . .	Blake
Glenn Strange	. . . . .	Giant
Alexander Pollard	. . . . .	Butler
Sam Flint	. . . . .	Dr. Adams
Ace	. . . . .	Himself
Ray Corrigan	. . . . .	Gorilla

Synopsis:
The evil Dr. Markoff is a scientist experimenting with a cure for the rare disfiguring disease acromegaly. At a concert by pianist Lawrence he sees a beautiful girl who reminds him of his late wife. Backstage he discovers that she is Lawrence's daughter Patricia. He sets out to woo her, but after she spurns his advances he deliberately infects her father with acromegaly with the plan of forcing him to "give" his daughter to him in return for a cure.

Production Notes:
Filmed from early February through February 14, 1944.

344

The Hairy Ape

Produced by Jules Levey Productions. Released by United Artists Corp. on June 16, 1944. Copyright Jules Levey Productions, June 16, 1944, LP12801. Running Time, 90 minutes. *Directed by* Alfred Santell; *produced by* Jules Levey; *associate producer*, Joseph H. Nadel; *screenplay by* Robert D. Andrews and Decla Dunning; *musical director*, Eddie Paul; *music score composed by* Michel Michelet; *director of photography*, Lucien Andriot, a.s.c.; *art director*, James Sullivan; *assistant director*, Sam Nelson; *supervising editor*, William Ziegler; *film editor*, Harvey Manger; *sound engineer*, Corson Jowett; *special effects*, Harry Redmond; *set dressing*, Howard Bristrol; *make-up artist*, Bob Mark; *hair stylist*, Nina Roberts; *Eugene O'Neill's prize winning play.*

Cast:

William Bendix	. . . . .	Hank Smith
Susan Hayward	. . . . .	Mildred Douglas
John Loder	. . . . .	Tony Lazar
Dorothy Comingore	. . . . .	Helen Parker
Roman Bohnen	. . . . .	Paddy
Tom Fadden	. . . . .	Long
Alan Napier	. . . . .	MacDougald
Charles Cane	. . . . .	Gantry
Charles La Torre	. . . . .	Portuguese proprietor
Ray Corrigan	. . . . .	Gorilla

Also featuring: Don Zolava, Mary Zavian, George Sorel, Paul Weigel, Egon Brecher, Gisela Werbiseck, Carmen Rachel, Johnny Lee, Dick Baldwin, Ralph Dunn, William Halligan, Tommy Hughes, Bob Perry, Ruth Robinson, Rod De Medici, and Eddie Kane.

Synopsis:

Hank Smith, a brutish stoker on board a freighter, is appalled when Mildred Douglas, a society girl forced by circumstance to travel as a passenger, visits the stokehold and recoils at the filthy, sweating Hank. A powerhouse of a man with a primitive confidence, Hank has never been looked down on before nor suffered the insult "hairy ape" flung at him by the rich girl. At first he seeks vengeance for the insult, but broods over it until more than anything, he desires to understand it. When the ship reaches port, he seeks her out in her upper class surroundings, determined to grasp the meaning of the encounter.

Production Notes:

Filmed from January 10 to late February 1944. Retakes done on April 18, 1944.

UNIVERSAL *presents*

JUNGLE WOMAN
COPYRIGHT MCMXLIV BY UNIVERSAL PICTURES COMPANY, INC.

With
EVELYN ANKERS
J. CARROL NAISH
SAMUEL S. HINDS
LOIS COLLIER
MILBURN STONE
DOUGLASS DUMBRILLE
and
ACQUANETTA

Screenplay by
BERNARD SCHUBERT
HENRY SUCHER
EDWARD DEIN

Original Story by
HENRY SUCHER

Director of Photography ... JACK MACKENZIE, a.s.c.
Musical Director ... PAUL SAWTELL
Art Direction ... JOHN B. GOODMAN
ABRAHAM GROSSMAN
Director of Sound ... BERNARD B. BROWN
Technician ... JESS MOULIN
Set Decorations ... RUSSELL A. GAUSMAN
E.R. ROBINSON
Film Editor ... RAY SNYDER
Gowns ... VERA WEST
Dialogue Director ... EMORY HORGER

WE HEREBY MAKE GRATEFUL
ACKNOWLEDGMENT TO MR. CLYDE
BEATTY FOR HIS COOPERATION
AND INIMITABLE TALENT IN
STAGING THE THRILLING ANIMAL
SEQUENCES IN THIS PICTURE

Associate Producer
WILL COWAN

Directed by
REGINALD LeBORG

The End
A UNIVERSAL PICTURE

The Players
Beth .... EVELYN ANKERS
Dr. Fletcher ... J. CARROL NAISH
Coroner .... SAMUEL S. HINDS
Joan Fletcher .... LOIS COLLIER
Fred Mason .. MILBURN STONE
District Attorney
DOUGLASS DUMBRILLE
Bob Whitney ... RICHARD DAVIS

Miss Gray ...... NANA BRYANT
Dr. Meredith .. PIERRE WATKIN
George .... CHRISTIAN RUB
Caretaker ...... ALEC CRAIG
Willie .. EDWARD M. HYANS, Jr.
Joe, Fingerprint Man ..
RICHARD POWERS
and ACQUANETTA as Paula

Jungle Woman

Produced and Released by Universal Pictures Co., Inc. on July 7, 1944. Copyright Universal Pictures Co., Inc., June 14, 1944, LP12746. Running Time, 60-65 minutes. *Directed by* Reginald LeBorg; *associate producer*, Will Cowan; *screenplay by* Bernard Schubert, Henry Sucher, and Edward Dein; *original story by* Henry Sucher; *director of photography*, Jack Mackenzie, a.s.c.; *musical director*, Paul Sawtell; *art direction*, John B. Goodman and Abraham Grossman; *director of sound*, Bernard B. Brown; *technician*, Jess Moulin; *set decorations*, Russell A. Gausman and E. R. Robinson; *film editor*, Ray Snyder; *gowns*, Vera West; *dialogue director*, Emory Horger.

Cast:

Evelyn Ankers	. . . . .	Beth
J. Carrol Naish	. . . . .	Dr. Fletcher
Samuel S. Hinds	. . . . .	Coroner
Lois Collier	. . . . .	Joan Fletcher
Milburn Stone	. . . . .	Fred Mason
Douglass Dumbrille	. . . . .	District Attorney
Richard Davis	. . . . .	Bob Whitney
Nana Bryant	. . . . .	MIss Gray
Pierre Watkin	. . . . .	Dr. Meredith
Christian Rub	. . . . .	George
Alec Craig	. . . . .	Caretaker
Edward M. Hyans, Jr.	. . . . .	Willie
Richard Powers	. . . . .	Joe, Fingerprint Man
Acquanetta	. . . . .	Paula
Ray Corrigan	. . . . .	Gorilla

Also featuring: .

Synopsis:
Paula the ape woman is alive and well. She is at an old sanitarium run by Dr. Fletcher. She reverts to her true gorilla form every so often in order to kill somebody.

Production Notes:
Filmed between February 14 and late February 1944, this film is a sequel to "Captive Wild Woman". The following appeared in the opening credits: "We hereby make grateful acknowledgment to Mr. Clyde Beatty for his cooperation and inimitable talent in staging the thrilling animal sequences in this picture." At the end of the film appeared "The evil that man has wrought shall in the end destroy itself". . . The film utilized a lot of flashback sequences taken from "Captive Wild Woman". All of Corrigan's scenes in this movie are from that film.

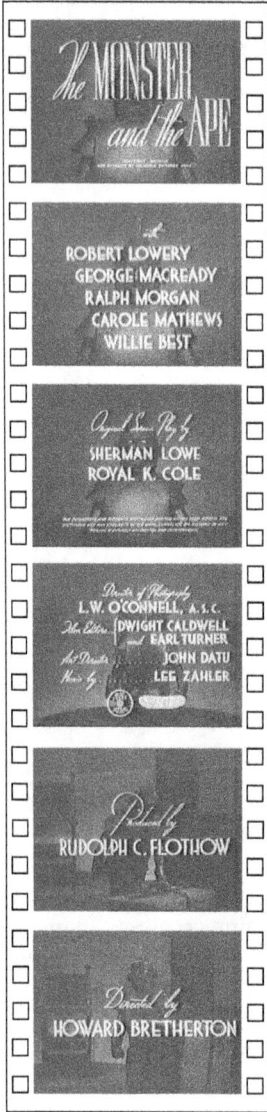

348

The Monster and the Ape

Produced and Released by Columbia Pictures Corp. on April 20, 1945. Copyright Columbia Pictures Corp. (see below) Running Time, 295 minutes, 15 Chapters. *Directed by* Howard Bretherton; *produced by* Rudolph C. Flothow; *original screen play by* Sherman Lowe and Royal K. Cole; *director of photography*, L. W. O'Connell, a.s.c.; *film editors*, Dwight Caldwell and Earl Turner; *art director*, John Datu; *music by* Lee Zahler.

Cast:

Robert Lowery	Ken Morgan
George Macready	Professor Ernst
Ralph Morgan	Professor Franklin Arnold
Carole Mathews	Babs Arnold
Willie Best	Flash
Ray Corrigan	Thor the Gorilla

Also featuring: Jack Ingram, Anthony Warde, Ted Mapes, Eddie Parker, Stanley Price, Charles King, Kenneth MacDonald, and Bud Osborne.

Episode Titles:

1. The Mechanical Terror — copyright April 20, 1945 L13399
2. The Edge of Doom — copyright April 27, 1945 L13408
3. Flames of Fate — copyright May 4, 1945 L13400
4. The Fatal Search — copyright May 11, 1945 L13401
5. Rocks of Doom — copyright May 18, 1945 L13402
6. A Friend in Disguise — copyright May 25, 1945 L13403
7. A Scream in the Night — copyright June 2, 1945 L13409
8. Death in the Dark — copyright June 9, 1945 L13410
9. The Secret Tunnel — copyright June 16, 1945 L13411
10. Forty Thousand Volts — copyright June 23, 1945 L13412
11. The Mad Professor — copyright June 30, 1945 L13413
12. Shadows of Destiny — copyright July 7, 1945 L13414
13. The Gorilla at Large — copyright July 14, 1945 L13415
14. His Last Flight — copyright July 21, 1945 L13416
15. Justice Triumphs — copyright July 28, 1945 L13417

Synopsis:

At the Bainbridge Research Foundation, Professor Franklin Arnold displays his Metalogen Man, a robot, to Professor Ernst and three other colleagues. Shortly afterward, the three associates are killed by Thor, a huge ape trained by Ernst, and Arnold, his daughter Babs and Ken Morgan, a representative of the company for whom the robot was made, find that it has been stolen.

Production Notes:

Exterior shots filmed at the Columbia Ranch and Bronson Canyon Caves.

"THE EDGE OF DOOM"
Chapter 2
"THE MONSTER AND THE APE"
A COLUMBIA SERIAL REPRINT

THE MONSTER AND THE APE

with
ROBERT LOWERY
GEORGE MACREADY
RALPH MORGAN
CAROLE MATHEWS

Original Screen Play by
SHERMAN LOWE and ROYAL K. COLE
Produced by RUDOLPH C. FLOTHOW
Directed by HOWARD BRETHERTON

+ Chapter 6 +
A FIEND IN DISGUISE

A COLUMBIA SUPER-SERIAL (Reprint)

352

White Pongo

Produced by Sigmund Neufeld Productions Inc. Released by PRC Pictures Inc. on November 2, 1945. Copyright PRC Pictures Inc. August 10, 1945 LP13598. Running Time, 74-77 minutes, 8 reels. *Directed by* Sam Newfield; *produced by* Sigmund Neufeld; *screenplay and original story by* Raymond L. Schrock; *production manager*, Bert Sternbach; *director of photography*, Jack Greenhalgh, a.s.c.; *special effects*, Ray Mercer; *musical director*, Leo Erdody; *sound engineer*, John Carter; *film editor*, Holbrook N. Todd; *art director*, Edward C. Jewell; *set dresser*, Elias H. Reif; *master of properties*, Eugene C. Stone; *costumed by* James H. Wade.

Cast:

Richard Fraser	. . . . .	Jeffrey Bishop
Maris Wrixon	. . . . .	Pamela Bragdon
Lionel Royce	. . . . .	Dr. Peter Van Doom
Al Eben	. . . . .	Hans Kroegert
Gordon Richards	. . . . .	Sir Harry Bragdon
Michael Dyne	. . . . .	Clive Carswell
George Lloyd	. . . . .	Baxter
Larry Steers	. . . . .	Dr. Kent
Milton Kibbee	. . . . .	Gunderson
Egon Brecher	. . . . .	Dr. Gerig
Joel Fluellen	. . . . .	Mumbo Jumbo
Ray Corrigan	. . . . .	Gorilla
Rod Cameron		Gorilla

Also featuring: Jack Perrin.

Synopsis:
In the jungles of the Belgian Congo, Gunderson is being held prisoner by the Negrito tribe. Dr. Gerig, an aging scientist, frees Gunderson and gives him the diary of a dead comrade, Dr. Friedrich Dierdoff. While fleeing, Gunderson sees an albino gorilla. In England, Dr. Peter Van Doom reads the diary and is convinced that the albino gorilla is the missing link. An expedition is formed to find the albino/pongo gorilla.

Production Notes:
Exterior locations were shot at the Baldwin Ranch, now known as the Los Angeles County Arboretum in Arcadia. Both the white and black gorillas were portrayed by Corrigan. When both the black and the white gorilla appeared in the same scene, Corrigan portrayed the black gorilla and Rod Cameron was the white gorilla.

IN THE POWER OF THE MISSING LINK!

PRC presents

WHITE PONGO

with

RICHARD **FRASER** · MARIS **WRIXON**

LIONEL ROYCE · AL EBEN

GORDON RICHARDS

MICHAEL DYNE

GEORGE LLOYD

PRC

Screenplay and Original Story by RAYMOND L. SCHROCK
Produced by SIGMUND NEUFELD · Directed by SAM NEWFIELD

357

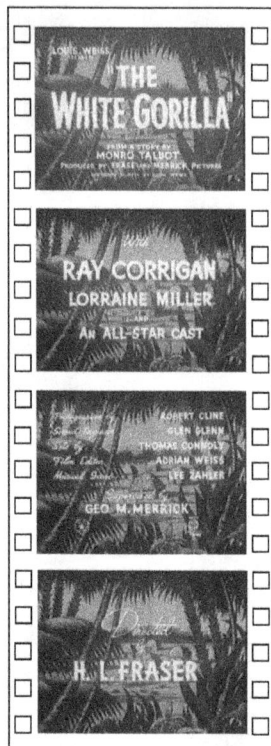

The White Gorilla

Produced by Louis Weiss. Released on the States Rights Market in 1946. Copyright Louis Weiss, July 12, 1945 LP13381. Running Time, 62 minutes, 6 reels. *Directed by* H. L. Fraser; *produced by* Frase and Merrick Pictures; *from a story by* Monro Talbot; *photographed by* Robert Cline; *sound engineer,* Glen Glenn; *sets by* Thomas Connoly; *film editor,* Adrian Weiss; *musical score,* Lee Zahler; *supervised by* George M. Merrick.

Cast:

Ray Corrigan	. . . . .	Steve Collins; Nbonga, the black gorilla; and Narrator
Lorraine Miller	. . . . .	Ruth Stacey
Charles King	. . . . .	J. Morgan
Francis Ford	. . . . .	Stacey
George Lewis	. . . . .	Stacey's cohort

Also featuring in stock footage: Frank Merrill, Bobby Nelson, Eugenia Gilbert, Albert J. Smith.

Synopsis:
A white gorilla is snubbed by black gorillas because he is the wrong color. Cut off from his tribe he becomes lonely and angry. After upsetting hunters and natives, the white gorilla battles the king of the black gorillas.

Production Notes:
The white gorilla, Konga, was portrayed by Corrigan in scenes in which Corrigan did not appear as himself or as Nbonga. Where he appeared with the Konga, the white gorilla was portrayed by an unknown actor. A large amount of this film consists of footage from "Perils of the Jungle" (1927).

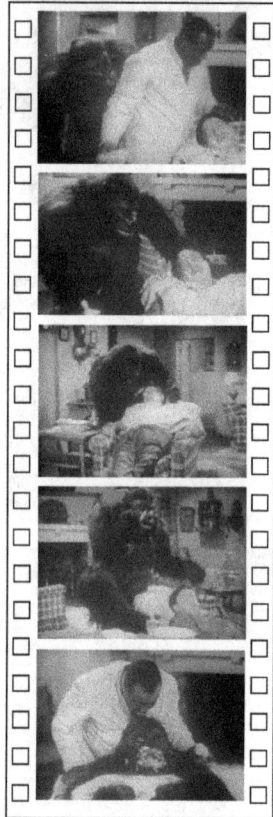

Tall, Dark and Gruesome

Produced and Released by Columbia Pictures Corp. on April 15, 1948. Copyright Louis Weiss, July 12, 1945 LP13381. Running Time, 16 minutes, 2 reels. *Directed by* Del Lord; *produced by* Hugh McCollum; *story and screenplay by* Clyde Bruckman; *director of photography,* Ira H. Morgan, a.s.c.; *art director,* Charles Clague; *film editor,* Henry DeMond.

Cast:

Hugh Herbert	. . . . .	Hugh Sherlock
Dudley Dickerson	. . . . .	Dudley
Ray Corrigan	. . . . .	Gorilla

Also featuring: Charles C. Wilson, Christine McIntyre, Myron Healey, and Heinie Conklin.

Synopsis:

Sherlock, a playwright, is having trouble working in the city with riveters outside his residence. So, they pack up and head for the mountains. A crate with a gorilla inside is delivered there. The ape escapes and causes problems with Sherlock and his servant.

Production Notes:

Filmed entirely on a sound stage. Corrigan seems to have a lot of fun with Hugh Herbert and shaving him. He ends up being shaved by the butler.

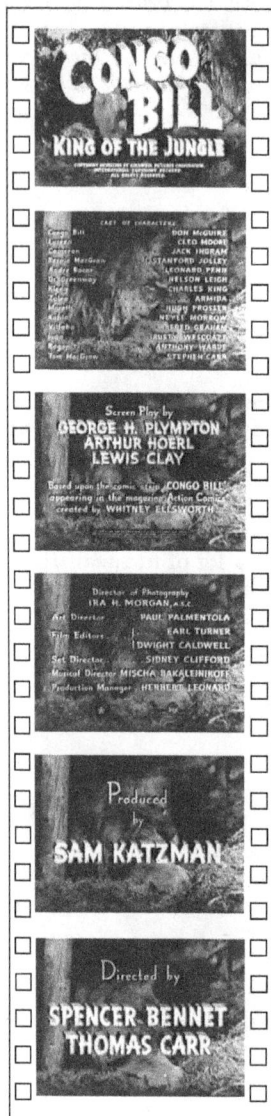

364

Congo Bill

Produced and Released by Columbia Pictures Corp. in October 1948. Copyright Columbia Pictures Corp. (see below). Running Time, 12 Chapters, 2 reels each. *Directed by* Spencer Bennet and Thomas Carr; *produced by* Sam Katzman; *screen play by* George H. Plympton, Arthur Hoerl, and Lewis Clay; *based upon the comic strip CONGO BILL appearing in the magazine Action Comics created by Whitney Ellsworth; director of photography,* Ira H. Morgan, a.s.c.; *art director,* Paul Palmentola; *film editors,* Earl Turner and Dwight Caldwell; *set director,* Sidney Clifford; *musical director,* Mischa Bakaleinikoff; *production manager,* Herbert Leonard.

Cast:

Don McGuire	. . . .	Congo Bill
Cleo Moore	. . . .	Lureen
Jack Ingram	. . . .	Cameron
I. Stanford Jolley	. . . .	Bernie MacGraw
Leonard Penn	. . . .	Andre Bocar
Nelson Leigh	. . . .	Dr. Greenway
Charles King	. . . .	Kleeg
Armida	. . . .	Zalea
Hugh Prosser	. . . .	Morelli
Neyle Morrow	. . . .	Kahla
Fred Graham	. . . .	Villabo
Rusty Wescoatt	. . . .	Ivan
Anthony Warde	. . . .	Rogan
Stephen Carr	. . . .	Tom MacGraw
Ray Corrigan	. . . .	Gorilla

Also featuring:

Episode Titles:

1. The Untamed Beast	copyright October 12, 1948 LP1853
2. Jungle Gold	copyright October 13, 1948 LP1889
3. A Hot Reception	copyright October 26, 1948 LP1876
4. Congo Bill Springs a Trap	copyright November 2, 1948 LP1892
5. White Shadows in the Jungle	copyright November 9, 1948 LP1903
6. The White Queen	copyright November 17, 1948 LP1926
7. Black Panther	copyright November 23, 1948 LP1938
8. Sinister Schemes	copyright November 30, 1948 LP1957
9. The Witch Doctor Strikes	copyright December 7, 1948 LP1992
10. Trail of Treachery	copyright December 14, 1948 LP1997
11. A Desperate Chance	copyright December 22, 1948 LP2018
12. The Lair of the Beast	copyright December 28, 1948 LP2028

Synopsis:

Congo Bill, a tamer of wild animals, intends to find Ruth Culver, a missing woman who has just inherited the Culver Circus, worth half a million dollars. He has heard of the existence somewhere in Africa of a white queen who might be Ruth. Once on the African continent, Congo Bill's safari gets attacked several times. The man behind all that is none other than Andre Bocar, a trafficker in cahoots with Bernie MacGraw, who hopes to capture the Culver inheritance. With the help of Cameron, a mysterious stranger, Congo Bill manages to locate Lureen, the white queen, who turns out to be Ruth Culver as the tamer had guessed. But trouble is not at an end yet. Indeed Nagu, the witch doctor, who smuggles gold with Bocar, tries to get rid of Congo Bill. To no avail, for Bill and Cameron (who happens to be a colonial officer) recover the gold and capture Bocar. Congo Bill returns to the USA with Lureen/Ruth with a view to creating new circus, even bigger than the former one.

Production Notes:
Exteriors shot at Jungleland, Iverson Movie Ranch, and Ray Corrigan Ranch. Corrigan portrayed the gorilla in the first two chapters of the serial. Another actor, identity unknown, portrayed the gorilla in the rest of the serial.

CONGO BILL
KING OF THE JUNGLE

Based upon the comic strip, "Congo Bill," appearing in "Action Comics" magazine, created by WHITNEY ELLSWORTH

with

DON McGUIRE
(as Congo Bill)

CLEO MOORE
JACK INGRAM
I. STANFORD JOLLEY

Screenplay by
GEORGE H. PLYMPTON, ARTHUR HOERL and LEWIS CLAY
Directed by SPENCER BENNET and THOMAS CARR
Produced by SAM KATZMAN
A COLUMBIA SUPER-SERIAL Reprint

Chapter 11.
"A Desperate Chance"

367

ROBERT L. LIPPERT
Presents

"RENEGADE GIRL"

Starring

ANN ALAN
SAVAGE CURTIS

EDWARD BROPHY
RUSSELL WADE

with
JACK HOLT · CLAUDIA DRAKE
RAY CORRIGAN · JOHN KING
and
CHIEF THUNDER CLOUD
EDMUND COBB
RICHARD CURTIS
NICK THOMPSON
HARRY CORDING
ERNIE ADAMS
JAMES MARTIN

Original Screenplay
EDWIN V. WESTRATE

Director of Photography
JAMES BROWN, Jr. A.S.C.
Supervising Editor . . . . ARTHUR A. BROOKS
Production Manager . . . CARL HITTLEMAN
Musical Director . . . . DAVID CHUDNOW
Musical Score . . . . . DARRELL CALKER
Sound Recorder . . . . MAX HUTCHINSON

Associate Producer
SAMUEL K. DECKER

Produced and Directed
by
WILLIAM BERKE

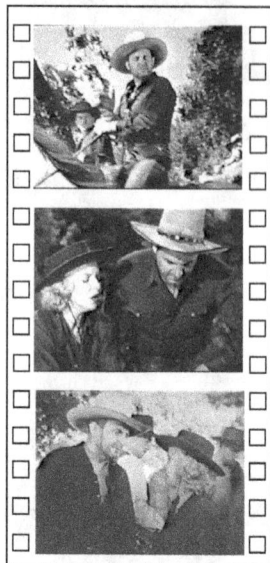

Fine performances by Alan Curtis and Ann Savage, exciting action with a fine historical background, and impressive outdoor settings—all combined with a highly unusual and exciting story go to make "Renegade Girl." cmpanion feature on the Paramount Friday program, an entertaining picture.

Renegade Girl

Produced by Affiliated Productions, Inc. Released by Screen Guild Productions, Inc. on December 25, 1946. Copyright November 15, 1946, Screen Guild Productions, Inc., LP779. Running time 65 minutes, 5,871 feet. *Directed by* William Berke; *produced by* William Berke; *president*, Robert L. Lippert; *original screenplay by* Edwin V. Westrate; *director of photography*, James Brown, Jr. A.S.C.; *supervising editor*, Arthur A. Brooks; *production manager*, Carl Hittleman; *musical director*, David Chudnow; *musical score*, Darrell Calker; *sound recorder*, Max Hutchinson; *associate producer*, Samuel K. Decker.

Cast:

Ann Savage	. . . . Jean Shelby
Alan Curtis	. . . . Captain Fred Raymond
Edward Brophy	. . . . Bob Crandall
Russell Wade	. . . . Jerry Long
Jack Holt	. . . . Major Barker
Claudia Drake	. . . . Mary Manson
Ray Corrigan	. . . . Bill Quantrill
John King	. . . . Corporal Brown
Chief Thunder Cloud	. . . . Chief White Cloud
Edmund Cobb	. . . . Sergeant James
Richard Curtis	. . . . Joe Barnes
Nick Thompson	. . . . Tom Starr
Harry Cording	. . . . Mustached raider
Ernie Adams	. . . . Ted
James Martin	. . . . Bob Shelby

Synopsis:

Jean Shelby, beautiful Southern girl in whose veins flows a trace of hot Indian blood, has a brother, Bob, who is a member of a gang of Rebel guerillas headed by William Quantrill. These guerillas, in the latter days of the Civil War, continue to harass the Yankee military occupants of the Missouri border region, whom they consider to be invaders. Through the offices of a blood enemy of the Shelby's, a turncoat Cherokee named White Cloud, who is in the pay of the Union Army, Bob and Quantrill are killed. Jean falls in love with a Union Army captain, Fred Raymond, who returns her affections. However, she is led to believe that he has betrayed her and in bitterness she joins the remnants of the Quantrill gang. As their leader, she plots a series of brutal raids against persons and property they consider to be fair prey. The gang members, however, fall out over which of them shall have Jean and this culminates in a gun battle in which the outlaws virtually whipe themselves out. Jean and Fred are reunited, and she discovers that he has been faithful to her. Because of her outlaw past, however, she realizes they cannot marry, so she dashes off alone to confront and kill White Cloud, whose Indian band is raiding in the vicinity. Fred discovers her purpose and leads a band of Union soldiers to her aid. The find her at the scene of a cabin under attack by White Cloud's band. The Indians are routed, but Jean has suffered fatal wounds and dies in Fred's arms at the fadeout.

369

Production Notes:
Filmed during mid-September 1946 with location scenes photographed at the west Morrison Agoura Ranch and the Ray Corrigan Ranch. When the actor who was signed to play Quantrill failed to show up the first day of shooting, producer/director Berke selected an old friend, Ray Corrigan, at whose ranch they were filming that day, to step into the role of Quantrill. Ann Savage was injured while performing a stunt scene on location where she was called upon to fall from an embankment and roll more than 15 feet to the foot of a huge oak tree. James Martin also was injured during a riding scene when he was thrown from the saddle after his horse stepped into a hole. He fractured a rib.

PLUS

Outdoor thrills with Quantrill's Raiders in . . .

"RENEGADE GIRL"

Alan CURTIS
Ann SAVAGE
Edward BROPHY
Jack HOLT

A LEADER
AMONG
OUTLAWS...
Yet just a Woman in Love!

AFFILIATED
PRODUCTIONS
presents

RENEGADE GIRL

WITH ALAN CURTIS · ANN SAVAGE
EDWARD BROPHY · RUSSELL WADE

JACK HOLT · RAY CORRIGAN

Producer-Director WILLIAM BERKE
Original Screenplay by EDWIN V. WESTRATE

Distributed by SCREEN GUILD PRODUCTIONS

371

FILM CLASSICS, INC.
Unknown
ISLAND
Color by CINECOLOR
VIRGINIA GREY
PHILIP REED
RICHARD DENNING
BARTON MacLANE
ROBERT T. SHANNON
ROBERT T. SHANNON
JACK HARVEY
ALBERT J. COHEN
JACK BERNHARD

Unknown Island

Produced by Albert Jay Cohen Productions, Inc. Released by Film Classics Inc. in November 1948. Copyright by Albert Jay Cohen Productions, Inc., December 1, 1948 LP2087. Running time 75-79 minutes, 8 reels. *Directed by* Jack Bernhard; *produced by* Albert J. Cohen; *screenplay by* Robert T. Shannon and Jack Harvey; *original story by* Robert T. Shannon; *director of photography,* Fred Jackman, Jr.; *camera operator,* Robert Gough; *stills,* Milton Gold; *special effects photographed and created by* Howard A. Anderson and Ellis Burman; *color director,* Henry J. Staudig; *art director,* Jerome Pycha, Jr.; *film editor,* Harry Gerstad; *set decorator,* Robert Priestly; *music by* Ralph Stanley; *sound by* Max Hutchinson; *makeup supervisor,* Harry Ross; *production manager,* R. E. Abel; *script supervisor,* Mary Gibsone; *grip,* John Livesley.

Cast:

Virginia Grey	. . . .	Carol Lane
Philip Reed	. . . .	Ted Osborne
Richard Denning	. . . .	John Fairbanks
Barton MacLane	. . . .	Captain Tarnowski
Richard Wessel	. . . .	Sanderson
Daniel White	. . . .	Edwards
Philip Nazir	. . . .	Golab
Ray Corrigan	. . . .	Giant Sloth

Also featuring: Snub Pollard and Harry Wilson.

Synopsis:
Adventure-seeker Ted Osborne has convinced his finacee Carol to finance his expedition to an uncharted South Pacific island supposedly populated with dinosaurs. Piloting their ship is Captain Tarnowski, a ruthless alcoholic suffering from malaria-induced bouts of insanity. When they arrive at the island, they discover that the stories they have heard are all true.

Production Notes:
Filmed in Cinecolor. Some exteriors of the fighting monsters were filmed in the Palmdale area as well as the Ray Corrigan Ranch. A few scenes of the coastline were shot in the Southern California area.

Crime on Their Hands

Produced and Released by Columbia Pictures Corp. on December 9, 1948. Copyright Columbia Pictures Corp., December 9, 1948, LP2051. Running Time, 18 minutes. *Directed by* Edward Bernds; *produced by* Hugh McCollum; *story and screenplay by* Elwood Ullman; *director of photography*, Henry Freulich, a.s.c.; *art director*, Charles Clague; *film editor*, Henry DeMond.

Cast:

Shemp	. . . . .	Shemp
Larry	. . . . .	Larry
Moe	. . . . .	Moe
Kenneth MacDonald	. . . . .	Dapper Malone
Christine McIntyre	. . . . .	Bea
Charles C. Wilson	. . . . .	J. L. Cameron
Lester Allen	. . . . .	Runty
Ray Corrigan	. . . . .	Gorilla

Also featuring: Heinie Conklin, George Lloyd, Frank O'Connor, Cy Schindell, and Blackie Whiteford.

Synopsis:
The Three Stooges are janitors working in a newspaper office. When an anonymous caller phones in a tip about the theft a famous diamond, the boys decide to become reporters and go after the crooks. They find the crooks, but Shemp accidentally swallows the diamond which was hidden in a bowl of candy. The crooks want to cut the diamond out, but the boys foil them with the help of a friendly gorilla.

Production Notes:
No exterior filming. This short was remade as "Hot Ice" in 1955.

The Lost Tribe

Produced by The Sam Katzman Corp. Released by Columbia Pictures Corp. on May 3, 1949. Copyright Columbia Pictures Corp. April 28, 1949 LP2247. Running Time, 71-72 minutes. *Directed by* William Berke; *produced by* Sam Katzman; *screen play by* Arthur Hoerl and Don Martin; *story by* Arthur Hoerl; *based upon the newspaper feature JUNGLE JIM owned and copyrighted by King Features Syndicate and which appears regularly in The Comic Weekly*; *director of photography*, Ira H. Morgan, a.s.c.; *art director*, Paul Palmentola; *film editor*, Aaron Stell; *set decorator*, Sidney Clifford; *musical director*, Mischa Bakaleinikoff.

Cast:

Johnny Weissmuller	. . . . .	Jungle Jim
Myrna Dell	. . . . .	Norina
Elena Verdugo	. . . . .	Li Wanna
Joseph Vitale	. . . . .	Calhoun
Ralph Dunn	. . . . .	Captain Rawling
Paul Marion	. . . . .	Chot
Nelson Leigh	. . . . .	Zoron
George J. Lewis	. . . . .	Whip Wilson
Ray Corrigan	. . . . .	Gorilla

Also featuring: Emil Sitka, Jody Gilbert, John Merton, Gil Perkins, George DeNormand, Wally West, Charles Schaeffer, Wally West, Blackie Whiteford, Rube Schaffer, Billy Jones, Charles Gemorra, D. Drager, C. Campbell, and J. Marlow.

Synopsis:

A lost treasure is located somewhere in the faraway land of Dzamm. Villains Calhoun and Rawling plot to steal the treasure, but Jungle Jim won't let that happen. Our hero summons forth an army of gorillas to fight off the bad guys.

Production Notes:

Filmed between September 8 and 20, 1948. Exteriors were shot at Portuguese Bend and Corriganville (the Ray Corrigan Ranch). This was one of the last few times that Corrigan appeared in one of his ape costumes (he owned several) on film. Other actors portraying gorillas are Emil Sitka, D. Drager, C. Campbell, and J. Marlow (information contained in a Call Sheet for September 14, 1948). Stuntman Billy Jones was injured when he jumped, dressed as a gorilla, from an archway onto stunt doubles 10 feet below and they failed to break his fall. He was out of work for several weeks.

Next Page Top: Several actors were hired to portray gorillas in this film, including Corrigan and Emil Sitka.

CALL

COLUMBIA PICTURES CORPORATION

Director...... WM.BERKE ...... Picture.. #942 - JUNGLE JIM'S ADVENTURE

Date..... TUESDAY SEPT. 14,1948 ..... Time...... 8:30 AM SHOOTING   A.M. P.M.

NOTE: NOTIFICATION AT 5:00PM 9/13 AS TO WHETHER THIS CALL IN EFFECT. NOTIFICATION AT
     6:00 AM.THIS CALL IN EFFECT FOR ALL TALENT UNLESS CHANGED AT 6:00 AM.
NOTE: CAST & CREW REPORT TO COLUMBIA RANCH
LOCATION: CORRIGAN'S RANCH(VENDETTA ST)
EXT. VILLAGE OF DZAAM & TEMPLE(D)SEQ 9½ SCS 410-469 CONT.COMPL. OF NOT FIN
EXT. DZAAM TEMPLE(D)SEQ 2, SCS 92-97
EXT.   "   " (D)SEQ 4, SCS 120-125

CAST: 7:00 AM LV -8:00 AM WARD. & MAKEUP ON LOC 8:30 AM READY

JOHNNY WEISSMULLER	JIM	
RALPH DUNN	RAWLING	
GEO. LEWIS	WILSON	
JOE VITALE	CALHOUN	
RUBE SCHAEFFER	LERCH	
GEO. DENORMAND	CULLEN	
PAUL MARION	CHOT	
AL WYATT	JORY	
WALLY WEST	ECKLE	
ELENA VERDUGO	LAWANNA	6:00 AM HAIRDR.
GIL PERKINS	DOJECK	
NELSON LEIGH	ZOROM	6:00 AM MAKEUP

STANDINS: WEEKLY 7:00 AM LV RANCH

P.WEISSMULLER	S.I. WEISSMULLER
L.LANDI	S.I. UTILITY
P.BARIBAULT	S.I. "

BITS: KAY NOTIFY 7:00 AM LV-8:00 AM WARD ON LOC-9:00 AM READY IF NOT FIN

R.CORRIGAN	GORILLA
D.DRAGER	"
C.CAMPBELL	"
J.MARLOW	"
EMIL SITKA	"

ATMOSPHERE: 7:00 AM LV WARD FURN COL.NOTIFY
4 seamen(wkly)(Whiteford,Laidlaw,Dorrington,Martin)
33 extras as recalled-will cut if not fin
5 children "

DOUBLES: 7:00 AM LV RANCH 8:00 AM MAKEUP WARD ON LOC. KAY NOTIFY

PAUL STADER(WKLY)	STUNT DBLE WEISSMULLER		
C.SAXW	" " VITALE		
B.WOLFE	" " DUNNE	LIVESTOCK:	8:00 AM ON LOC
D.GREEN	" " NATIVE	3 boats	
J.DAHEIM	" " "	3 sheep	
P.KEOLOHA	" "		

Above is a Call Sheet for September 14, 1948, the day that the gorilla attack on the village of Dzaam was filmed at Corrigan's Movie Ranch. In the listing of actors, under "Bits", you find the five actors who performed as gorillas in the film, with Corrigan as the first. Emil Sitka used one of Corrigan's costumes.

Microspook

Produced by Hugh McCollum Productions. Released by Columbia Pictures Corp. on June 9, 1949. Copyright by Columbia Pictures Corp, June 9, 1949 LP2386. Running time, 16 minutes, 2 reels. *Directed by* Edward Bernds; *produced by* Hugh McCollum; *written by* Edward Bernds; *film editor,* Henry DeMond.

Cast:

Harry von Zell	. . . . .	Harry von Zell
Christine McIntyre	. . . . .	Jean
Emil Sitka	. . . . .	George
Dudley Dickerson	. . . . .	Zack
Jimmy Aubrey	. . . . .	Blinky
Harry Tyler	. . . . .	Station boss
Ray Corrigan	. . . . .	Congo the Gorilla

Synopsis:
His radio station co-workers are so annoyed at being the victims of announcer Harry Von Zell's endless practical joking, they decide to get even by selling the sponsor on having Von Zell do a broadcast from a haunted house. They then sneak in to scare him with a gorilla costume worn by one of them, only to find that an escaped gorilla and his keeper are already there.

Production Notes:
Filmed in mid-August 1948 at the Darmour Studio. Emil Sitka met Corrigan on this film shoot and they became friends. The next month, Corrigan invited Sitka to portray a gorilla in "The Lost Tribe". Below, Sitka meets Corrigan's gorilla.

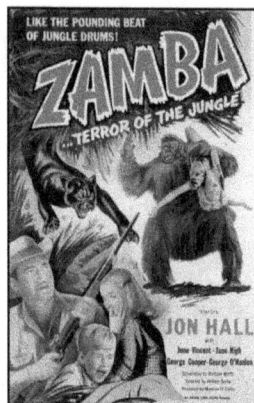

Zamba

Produced by Fortune Film Corp. Released by Eagle-Lion Films, Inc. in September 1949. Copyright Fortune Film Corp., September 9, 1949, LP2623. Running time, 70-71 minutes, 6,395 feet, 8 reels. *Directed by* William Berke; *produced by* Maurice H. Conn; *associate producer*, Harry Hendel; *screenplay by* Barbara Worth; *from the original story The Girl and the Gorilla by* Maurice H. Conn; *music by* Raoul Kraushaar; *director of photography*, James S. Brown, Jr., a.s.c.; *film editor*, Martin G. Cohn; *special effects*, Ray Mercer, a.s.c.; *sound effects editor*, Quinn Martin; *sound recorder*, Garry Harris; *art director*, Fred Preble; *set decorator*, Elias H. Reif; *assistant director*, Al Westen; *dialogue director*, Irvin Berwick; *production manager*, Robert Beche.

Cast:

Jon Hall	. . . . .	Steve O'Malley
June Vincent	. . . . .	Jenny Duncan
George Cooper	. . . . .	Doug
Jane Nigh	. . . . .	Caro
George O'Hanlon	. . . . .	Marvin
N'Bonga (Ray Corrigan)	. . . . .	Zamba
Beau Bridges	. . . . .	Tommy Duncan
Pierre Watkin	. . . . .	Benton
Harry Lauter	. . . . .	Jim
Alphonse Martel	. . . . .	Gaston
Darby Jones	. . . . .	Keega
Theron Jackson	. . . . .	Kayla
Ernest Whitman	. . . . .	Bit part

Synopsis:
Jenny Duncan and her six-year-old son, Tommy, are flying over the Belgian Congo when they are forced to bail out and become separated. Jenny is rescued by a safari headed by two wild-animal collectors, but Tommy is not found. He has amnesia and is lost, but is adopted by Zamba, a huge gorilla. Jenny returns with a searching party, while Zamba, the gorilla protector, is determined to protect Tommy from outsiders.

Production Notes:
Filmed from mid-September to early October 1948 at the Nassour Studios. Exteriors were shot at the Ray Corrigan Ranch (soon to be Corriganville).

COLUMBIA

Adventures of Sir Galahad

Produced by Sam Katzman

Directed by Spencer Bennet

Chapter 7 Unknown Betrayer

Chapter 8 Perilous Adventure

Chapter 9 Treacherous Magic

Adventures of Sir Galahad

Produced and Released by Columbia Pictures Corp. on December 22, 1949. Copyright Columbia Pictures Corp. (see below). Running Time, 15 Chapters, 2 reels each. *Directed by* Spencer Bennet; *produced by* Sam Katzman; *written for the screen by* George H. Plympton, Lewis Clay, and David Mathews; director of photography, Ira H. Morgan, a.s.c.; *art director*, Paul Palmentola; *film editors*, Earl Turner and Dwight Caldwell; *set decorator*, Sidney Clifford; *set continuity by* Robert Walker; *musical director*, Mischa Bakaleinikoff; *production manager*, Herbert Leonard.

Cast:

George Reeves	.....	Sir Galahad
Charles King	.....	Sir Bors
William Fawcett	.....	Merlin, the Magician
Pat Barton	.....	Morgan le Fay
Hugh Prosser	.....	Sir Lancelot
Lois Hall	.....	Lady of the Lake
Nelson Leigh	.....	King Arthur
Jim Diehl	.....	Sir Kay
Don Harvey	.....	Bartog
Marjorie Stapp	.....	Queen Guinevere
John Merton	.....	Ulric
Pierce Lyden	.....	Cawker
Ray Corrigan	.....	One-Eyed Proprietor

Also featuring: Rick Vallin, Leonard Penn, Frank Ellis, Al Ferguson, Paul Frees, and Rusty Wescoatt.

Chapter Titles:

1. The Stolen Sword — copyright Dember 22, 1949 LP2708
2. Galahad's Daring — copyright December 29, 1949 LP2755
3. Prisoners of Ulric — copyright January 5, 1950 LP2767
4. Attack on Camelot — copyright not registered
5. Galahad to the Rescue — copyright January 19, 1950 LP2768
6. Passage of Peril — copyright January 17, 1950 LP2839
7. Unknown Betrayer — copyright January 24, 1950 LP2840
8. Perilous Adventure — copyright January 31, 1950 LP2884
9. Treacherous Magic — copyright February 7, 1950 LP2841
10. The Sorcerer's Spell — copyright February 14, 1950 LP2842
11. Valley of No Return — copyright February 21, 1950 LP2883
12. Castle Perilous — copyright February 28, 1950 LP2885
13. The Wizard's Revenge — copyright March 6, 1950 LP2889
14. Quest for the Queen — copyright March 14, 1950 LP2915
15. Galahad's Triumph — copyright March 21, 1950 LP2916

Synopsis:

Sir Galahad is refused admission to King Arthur's Round Table until he regains the missing magic sword "Excalibur". Ulric invades England. Galahad, aided by Sir Bors, attempts to retrieve "Excalibur" from Bartog, Ulric's chief aide, who has gotten it from a mysterious Knight. Merlin the Magician harasses Galahad at every turn, while Morgan le Fey, Arthur's sister and also a magician, helps Galahad fight both Merlin's magic and the Saxons. The Black Knight, a traitor within Camelot, is conspiring with the Saxons and a band of outlaws to overthrow King Arthur. When Queen Guinevere is seized by the traitors, Merlin relents and sends Galahad to the Lady of the Lake, who gives him "Excalibur."

Production Notes:
Exteriors were shot at the Columbia Ranch and Corriganville (Ray Corrigan Ranch).

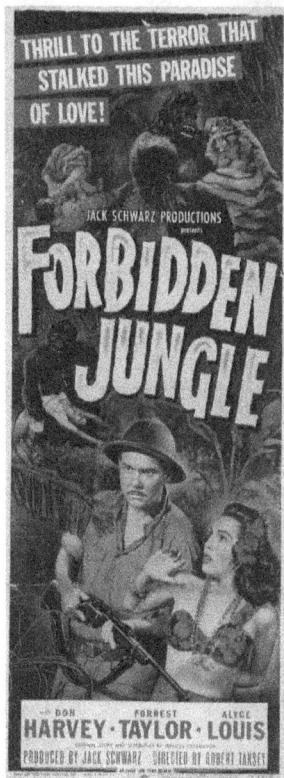

Forbidden Jungle

Produced by Jack Schwarz Productions, Inc. Released by Eagle-Lion Films, Inc. in March 1950. Copyright March 31, 1950, Jack Schwarz Productions, LP8. Running time, 66-67 minutes, 5,947 feet, 7 reels. *Directed by* Robert Tansey; *produced by* Jack Schwarz; *original story and screenplay by* Frances Kavanaugh; *musical supervision,* David Chudnow; *original music,* Darrel Calker; *production manager,* Arthur Hammond; *film editor,* Reg Browne; *wardrobe,* Albert Diano; *makeup,* Kiva Hoffman; *photography,* Clark Ramsey; *sound engineer,* T. T. Triplett; *set dressing,* Harry Reif; *set designer,* Fred Preble; *sound by* Academy Sound System; *animal trainer,* William Richards.

Cast:

Don Harvey	. . . .	Tom Burton
Forrest Taylor	. . . .	Trader Kirk
Alyce Louis	. . . .	Nita
Robert Cabal	. . . .	Tawa
Tamba	. . . .	Tamba
Ray Corrigan	. . . .	Gigi, the gorilla

Synopsis:
A well-known explorer, Tom Burton, accepts an assignment to track down a jungle boy for a wealthy American who believes the boy is his grandson. Burton penetrates a part of the African jungle rarely visited by white men and encounters Trader Kirk, ruler of the natives. Kirk and his daughter, Nita, try to dissuade Burton from his dangerous mission. When they fail, Nita races ahead to warn the boy, Tawa. The latter becomes curious about the white explorer and decides to see him. He saves the explorer's life when a lion attacks him. They become friends and Tawa leads Burton safely to the edge of the jungle, while he remains behind with his animal friends.

Production Notes:
Production began on August 8, 1949 at the Motion Pictures Center Studios.

The Fuller Brush Girl

Produced and Released by Columbia Pictures Corp. in September, 1950. Copyright January 10, 1950, Columbia Pictures Corp., LP441. Running time, 85-85 minutes, 7,579 feet. *Directed by* Lloyd Bacon; *written by* Frank Tashlin; *director of photography*, Charles Lawton, Jr., A.S.C.; *art director*, Robert Peterson; *film editor*, William Lyon; *assistant director*, Earl Bellamy; *gowns by* Jean Louis; *makeup*, Clay Campbell; *hair styles by* Helen Hunt; *sound engineer*, Lambert Day; *musical score by* Heinz Roemheld; *musical director*, Morris Stoloff.

Cast:

Lucille Ball	Sally Elliott
Eddie Albert	Humphrey Briggs
Carl Benton Reid	Christy
Gale Robbins	Ruby Rawlings
Jeff Donnell	Jane Bixby
Jerome Cowan	Harvey Simpson
John Litel	Watkins
Fred Graham	Rocky Mitchell
Lee Patrick	Claire Simpson
Arthur Space	Inspector Rodgers
Ray Corrigan	Gorilla

Also featuring: Sid Tomack, Billy Vincent, Lorin Raker, Lelah Tyler, Sarah Edwards, Lois Austin, Isabel Randolph, Isabel Withers, Donna Boswell, Gregory Marshall, Gail Bonney, Joet Robinson, Shirley Whitney, Mary Treen, Sumner Getchell, William Tannen, Bobby Hyatt, Charles Sherlock, Jay Barney, Russ Conway, John Doucette, Charles Hamilton, Joseph Palma, Cy Malis, Frank Wilcox, Jean Willes, Myron Healey, Jack Little, James L. Kelly, Raoul Freeman, Bud Osborne, George Lloyd, Cliff Clark, Paul E. Burns, Syd Saylor, Joseph Crehan, Charles Sullivan, Shirley Ballard, Barbara Pepper, Paul Bryar, Red Skelton.

Synopsis:

Sally Elliott and Humphrey Briggs want to get married and buy a house, but cannot afford it even with their combined salaries from the Maritime Steamship Company, where Sally is a switchboard operator, and Humphrey is a file clerk. After the cargo supervisor is fired, Sally encourages the timid Humphrey to apply for the job. Unknown to Sally and Humphrey, Harvey Simpson, the head of the company, is smuggling diamonds and wants to replace the former supervisor with a stupid man, like the unassuming Humphrey. On the strength of his new position, Humphrey puts a down payment on a house. At the office, Sally's friend, Jane Bixby, a Fuller Brush saleswoman, stops by to demonstrate the cosmetics she is selling. While trying the cosmetics, Sally manages to blow up the switchboard and is fired. Jane then convinces her to apply for a job as a Fuller Brush Girl. Her attempts at selling cosmetics door-to-door are disastrous. Things get worse when one of her customers is murdered and she becomes the prime suspect..

391

Production Notes:
Filmed September 6 to October 15, 1949. Columbia Ranch was used for many of the exterior shots. However, some real-life residences and streets were also used. Ray Corrigan appeared as the gorilla. The scenes may be stock footage from a prior Columbia Pictures film.

Pygmy Island

Produced and Released by Columbia Pictures Corp. in November 1950. Copyright January 11, 1950, Columbia Pictures Corp., LP968. Running time, 69 minutes, 6,190 feet. *Directed by* William Berke; *produced by* Sam Katzman; *written for the screen by* Carroll Young; *director of photography*, Ira H. Morgan, a.s.c.; *art director*, Paul Palmentola; *film editor*, Jerome Thoms; *set decorator*, Sidney Clifford; *musical director*, Mischa Bakaleinikoff; *unit manager*, Herbert Leonard.

Cast:

Johnny Weissmuller	. . . .	Jungle Jim
Ann Savage	. . . .	Capt. A. R. Kingsley
David Bruce	. . . .	Major Bolton
Steven Geray	. . . .	Leon Marko
William Tannen	. . . .	Kruger
Tris Coffin	. . . .	Novak
Billy Curtis	. . . .	Makuba

Also featuring: Tommy Farrell, Pierce Lyden, Rusty Wescoatt, Billy Barty, Ray Corrigan.

Synopsis:

Captain A. R. Kingsley is missing in Africa on a secret mission. Jungle Jim finds her dog tags among the remains of a dead pygmy. He joins a U.S. military investigation to locate her and to search for a recently discovered kind of rope made from the ngoma plant that will not burn or break. The Bush Devil cult is terrorizing the pygmies, seeking to scare them out of the ngoma territory. It is up to Jungle Jim to stop them.

Production Notes:

Filmed between June 5 and 15, 1950, at Corriganville and the Arboretum. Once again, Corrigan dons one of his gorilla costumes.

Trail of Robin Hood

Produced and Released by Republic Pictures Corp. on December 15, 1950. Copyright November 30, 1950, Republic Pictures Corp., LP571. Running time, 66-67 minutes, 5,994 feet. *Directed by* William Witney; *associate producer*, Edward J. White; *written by* Gerald Geraghty; *director of photography*, John MacBurnie; *art director*, Frank Arrigo; *music*, Nathan Scott; *film editor*, Tony Martinelli; *sound*, T. A. Carman; *costume supervision*, Adele Palmer; *set decorations*, John McCarthy, Jr., and James Redd; *special effects*, Howard and Theodore Lydecker; *makeup supervision*, Bob Mark; *optical effects*, Consolidated Film Industries.

Cast:

Roy Rogers	. . . . .	Roy Rogers
Trigger	. . . . .	Trigger
Penny Edwards	. . . . .	Toby Aldridge
Gordon Jones	. . . . .	Splinters McGonigle
Rex Allen	. . . . .	Rex Allen
Allan "Rocky" Lane	. . . . .	Allan "Rocky" Lane
Monte Hale	. . . . .	Monte Hale
William Farnum	. . . . .	William Farnum
Tom Tyler	. . . . .	Tom Tyler
Ray Corrigan	. . . . .	Ray "Crash" Corrigan
Kermit Maynard	. . . . .	Kermit Maynard
Tom Keene	. . . . .	Tom Keene
Jack Holt	. . . . .	Jack Holt
Emory Parnell	. . . . .	J. Corwin Aldridge
Clifton Young	. . . . .	Mitch McCall
James Magill	. . . . .	Murtagh
Carol Nugent	. . . . .	Sis
George Chesebro	. . . . .	George Chesebro
Edward Cassidy	. . . . .	Sheriff
Foy Willing and The Riders of the Purple Sage	. . . . .	Themselves

Also featuring: Virginia Carroll, Clarence Straight, Ken Terrell, Lane Bradford, and Stanley Blystone.

Synopsis:
Retired actor, Jack Holt, is raising Christmas trees to sell at cost. A commercial company headed by J. C. Aldridge is buying all competitors, but can't get Holt to sell. Unknown to Aldridge, his foreman has his men sabotaging Holt's operation. When there is a murder, Aldridge comes to investigate, taking a job as a tree cutter. Roy fights to help Holt and to find the murderer.

Production Notes:
Filmed from mid-June to mid-July 1950. Exteriors were shot at Iverson Movie Ranch, Cedar Lake, Chatsworth Lake, and the Republic Studios backlot.

ROY
ROGERS
KING OF THE COWBOYS

TRIGGER
THE SMARTEST HORSE IN THE MOVIES

Trail of
ROBIN HOOD
in TRUCOLOR

REX ALLEN
"THE ARIZONA COWBOY"

ALLAN "Rocky" LANE

MONTE HALE

WILLIAM FARNUM · TOM TYLER
RAY CORRIGAN · KERMIT MAYNARD
TOM KEENE

with PENNY EDWARDS · GORDON JONES

JACK HOLT · FOY WILLING and the RIDERS of the PURPLE SAGE

DIRECTED BY WILLIAM WITNEY · WRITTEN BY GERALD GERAGHTY

399

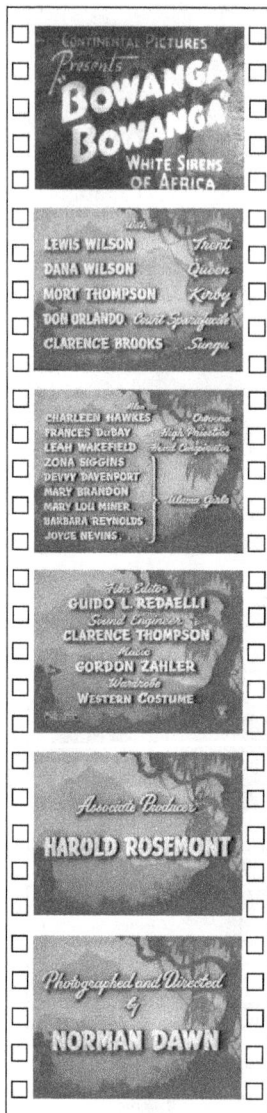

CONTINENTAL PICTURES
Presents
BOWANGA
BOWANGA
WHITE SIRENS
OF AFRICA

LEWIS WILSON — Trent
DANA WILSON — Queen
MORT THOMPSON — Kirby
DON ORLANDO — Count Springfield
CLARENCE BROOKS — Sungu

CHARLEEN HAWKES
FRANCES DeBAY
LEAH WAKEFIELD
ZONA SIGGINS
DEVVY DAVENPORT
MARY BRANDON
MARY LOU MINER
BARBARA REYNOLDS
JOYCE NEVINS

Film Editor
GUIDO L. REDAELLI
Sound Engineer
CLARENCE THOMPSON
Music
GORDON ZAHLER
Wardrobe
WESTERN COSTUME

Associate Producer
HAROLD ROSEMONT

Photographed and Directed
by
NORMAN DAWN

Produced by
MORRIS M. LANDRES

White Sirens of Africa

Produced by Continental Pictures, Inc. Released by Famous Pictures Film Exchange by September 1951. No record of copyright. *Directed by* Norman Dawn; *produced by* Morris M. Landres; *film editor*, Guido L. Redaelli; *sound engineer*, Clarence Thompson; *music*, Gordon Zahler; *wardrobe*, Western Costume; *associate producer*, Harold Rosemont; *photographed by* Norman Dawn.

Cast:

Lewis Wilson	Trent
Dana Wilson	Queen
Mort Thompson	Kirby
Don Orlando	Count Sparafucile
Clarence Brooks	Sungu
Charleen Hawkes	Owoona
Frances DuBay	High priestess
Leah Wakefield	Head conspirator
Zona Siggins	Ulama girl
Devvy Davenport	Ulama girl
Mary Brandon	Ulama girl
Mary Lou Miner	Ulama girl
Barbara Reynolds	Ulama girl
Joyce Nevins	Ulama girl
Ray Corrigan	Gorilla

Synopsis:
Kirby and Count Sparafucile are on a safari in Africa, when they suddenly discover a battered white man who stumbles out of the jungle only to collapse at their feet. After reviving the man, he tells them an old jungle legend about a tribe of white warrior women living on the top of a nearby mountain. As amazing as this seems, he claims to have actually seen these Amazons, and wants Kirby and the Count to join him in returning to their village. The pair agree to go along with him, They soon find the Amazons. Their leader takes a liking to one of the white explorers.

Production Notes:
Corrigan portrayed a gorilla in two short scenes, stock footage from "The White Gorilla"; newer footage of the gorilla with the girl is not Corrigan. This film has appeared under a variety of titles. Originally appeared in 1951 as "White Sirens of Africa". By the following year, it was "Bowanga, Bowanga, White Sirens of Africa". It has also been titled "Wild Women" and "Untamed Women".

Fraidy Cat

Produced and Released by Columbia Pictures Corp. on December 19, 1951. Copyright Columbia Pictures Corp., December 19, 1951, LP1366. Running Time, 16 minutes, 2 reels. *Directed by* Jules White; *produced by* Jules White; *screenplay by* Jules White; *story by* Felix Adler; *director of photography*, Henry Freulich, a.s.c.; *art director*, Charles Clague; *film editor*, Edwin Bryant, a.c.e.

Cast:

Joe Besser	. . . . .	Joe Besser
Jim Hawthorne	. . . . .	Hawthorne
Tom Kennedy	. . . . .	I. Katchum
Joe Palma	. . . . .	Thief
Eddie Baker	. . . . .	Thief
Ray Corrigan	. . . . .	Gorilla

Synopsis:
Wide Awake Detective Agency investigators, Besser and Hawthorne, have failed to solve the Ape Man Gang robberies. Given one more chance by their boss, I. Katchum, they are guarding an antique store at night when they encounter the gang and a real gorilla.

Production Notes:
A remake of The Three Stooges' 1943 "Dizzy Detectives" and was remade in 1955 as "Hook A Crook".

404

The Great Adventures of Captain Kidd

Produced and Released by Columbia Pictures Corp. on September 17, 1953. Copyright Columbia Pictures Corp. (see below). Running Time, 230 minutes, 15 Chapters, 2 reels each. *Directed by* Derwin Abbe and Charles S. Gould; *produced by* Sam Katzman; *story and screen play by* Arthur Hoerl and George H. Plympton; *director of photography*, William Whitley; *art director*, Paul Palmentola; *film editor*, Earl Turner; *set decorator*, Sidney Clifford; *special effects*, Jack Erickson; *set continuity by* Moree Herring; *assistant director*, Leonard Katzman; *sound engineer*, Josh Westmoreland; *musical director*, Mischa Bakaleinikoff; *production manager*, Herbert Leonard.

Cast:

Richard Crane	Richard Dale
David Bruce	Alan Duncan
John Crawford	Captain Kidd
George Wallace	Buller
Lee Roberts	Devry
Paul Newlan	Long Ben Avery
Nick Stuart	Dr. Brandt
Terry Frost	Moore
John Hart	Jenkins
Marshall Reed	Captain Culliford
Eduardo Cansino, Jr.	Native
Willetta Smith	Princess
Ray Corrigan	Henchman leader

Chapter Titles:

1. Pirate vs. Man-of-War — copyright September 17, 1953 LP3075
2. The Fatal Shot — copyright September 24, 1953 LP3114
3. Attacked by Captain Kidd — copyright October 1, 1953 LP3110
4. Captured by Captain Kidd — copyright October 8, 1953 LP3102
5. Mutiny on the Adventure's Galley — copyright October 15, 1953 LP3122
6. Murder on the Main Deck — copyright October 22, 1953 LP3123
7. Prisoners of War — copyright October 29, 1953 LP3166
8. Mutiny Unmasked — copyright November 5, 1953 LP3165
9. Pirate Against Pirate — copyright November 12, 1953 LP3164
10. Shot from the Parapet — copyright November 19, 1953 LP3186
11. The Flaming Fortress — copyright November 26, 1953 LP3203
12. Before the Firing Squad — copyright December 3, 1953 LP3204
13. In the Hands of the Mohawks — copyright December 10, 1953 LP3205
14. Pirate Gold — copyright December 17, 1953 LP3206
15. Captain Kidd's Last Chance — copyright December 24, 1953 LP3207

Synopsis:

The British Admirality assigns two officers, Richard Dale and Alan Duncan, to gather evidence to convict Captain Kidd of piracy. They sail for New York to learn the whereabouts of Kidd, and posing as ordinary seamen, they join his crew. They learn that Kidd, the legendary swashbuckler of the seven seas, is not a a villain who scourges and plunders at will, but a man whose loyalty to England knows no bounds; a maritime adventurer who attacks only enemy French vessels and those of the pirates that sail against the British Empire. But can they keep him from being betrayed by his enemies and hanged?

Production Notes:
Exteriors were filmed at the Iverson Movie Ranch and Columbia Ranch.

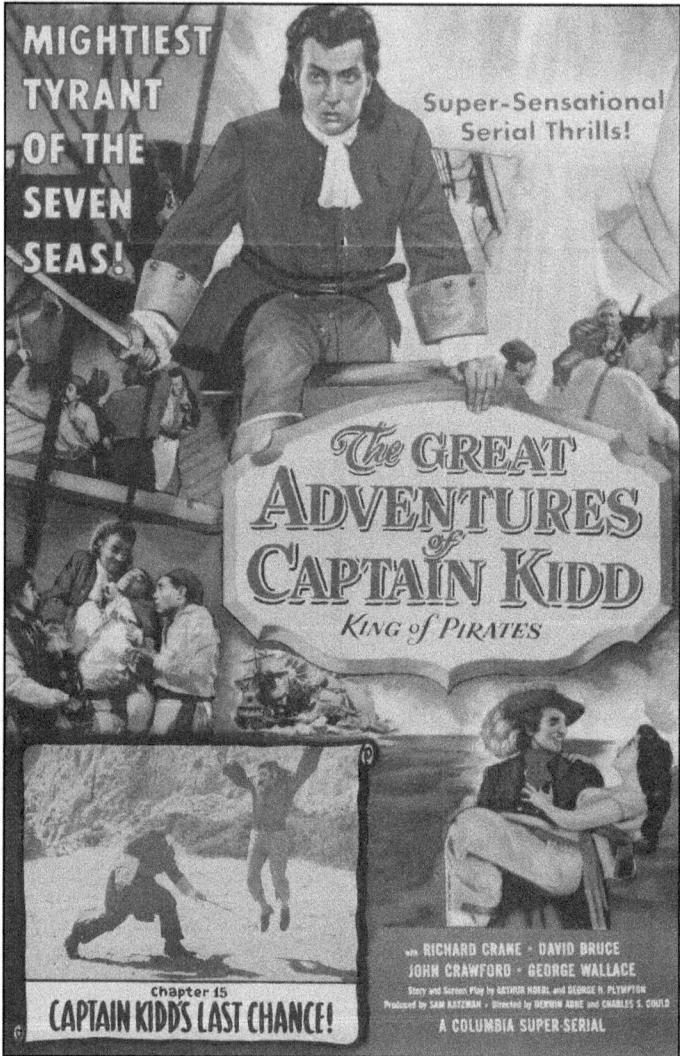

COLUMBIA
JOHNNY WEISSMULLER
JUNGLE JIM
KILLER APE
CAROL THURSTON
MAX PALMER
BURT WENLAND
NESTOR PAIVA
PAUL MARION
EDDIE FOSTER
RORY MALLINSON
RAY CORRIGAN
NICK STUART
TAMBA
CARROLL YOUNG ARTHUR HOERL
CARROLL YOUNG
PRODUCED BY
SAM KATZMAN
DIRECTED BY
SPENCER G. BENNET

Killer Ape

Produced by the Katzman Corporation. Released by Columbia Pictures Corporation in December 1953. Copyright January 12, 1953 by Columbia Pictures Corp, LP3053. Running time, 68 minutes, 7 reels. *Directed by* Spencer G. Bennet; *produced by* Sam Katzman; *screen play by* Carroll Young and Arthur Hoerl; *story by* Carroll Young; *based upon the newspaper eature JUNGLE JIM, owned and copyrighted by King Features Syndicate, and which appears regularly in THE COMIC WEEKLY; director of photography*, William Whitley; *art director*, Paul Palmentola; *film editor*, Gene Havlick, a.c.e.; *set decorator*, Sidney Clifford; *assistant director*, Carter DeHaven, Jr; *sound engineer*, Josh Westmoreland; *musical director*, Mischa Bakaleinikoff; *unit manager*, Herbert Leonard.

Cast:

Johnny Weissmuller	. . . . . Jungle Jim
Carol Thurston	. . . . . Shari
Max Palmer	. . . . Ape-man
Burt Wenland	. . . . Ramada
Nestor Paiva	. . . . Dr. Andrews
Paul Marion	. . . . . Mahara
Eddie Foster	. . . . . Achmed
Rory Mallinson	. . . . . Perry
Ray Corrigan	. . . . Norley
Nick Stuart.	. . . . . Maron
Tamba	. . . . . Tamba

Synopsis:
Jungle Jim is accused of killing a native who has been providing a scientist with innocent animals to be used in his mad experiments. Turns out that the real killer is a giant Ape-man.

Production Notes:
Filmed between February 3 and 12, 1953 at the Ray Corrigan Ranch. Now that Corrigan had given up his gorilla sideline (he sold one of his costumes to Steve Calvert), the remainder of his screen appearances will be as an actor.

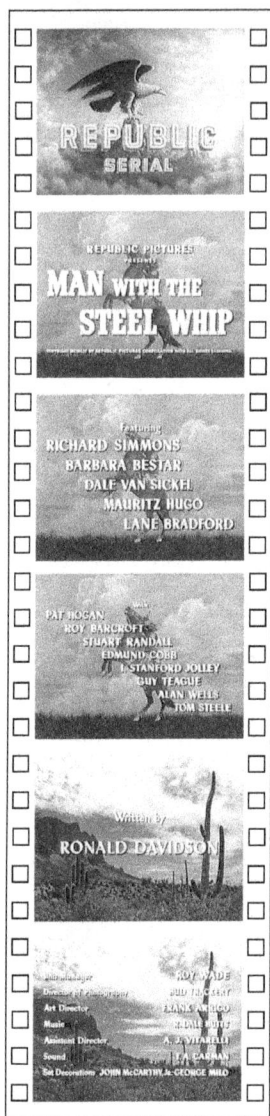

REPUBLIC SERIAL

REPUBLIC PICTURES
PRESENTS

MAN WITH THE
STEEL WHIP

Featuring
RICHARD SIMMONS
BARBARA BESTAR
DALE VAN SICKEL
MAURITZ HUGO
LANE BRADFORD

PAT HOGAN
ROY BARCROFT
STUART RANDALL
EDMUND COBB
I. STANFORD JOLLEY
GUY TEAGUE
ALAN WELLS
TOM STEELE

Written by
RONALD DAVIDSON

Film Editor
Special Effects
HOWARD and THEODORE LYDECKER
Makeup Supervision
Optical Effects
CONSOLIDATED FILM INDUSTRIES

Associate Producer and Director
FRANKLIN ADREON

Chapter Five
THE STONE
GUILLOTINE

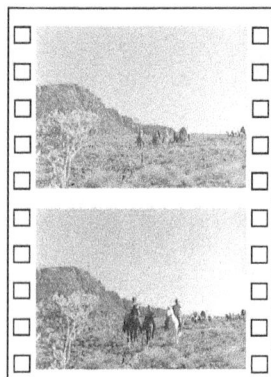

Man With The Steel Whip

Produced and Released by Republic Pictures Inc. on July 19, 1954. Copyright Republic Pictures Inc., Trailer and Chapters 1-12, July 19, 1954 LP4192. Running Time, 167 minutes, 12 Chapters, 2 reels each. *Directed by* Franklin Adreon; *associate producer*, Franklin Adreon; *written by* Ronald Davidson; *unit manager*, Roy Wade; *director of photography*, Bud Thackery; *art director*, Frank Arrigo; *music*, R. Dale Butts; *assistant director*, A. J. Vitarelli; *sound*, T. A. Carman; *set decorations*, John McCarthy, Jr. and George Milo; *film editors*, Cliff Bell, a.c.e. and Joseph Harrison; *special effects*, Howard and Theodore Lydecker; *makeup supervision*, Bob Mark; *optical effects*, Consolidated Film Industries.

Cast:

Richard Simmons	Jerry Randall/El Latigo
Barbara Bestar	Nancy Cooper
Dale Van Sickel	Crane
Mauritz Hugo	Barnett
Lane Bradford	Tosco
Pat Hogan	Indian Chief
Roy Barcroft	Sheriff
Stuart Randall	Harris
Edmund Cobb	Lee
I. Stanford Jolley	Sloane
Guy Teague	Price
Alan Wells	Quivar
Tom Steele	Tom/Gage

Chapter Titles:
1. The Spirit Rider
2. Savage Fury
3. Mask of El Latigo
4. The Murder Cave
5. The Stone Guillotine
6. Flame and Battle
7. Double Ambush
8. The Blazing Barrier
9. The Silent Informer
10. Window of Death
11. The Fatal Masquerade
12. Redskin Raiders

Synopsis:
Saloon owner Barnett wants the Indian reservation land on which he knows there is gold. He organizes a gang, aided by some renegade Indians, to raid and terrorize close-by settlers, hoping to arouse them to drive off the Indians. Rancher Jerry Randall, accompanied by school teacher Nancy Cooper, set out to defeat the gang. In order to win the loyalty of the innocent tribe members, Randall masquerades as a legendary friend of the Indians, El Latigo.

Production Notes:
Filmed between March 2 and March 22, 1954. Stock footage from "The Painted Stallion" was used in Chapter Five with distant shots of Corrigan, but no close-ups.

Panther Girl of the Kongo

Produced and Released by Republic Pictures Corp. on January 3, 1955. Copyright Republic Pictures Corp., Trailer and Chapters 1-12, January 3, 1955 LP4564. Running Time, 167 minutes, 12 chapters, 2 reels each. *Directed by* Franklin Adreon; *associate producer*, Franklin Adreon; *written by* Ronald Davidson; *unit manager*, Roy Wade; *director of photography*, Bud Thackery; *art director*, Frank Hotaling; *music*, R. Dale Butts; *assistant director*, Leonard Kunody; *set decorations*, John McCarthy, Jr. and Edward G. Boyle; *film editor*, Cliff Bell, a.c.e.; *special effects*, Howard and Theodore Lydecker; *sound*, Roy Meadows; *makeup supervision*, Bob Mark; *optical effects*, Consolidated Film Industries.

Cast:

Phyllis Coates	. . . .	Jean Evans
Myron Healey	. . . .	Larry Sanders
Arthur Space	. . . .	Dr. Morgan
John Day	. . . .	Cass
Mike Ragan	. . . .	Rand
Morris Buchanan	. . . .	Tembo
Roy Glenn, Sr.	. . . .	Chief Danka
Archie Savage	. . . .	Ituri
Ramsay Hill	. . . .	Comm. Stanton
Naaman Brown	. . . .	Orto
Dan Ferniel	. . . .	Ebu
James Logan	. . . .	Const. Harris

Chapter Titles:
1. The Claw Monster
2. Jungle Ambush
3. The Killer Beast
4. Sands of Doom
5. Test of Terror
6. High Peril
7. Double Trap
8. Crater of Flame
9. River of Death
10. Blasted Evidence
11. Double Danger
12. House of Doom

Synopsis:
Jean Evans of an international wildlife foundation has made herself at home in Africa as the elephant-riding, vine-swinging, miniskirted "Panther Girl". On safari to film animals, Jean encounters something strange—a giant crayfish monster. Turns out that scientist Morgan, with help from his gang, is creating the giant creatures in hopes of scaring everyone out of the district so that they can secretly mine diamonds.

Production Notes:

Filmed between August 16 and September 4, 1954. Corrigan portrayed a gorilla in stock footage from "Darkest Africa" (Bonga); new footage of the gorilla is Steve Calvert in Corrigan's old gorilla suit.

Apache Ambush

Produced and Released by Columbia Pictures Corporation on September 1, 1955. Copyright Columbia Pictures Corp., August 26, 1955, LP5311. Running time, 67-68 minutes, 7 reels. *Directed by* Fred F. Sears; *produced by* Wallace MacDonald; *story and screen play by* David Lang; *director of photography*, Fred Jackman, Jr., a.s.c.; *art director*, Paul Palmentola; *film editor*, Jerome Thoms, a.c.e.; *set decorator*, Frank Tuttle; *assistant director*, Charles S. Gould; *sound*, Don McKay; *music conducted by* Mischa Bakaleinikoff.

Cast:

Bill Williams	James Kingston
Richard Jaeckel	Lee Parker
Alex Montoya	Joaquin Jironza
Movita	Rosita
Adelle August	Ann Parker
Tex Ritter	Trager
Ray "Crash" Corrigan	Hank Calvin
Ray Teal	Sgt. Tim O'Roarke
Don Harvey	Tex McGuire
James Griffith	President Abraham Lincoln
James Flavin	Col. Marshall
George Chandler.	Chandler
Forrest Lewis	Silas Parker
George Keymas	Tweedy

Also featuring: Harry Lauter, Henry Escalante, Bill Hale, Robert Foulk, Victor Millan, Clayton Moore, John Zaremba, Don Carlos, Edmund Cobb, Frank Sully, Ed Hinton, Joseph Breen, Robert B. Williams, Leonard Geer, Lane Chandler, Jack Perrin, Guy Teague, Iron Eyes Cody, Chris Alcaide, Steven Ritch, J. W. Cody, Chuck Cason, and Harry Strang.

Synopsis:
Just after the Civil War, President Abraham Lincoln asks two former enemies—a Union officer and a former Confederate—to drive a herd of cattle from Texas to Kansas, to help feed civilians who are short of food. The journey is complicated by marauding Apache Indians and a gang of Mexican bandits who want the new Henry repeating rifles that the drovers will be carrying.

Production Notes:
Filmed between March 28 and April 6, 1955. Exteriors shot at the Iverson Movie Ranch and the Sierra Railroad in Tuolumne County.

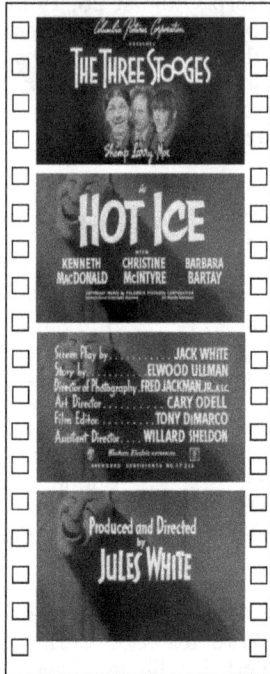

422

Hot Ice

Produced and Released by Columbia Pictures Corporation on October 6, 1955. Copyright Columbia Pictures Corp., August 26, 1955, LP5311. Running time, 16-17 minutes, 2 reels. *Directed by* Edward Bernds; *produced by* Jules White; *story and screen play by* David Lang; *director of photography*, Fred Jackman, Jr., a.s.c.; *art director*, Paul Palmentola; *film editor*, Jerome Thoms, a.c.e.; *set decorator*, Frank Tuttle; *assistant director*, Charles S. Gould; *sound*, Don McKay; *music conducted by* Mischa Bakaleinikoff.

Cast:

Shemp Howard	Shemp
Larry Fine	Larry
Moe Howard	Moe
Kenneth MacDonald	Dapper Malone
Christine McIntyre	Bea
Barbara Bartay	Girl in Bar
Clive Morgan	Inspector McCormick
James Logan	Dawson
Cy Schindell	Muscles
Joe Palma	Muscles
Lester Allen	Runty
Jimmy Aubrey	Hawkins
George Lloyd	Squid McGuffey
Blackie Whiteford	Cauliflower-eared Seaman
Budd Fine	Seaman
Johnny Kascier	Sailor in Bar
Harry Wilson	Bum in Bed
Ray Corrigan	Harold the gorilla

Synopsis:

The Three Stooges apply at Scotland Yard as detectives but end up as gardeners. They stumble across a note concerning a stolen diamond case. At a saloon, Shemp accidentally swallows the diamond. The crooks decide to cut the diamond out of Shemp but a gorilla intercedes.

Production Notes:

This short was a remake of "Crime On Their Hands" from 1948 and utilized stock footage of Corrigan as a gorilla.

Hook A Crook

Produced and Released by Columbia Pictures Corporation on November 24, 1955. Copyright Columbia Pictures Corp., August 26, 1955, LP5311. Running time, 16-17 minutes, 2 reels. *Directed by* Edward Bernds; *produced by* Jules White; *story and screen play by* David Lang; *director of photography*, Fred Jackman, Jr., a.s.c.; *art director*, Paul Palmentola; *film editor*, Jerome Thoms, a.c.e.; *set decorator*, Frank Tuttle; *assistant director*, Charles S. Gould; *sound*, Don McKay; *music conducted by* Mischa Bakaleinikoff.

Cast:

Joe Besser	.....	Joe Besser
Jim Hawthorne	.....	Hawthorne
Ray Corrigan	.....	Gorilla
Steve Calvert	.....	Gorilla
Dan Blocker	.....	Gorilla
Eddie Baker	.....	Thief
Barbara Bartay	.....	Fifi
Lela Bliss	.....	Mrs. Van Sickle
Dudley Dickerson	.....	Janitor
Tom Kennedy	.....	I. Katchum
Joe Palma	.....	Thief

Synopsis:
A gorilla has been trained to commit crimes and has stolen jewelry from a socialite. She calls in two detectives to recover her jewelry.

Production Notes:
This short was a remake of "Fraidy Cat" from 1951 and utilized stock footage of Corrigan and Steve Calvert as the gorilla. New shots of the gorilla had Dan Blocker in the ape suit.

Battle expedition seeking History's most fabulous sunken treasure!

Turn beautiful girl into killer...

SUPERNATURAL TERROR

FANTASTIC THRILLS

...as ZOMBIE VENGEANCE

Over-runs the screen!

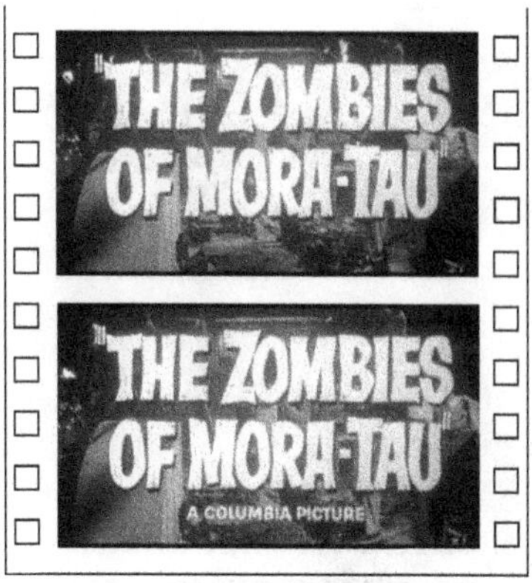

"THE ZOMBIES OF MORA-TAU

"THE ZOMBIES OF MORA-TAU
A COLUMBIA PICTURE

ZOMBIES OF MORA TAU

COLUMBIA PICTURES CORPORATION
presents
ZOMBIES
OF MORA TAU

WITH
GREGG PALMER
ALLISON HAYES
AUTUMN RUSSELL
JOEL ASHLEY
MORRIS ANKRUM
MARJORIE EATON
GENE ROTH
LEONARD GEER
KARL DAVIS
WILLIAM BASKIN

SCREEN PLAY BY
RAYMOND T. MARCUS
STORY BY
GEORGE PLYMPTON

Director of Photography BENJAMIN H. KLINE, A.S.C.
Art Director PAUL PALMENTOLA
Film Editor JACK OGILVIE, A.C.E.
Set Decorator SIDNEY CLIFFORD
Assistant Director JERROLD BERNSTEIN
Sound JOSH WESTMORELAND
Music Conducted by MISCHA BAKALEINIKOFF

PRODUCED BY
SAM KATZMAN
A
CLOVER
PRODUCTION

DIRECTED BY
EDWARD CAHN

IN THE DARKNESS OF AN ANCIENT
WORLD - - ON A SHORE THAT TIME HAS
FORGOTTEN - - THERE IS A TWILIGHT ZONE
BETWEEN LIFE AND DEATH.

HERE DWELL THOSE NAMELESS CREATURES
WHO ARE CONDEMNED TO PROWL THE LAND
ETERNALLY - THE WALKING DEAD.

ZOMBIES OF THE OCEAN DEEPS!

A TIDE
OF TERROR
FLOODS
THE
SCREEN!

ZOMBIES
OF MORA
TAU

WITH
GREGG PALMER
ALLISON HAYES
AUTUMN RUSSELL

428

Zombies of Mora Tau

Produced by Clover Production. Released by Columbia Pictures Corp., in March 1957. Copyright by Columbia Pictures Corp., January 3, 1957, LP8344. Running time, 68-69 minutes. *Directed by* Edward Cahn; *produced by* Sam Katzman; *screen play by* Raymond T. Marcus; *story by* George Plympton; *director of photography*, Benjamin H. Kline, a.s.c.; *art director*, Paul Palmentola; *film editor*, Jack Ogilvie, a.c.e.; *set decorator*, Sidney Clifford; *assistant director*, Jerrold Bernstein; *sound*, Josh Westmoreland; *music conducted by* Mischa Bakaleinikoff.

Cast:

Gregg Palmer	Jeff Clark
Allison Hayes	Mona Harrison
Autumn Russell	Jan Peters
Joel Ashley	George Harrison
Morris Ankrum	Jonathan Eggert
Marjorie Eaton	Mrs. Peters
Gene Roth	Sam
Leonard Greer	Johnny
Karl Davis	Zombie
William Baskin	Zombie

Also featuring: Ray Corrigan, Mel Curtis, and Frank Hagney.

Synopsis:
A sunken ship, diamonds, and zombies guarding the treasure. Adventurers try to salvage the diamonds.

Production Notes:
Filmed between October 29 and November 6, 1956. Exteriors were shot at the Baldwin Ranch, now the Los Angeles Country Arboretum.

COLUMBIA
COLUMBIA PICTURES CORPORATION
RORY CALHOUN
DOMINO KID
KRISTINE MILLER
ANDREW DUGGAN
YVETTE DUGAY
PETER WHITNEY
EUGENE IGLESIAS
ROBERT BURTON
SCREEN PLAY BY
KENNETH GAMET
HAL BILLER

PRODUCED BY
RORY CALHOUN
VICTOR M. ORSATTI
DIRECTED BY
RAY NAZARRO

RORY CALHOUN
DOMINO KID

The Domino Kid

Produced by Rorvic Productions and Calhoun-Orsatti Enterprises, Inc. Released by Columbia Pictures Corp. on October 1, 1957. Copyright January 10, 1957, by Calhoun-Orsatti Enterprises, Inc., LP9121. Running time, 73-74 minutes. *Directed by* Ray Nazarro; *produced by* Rory Calhoun and Victor M. Orsatti; *screenplay by* Kenneth Gamet and Hal Biller; *director of photography*, Irving Lippman; *art director*, Howard Richmond; *film editor*, Gene Havlick; *set decorators*, Maurice Mulcahy and George Sawley; *assistant director*, Floyd Joyer; *second assistant director*, Pat Corletto; *sound by* Jean Valentino and Lambert Day; *music conducted by* Mischa Bakaleinikoff; *costumes by* Izzy Berne; *sound editors*, John Newman and Don Harris; *script supervisor*, Bob Gary.

Cast:

Rory Calhoun	. . . . .	Domino Kid aka Cort Garand
Kristine Miller	. . . . .	Barbara Ellison
Andrew Duggan	. . . . .	Wade Harrington
Yvette Dugay	. . . . .	Rosita
Peter Whitney	. . . . .	Lafe Prentise
Eugene Iglesias	. . . . .	Juan Cortez
Robert Burton	. . . . .	Sheriff Travers

Also featuring: Bart Bradley, James Griffith, Roy Barcroft, Denver Pyle, Ray Corrigan, William Christensen, Don Orlando, Dennis Moore, Arline Anderson, Gloria Rhoads, Ricky Murray, Tom London, Don C. Harvey, Thomas Browne Henry, Harry Tyler, Frank Sully, Paul Burns, Rankin Mansfield, and Fred Graham.

Synopsis:
The Domino Kid hunts down and outguns four of the five rustlers who had killed his father and younger brother; he is unable to identify or find the fifth. Returned home to find wealthy Wade Harrington courting his sweetheart, Barbara Ellison, Domino decides to return to ranching. Forced into a showdown gun battle with Harrington, the Domino Kid unexpectedly finds himself bracketed in the gunsights of the fifth of the outlaw band, a target for gunmen on every side.

Production Notes:
Filmed between February 18 and 28, 1957. Exteriors shot at the Iverson Movie Ranch and the Columbia Ranch. Rory Calhoun and Ray Corrigan were best of friends and Rory was best man at Ray's marriage to Elaine DuPont in 1954.

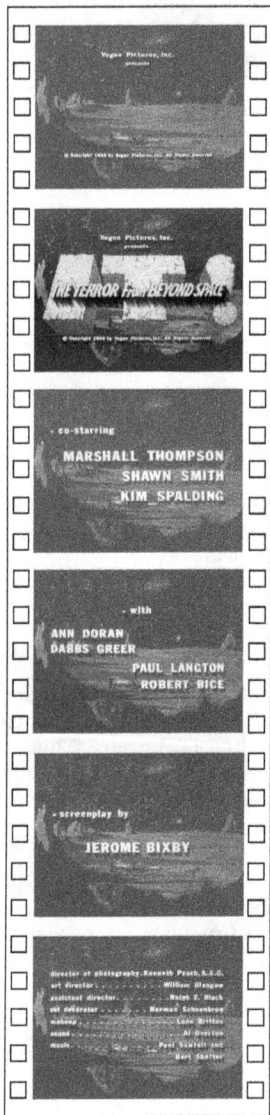

Vogue Pictures, Inc.
presents

IT!
THE TERROR From BEYOND SPACE

- co-starring
MARSHALL THOMPSON
SHAWN SMITH
KIM SPALDING

- with
ANN DORAN
DABBS GREER
PAUL LANGTON
ROBERT BICE

- screenplay by
JEROME BIXBY

director of photography: Kenneth Peach, A.S.C.
art director . . . . William Glasgow
assistant director . . . . . Ralph E. Black
set decorator . . . . Norman Schoenbrun
makeup . . . . Lane Britton
sound . . . . Al Overton
music . . . . Paul Sawtell and
Bert Shefter

supervising editor . . . . Grant Whytock, A.C.E.
effects editor . . . . Robert Carlisle
script supervision . . . . . George Rutter
property master . . . . . . Arthur Wasson
wardrobe . . . . Jack Masters

sound by
Ryder Sound Services

- produced by
ROBERT E. KENT

- directed by
EDWARD L. CAHN

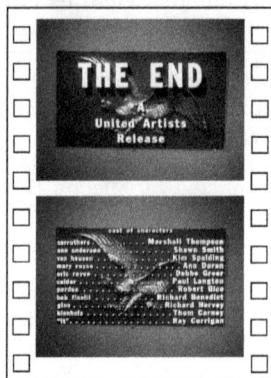

THE END
A
United Artists
Release

cast of characters
carruthers . . . . Marshall Thompson
ann anderson . . . . Shawn Smith
van heuser . . . . Kim Spalding
mary royce . . . . Ann Doran
eric royce . . . . Dabbs Greer
calder . . . . Paul Langton
purdue . . . . Robert Bice
bob finelli . . . . Richard Benedict
gino . . . . Richard Hervey
kienholz . . . . Thom Carney
"It" . . . . Ray Corrigan

It! The Terror From Beyond Space

Produced by Vogue Pictures, Inc. Released by United Artists in August 1958. Copyright August 13, 1958, Vogue Pictures, Inc., LP11864. Running time, 68 minutes. *Directed by* Edward L. Cahn; *produced by* Robert E. Kent; *screenplay by* Jerome Bixby; *director of photography*, Kenneth Peach, a.s.c.; *art director*, William Glasgow; *assistant director*, Ralph E. Black; *set decorator*, Herman Schoenbrun; *makeup*, Lane Britton; *sound*, Al Overton; *music*, Paul Sawtell and Bert Shefter; *supervising editor*, Grant Whytock; *effects editor*, Robert Carlisle; *script supervision*, George Rutter; *property master*, Arthur Wasson; *wardrobe*, Jack Masters; *sound by* Ryder Sound Services.

Cast:

Marshall Thompson	. . . . .	Col. Edward Carruthers
Shawn Smith	. . . . .	Ann Anderson
Kim Spalding	. . . . .	Commander Van Heusen
Ann Doran	. . . . .	Mary Royce
Dabbs Greer	. . . . .	Eric Royce
Paul Langton	. . . . .	Jim Calder
Robert Bice	. . . . .	Jack Purdue
Ray Corrigan	. . . . .	It

Also featuring: Richard Benedict, Richard Hervey, and Thom Carney.

Synopsis:
The first manned flight to Mars is marooned. When the rescue ship arrives, there is only one person alive—all of the others had been murdered. The survivor, Col. Carruthers is taken prisoner. Unbeknowst to the crew, the real killer is not Carruthers and has stolen aboard their ship. On the voyage back to Earth, the creature begins to attack.

Production Notes:
Filmed in mid-January 1958. According to Paul Blaisdell, who manufactured the "It" costume, he built it to fit his dimensions. When he learned that he was not going to play the monster, the suit had to be reworked to fit Corrigan's bulk (he was about a half foot or more taller than Blaisdell). When it was time to work on the headpiece, Corrigan either refused or had no time for the fitting. On set, the headpiece did not fit—it was too small. Corrigan's chin sticks out the mouth of the creature!

VoS-(18-6)-21

434

The Ribald Tales of Robin Hood

Produced by P. B. S. Co. and Mondo Films. Distributed by Entertainment Ventures, Inc. and Adam Academy of Adult Cinema. Not copyrighted. Released on October 29, 1969. Running time, 83 minutes. *Directed by* Richard Kanter; *produced by* Edward E. Paramore and John Harvey; *screenplay by* Richard Kanter; *associate producer*, Murray Perlstein; *original story by* Lawrence Morse; *director of photography*, Paul Hipp; *costumes*, Lee Fischer; *music*, Amphion Musicic; *sound mixer*, Sam Kopetzky; *makeup artist*, Mark Teller; *production manager*, Jax T. Carroll; *script girl*, Mindy Kanter; *head grip*, Paul Wilmoth; *titles*, Earl Marshall.

Cast:

Ralph Jenkins	. . . .	Robin Hood
Dee Lockwood	. . . .	Maid Marion
Lawrence Adams	. . . .	Prince John
Danielle Carver	. . . .	Lady Sallyforth
Scott Sizemore	. . . .	Young Robin
C. S. Poole	. . . .	The Sheriff
Frank Nathan	. . . .	Little John
James Brand	. . . .	Sir Guy
Eddie Nova	. . . .	Friar Tuck
Ray Benard	. . . .	Robin's father
Barbara Sanderson	. . . .	Robin's mother
L. Crandon	. . . .	Allan-a-Dale
Bambi Allen	. . . .	Polly
Paul Smith	. . . .	Will Scarlet
Terry Sands	. . . .	Tina

Also featuring: Capri, Karen Nichols, Ingred Young, Norma Vanden, Dee Howard, Wendel Swink.

Synopsis:
King Richard is imprisoned by the Normans. His evil brother, John, forcibly enters the castle of young Robin Hood's father, where his father is killed and his mother is raped and killed. As an adult, he gathers a Merry Band in Sherwood Forest and fights John's rule.

Production Notes:
A castle-like home in the Hollywood Hills and Hopetown Movie Ranch (formerly Corriganville/Ray Corrigan Ranch) are used for exteriors and some interiors.
Corrigan appears under his earlier alias of Ray Benard, the name he adopted in the late 1920's.

From Gusty, Grubby, Grabby 11th-Century England...An Area and Era of Unparalleled Earthiness Comes the Uncut, Uncloaked Version of one of Anglo-Saxondom's Best Loved Tales..!

The Ribald Tales of

Robin Hood

his Lusty Men and Bawdy Wenches

Peerlessly Portrayed in a Panoply of COLOR!

Starring RALPH JENKINS · DEE LOCKOOD · DANELLE CARVER

Produced by Edward E Paramore and John Harvey / Associate Producer Murray Perlstein / Directed by Richard Kanter
A PBS Production / Distributed by ENTERTAINMENT VENTURES, INC. / © MCMLXIX

Adults Only

Sex in America

The final film for Ray "Crash" Corrigan and/or Ray Benard, is "Sex in America" (1969 or 1971). A copy of the film could not be located for viewing. I found a listing, possibly for it, about 10 years ago in an archive. Unfortunately, I cannot locate that information in order to contact the archive.

THE
RAY "CRASH"
CORRIGAN
TELEVISION SHOWS

442

Crash Corrigan's Ranch

"Crash" Corrigan was the host of this weekly 30 minute variety show which aired from June 25, 1950 to September 16, 1950. There is no record of copyright registration for the series or individual shows. Regulars on the program included Georgia Lee, Bob Oates, Max "Alibi" Terhune, Buddy McDowell, Ralph Ward, and The Broome Boys with Billy Wolfe. A copy of a kinescope recording of the August 19, 1950 episode as well as the script from that episode still exist. The images at the left are from a vhs copy of the film.

```
A   CRASH CORRIGAN'S RANCH
M   (Program Title)

E
    (Advertiser)
R

I
    (Agency)
C

A   BOB OLSEN
    (Writer)
N

    SATURDAY - AUGUST 19, 1950
B   (Day and Date)

R   8:00-8:30PM
    (Time)
O

A

D   T E L E V I S I O N   P R O D U C T I O N   N O T E S
C

A   CHARACTERS AND CAST              PROPS AND SET

S   CRASH CORRIGAN                   PER SCRIPT
    GEORGIA LEE
T   BOB OATES
    MAX "ALIBI" TERHUNE
I   BUDDY MCDOWELL
    RALPH WARD
N   THE BROOME BOYS WITH BILLY WOLFE

G

    SOUND                            TITLE CARDS
C   ALARM CLOCK                      Per Script

O
                                     STUART PHELPS
M                                    (Production Director)

P

A
                                     RUSSELL FURSE AND DAN ECKLEY
    (Production Assistant)           (Agency Producer or Announcer)
N

Y

e
```

"THE CRASH CORRIGAN SHOW"
KTTV
APRIL 14, 1951
6:00-7:30 P.M.

VIDEO	AUDIO
FILM BIG OPENING (1:30)	THEME: (RECORDED)
L.S. OF CRASH RIDING ALONG ROAD EN ROUTE TO MAIN GATE.	ANNCR: (O.S.) Here comes CRASH CORRIGAN ! ! Along the old Stage Coach Road where every hoof beats out action, adventure, secrets and surprises of the old West!
L.S. OUTSIDE MAIN GATE, CROWD SCENE, CRASH GALLOPS IN WAVING.	You're at CORRIGANVILLE, famous 2000-acre movie ranch where you can walk in the footsteps of the stars!...down the streets of Frontier Town, Cavalry Fort, and the Spanish Village. This is where movies come
C.U. OF SIGN "CORRIGAN- VILLE"	to life!
	Welcome to the old West's last frontier!
L.S. REVERSE SHOT OF CROWD.	And this is you...wide-eyed and beaming with anticipation as you follow Crash on your first tour of his great ranch, down main street...past Sam's Saloon, the Wells-Fargo office and the General Store. You're about to enjoy 90 minutes of real out-in-the- open cowboy fun!
L.S. MAIN STREET; CRASH APPROACHES HITCHING RACK, DISMOUNTS, TIES HORSE AND STRIDES TOWARD TRADING POST.	Your host is none other than that famous star of "The Range Busters" and "Buckskin Rangers"---the real-life dare-devil, the popular bronc busting, roping and gun-toting movie star, "Crash" Corrigan, himself. Hi,
END OF FILM CLIP	Crash! 6:01:30
CUT TO:	

444

Crash Corrigan Show

"Crash" Corrigan was the host of this 90 minute show on KTTV (11) in Los Angeles from April 7, 1951 to August 18, 1951. Corrigan hosted the first half hour live and he demonstrated some aspect of filmmaking, such as stunts. During the final hour, a B-Western was shown. The show debuted on April 7th at 6 p.m. Beginning with the June 23rd show, the time shifted to 5 p.m. Eighteen of the twenty films shown on the show have been identified:

    4-7 "Santa Fe Bound"
    4-14 "Silver Trail"
    5-12 "Born to Battle"
    6-9 either "Tracy Rides" or "Coyote Trail"
    6-23 "Hometown Hayride"
    6-30 "Smoky Trails"
    8-11 special guests: Explorer Scouts of the Order of the Arrow
    8-11 "Arizona Roundup"

and "Texas Jack", "Santa Fe Riders", "Rio Rattlers", "Dude Wrangler", "Border Victory", "Silent Valley", "Wild Horse Valley", "Death Valley Raiders", "Where the Trail Ends", "Pal from Texas", and "Outlaw Trail".

tom porter's
TV Previews

FOR THE YOUNGER SET . . . RAY "CRASH" CORRIGAN, who got his nickname from his tackle-like method of downing the bad guys, starts a new show tonight at 6:00, Channel 11, for the edification of local "six-shootin'" tots and teens. Crash will have other Western stars as guests, and will demonstrate his ability at roping, riding, etc. for the benefit of aspiring young cow - punchers. But that's not all. A full-length Western film will round out the hour and a half show. To-night's cowboy thriller is "Santa Fe Bound" starring Tom Tyler, and Tom himself will be on hand to tell some tall tales of the Old West.

Crash Corrigan

Buckskin Rangers

Produced by Jerry Fairbanks, Inc. Running Time about 26 minutes. No copyright. *Directed by* Frank McDonald; *original story and screenplay*, William Nolte; *production supervisor*, Arnold Wesler; *photographed by* Kenneth Peach, a.s.c.; *supervising editor*, Richard Fritch; *film editor*, John C. Fuller; *sound*, Lawrence Aicholtz; *art director*, Oscar Yerg; *assistant director*, Tom Andre; *musical direction*, Edward Paul.

Cast:

Ray Corrigan	. . . . .	Crash Corrigan
Bill Hale	. . . . .	Buckskin Brown
Max Terhune	. . . . .	Alibi Terhune
Virginia Herrick	. . . . .	Carol Webster
Bob O-Dwyer	. . . . .	Tommy Webster
Ted Mapes	. . . . .	Sid Hanson
Kermit Maynard	. . . . .	Paul Baldwin
Dick Powers	. . . . .	Victor Gerard
Lane Bradford	. . . . .	Chet Duncan
Buff Brady	. . . . .	Earl
Joe Hooker	. . . . .	Floyd
Dusty Walker	. . . . .	Jeff

Synopsis:
Jess Webster has died. His daughter, Carol, and son, Tommy, come to take over his ranch. Victor Gerard seeks to gain control of the ranch, through hook or crook. The Buckskin Rangers help Carol and Tommy keep control of their ranch.

Production Notes:
Ray Corrigan, Bill Hale, and Max Terhune were the Buckskin Rangers. "Lady Tenderfoot" was the first episode to be filmed in a projected 26-episode color television series. Filming was scheduled to begin in early December 1950. Completely shot at Corriganville. How many episodes actually filmed is not known for sure. There is no record of the show in the Jerry Fairbanks Productions archive held by U.C.L.A. Probably only the initial show of the series. Fairbanks was going to syndicate the program himsef, so it is a little surprising that other episodes either were not filmed or have disappeared.

"let's dance"
THE al Jarvis SHOW

Appearing On

abc-tv

The Al Jarvis Show

Also known as "Let's Dance", Al Jarvis, a radio disc jockey, hosted this show from 1949. "Crash" Corrigan and Elaine DuPont appeared in one episode in 1952 of this show.

Hollywood Reel (4-14-52) Crash Corrigan will be seen guiding youngsters on a tour of his ranch on KTLA during Erskine Johnson's show.

CRASH CORRIGAN will be seen guiding youngsters on a tour of his ranch on KTLA · at 7:15 during Erskine Johnson's "Hollywood Reel."

Crash Corrigan's Rodeo Roundup (7-25-53 to 9-12-53) The "Rodeo Roundup" show was first telecast on June 6, 1953, and "Crash" Corrigan became the host on the July 25th episode. During Corrigan's time on the show, the rodeo was telecast live from Corriganville. It was a one hour show on Saturday afternoons at 4:30 p.m. on KNBH (4), a local Los Angeles television station.

Western Roundup (1-6-56 to 1-13-56) "Crash" was the host of this 30 minute show on KHJ (9) in Los Angeles. Air time was 4:30 p.m. to 5 p.m.

Movie Ranch (1-20-56 to 1-27-56) After two episodes of "Western Roundup", the title was changed to "Movie Ranch".

ROUNDUP TIME—Star of KNBH's (4) new Rodeo show Saturdays at 4:30 p.m. is Crash Corrigan.

You Bet Your Life

Also known as "The Groucho Marx Show", this quiz/comedy show ran from 1950 to 1961 on television. On the June 11, 1959, "Crash" was a contestant. He and his partner lost in the opening questions period.

Holiday (6-12-59) "Treasure Holiday at Corriganville" Thousands of treasure hunters head for Corriganville in search of buried loot.

Danger Is My Business (July 23, 1959) "Cowboy Stunt Man". "Crash" demonstrated stunt techniques. In one scene, he actually broke his nose.

```
                6:30
     4 CURT MASSEY (C)
       With Martha Tilton and
       Country Washburn.
     5 CLETE ROBERTS
     7 SEA ADVENTURE
   ★13 Col. John D. Craig pres.
       "Danger Is My Business"
       "Cowboy Stunt Man" fea-
       tures "Crash" Corrigan
       and team of movie stunt
       men at work.
                6:45
```

Opposite Page: A page from a celebrity cookbook

RAY CORRIGAN

Republic Pictures Corp.

Born in Milwaukee, Wisconsin on February 14, 1907. Height 6 ft. 2½ in. Weight 199 lbs. Grey eyes and dark brown hair. Real name Ray Bernard. One of the famous "Three Mesquiteers" whose films have been making Western picture history throughout the country, a trio that is becoming quite as well known as the Marx Brothers and bids fair to surpass all box office records for Western Pictures. Under contract to Republic Pictures Corp. for whom these films are made.

Like all folks who spend most of their time out of doors, particularly in the saddle, and pitch their tent wherever they happen to be, my favorite dish is:

STEAK WITH TOMATO SAUCE

Ask the butcher to cut the round steak about one inch in thickness and have him pound it well. Cut off the fat and place it in a large iron skillet to render.

Pound the steak yourself with the dull edge of the knife with salt, pepper and flour, on both sides.

Remove pieces of fat from the skillet and brown the steak on both sides, then lay it in a Dutch oven. Prepare the sauce as follows:

In the fat left in the skillet fry one large diced onion, one clove garlic (optional), a crumpled bay leaf, and a small bunch of finely chopped parsley. After these ingredients have browned, pour in a large can of puree of tomatoes, adding one teaspoon of chili powder. When this has cooked down to a semi-thickness,

add one small can of tomato juice; let simmer for a few minutes and pour the mixture over the steak. Cover the Dutch oven tightly and bake in a moderate oven until the meat is tender.

Before removing the meat from the Dutch oven, cut in pieces for serving.

2½ lbs. round steak	1 small bunch parsley
salt, pepper and onion	1 can puree of tomatoes
1 large onion (diced)	1 teaspoon chili powder
1 clove garlic (diced)	1 small can tomato juice
1 bay leaf	

[60]

Ray Corrigan

455

The Corriganville Story

Produced by Outdoor Amusements Inc. about 1960. Running Time, about 30 minutes. *Directed by* Buddy Noonan; *produced by* Buddy Noonan; *written by* Buddy Noonan; *assistant director,* David A. Smirnoff; *audio engineer,* David A. Smirnoff; *consultant,* Jim Turner, Hollywood Film Enterprises; *music and effects by* Audio Effects Company.

This early infomercial was hosted by Ray "Crash" Corrigan and told the story of his movie ranch, Corriganville. Outdoor Amusements Inc. leased Corriganville from Corrigan and it was also owned by Corrigan. Probably filmed around 1960.

The Last of the Corrigans (1961) Nothing is known about this show. It is listed in some filmographies of Corrigan and is said to co-star his son Tommy.

An Evening at the Inn (5-20-1962) a 30 minute live television show on KTLA (5) at 8 pm, hosted by KTLA's Stan Chambers with guests Noreen Corcoran, Ray Corrigan, Annette Funicello, Buck the Giant, Jimmie Jackson, Richard Lane, and J. P. Sloane.

People Will Talk (1963) a 30 minute game show on channel 4, in color, daily at noon, hosted by Dennis James.

THE
RAY "CRASH"
CORRIGAN
STAGE PLAYS

Juvenile Lead in Farce Awarded

Brian Gibbons, young screen actor, enacts the juvenile lead in the hot weather farce, "The Best Cure," by Belmont and Ashton, which opens at the Ben Bard Playhouse on Wilshire Boulevard next Wednesday. Others in the cast are William Begley, Ray Benard, Betty Black, Van Buren, Marilyn Reed, John Lawrence, Audrey Hall, Fredric Hohman. Elsie

Brian Gibbons

Kingsley, Dave Marshall, Gertrude Marson, Joyce Matthews, Wallace Pindell, Jill Ogden, Richard Stuart, Mildred Wilson and Wallace Warner.

The Best Cure

Produced and Performed in August 1935. Play by Belmont and Ashton.

Cast: Brian Gibbons, William Begley, Ray Benard, Betty Black, Van Buren, Marilyn Reed, John Lawrence, Audrey Hall, Fredric Hohman, Elsie Kingsley, Dave Marshall, Gertrude Marson, Joyce Matthews, Wallace Pindell, Jill Ogden, Richard Stuart, Mildred Wilson, Wallace Warner.

"Ray Benard" was a stage name for Raymond Benitz (birth name) who would be christened by Republic Pictures, "Crash" Corrigan. This was one of two plays in which Corrigan performed. A new play was put on each month by the Ben Bard Players. Ben Bard was a noted theatrical teacher.

Juvenile Actor
Rehearses Role
in "Rusty Keys"

Van Buren, juvenile actor, is rehearsing the juvenile lead in "The Rusty Keys," an original play by Sada Cowan, which will be presented by Ben Bard at his Playhouse about October 1. The play is a "League of Nations in a Garden," with a theme said to be pertinent at the present time and embodying many dramatic situations. Buren had a leading part in "The Rest Cure,"

Van Buren

which recently completed a long run at the Ben Bard Playhouse.

Others in the cast of "Rusty Keys" are Mati Afric, Jacklyn Alexander, William Begley, Lithe Belmont, Ray Benard, Kathleen Crespinel, Greta Diener, Marilyn Reed, John Lawrence, Dixie Francis, Wallace Gregory, Audrey Hall, Jack Jordan, Elsie Kingsley, Dave Marshall, Truda Marson, Dorothy Mason, Pauline Parker, Gwen Phillips, Wallace Pindell, Clarice Roma, Sylvia Rosenberg, Jill Ogden, Carolina Scott, Richard Stuart, Wallace Warner, Gaunt West, Mildred Wilson.

Student Players
Give 'Rusty Keys'

Ben Bard opened his production of "Rusty Keys," drama by Sada Cowan, last Tuesday, for a long run. Bard has assigned to Truda Marson, the role of Ivy Elliott, hard-bitten missionary whose bigotry and prejudice force her daughter into an elopement.

Others in the cast are Jacklyn Alexander, Lithe Belmont, Pauline Parker, R. A. G. Baird, Brian Gibbons,

Truda Marson

Bob Leeds, Dave Marshall, Joyce Matthews, Gwen Phillips, William Begley, Ray Benard, Brian Burke, Mati Afric, Gay Auburn, Dixie Francis, Audrey Hall, Dorothy Mason, Jill Ogden, Mildred Wilson, Kathleen Crespinel, Greta Diener, Dorothy King, Marilyn Reed, Carolina Scott, Elsie Kingsley, John Lawrence, Wallace Pindell, Jan Neu, Barbara Ray, Wallace Gregory and Wallace Warner.

Player to Enact
Two Characters

Mildred Wilson, Ben Bard player, will appear in the forthcoming production of "Rusty Keys" by Sada Cowan which will open at the Ben Bard Playhouse, on Wilshire Boulevard, Tuesday evening. Miss Wilson will portray Hope Barrington, the spirituelle young ingenue, and at other performances she will portray Phyllis Barrington, Hope's mother.

Others in the cast of "Rusty Keys" are Mati Afric, Jacklyn Alexander, William Begley, Lithe Belmont, Ray Benard, Kathleen Crespinel, Brian Gibbons, Marilyn Reed, John Lawrence, Dixie Francis, Wallace Gregory, Audrey Hall, Elsie Kingsley, Truda Marson, Dorothy Mason, Pauline Parker, Gwen Phillips, Clarice Roma, Sylvia Rosenberg, Jill Ogden, Carolina Scott, Wallace Warner, Gaunt West, Greta Diener and Wallace Pindell.

462

Rusty Keys

Produced and Performed in September 1935. Original play by Sada Cowan.

Cast: Van Buren, Mati Afric, Jacklyn Alexander, William Begley, Lithe Belmont, Ray Benard, Kathleen Crespinel, Greta Diener, Brian Gibons, Marilyn Reed, John Lawrence, Dixie Francis, Wallace Gregory, Audrey Hall, Jack Jordan, Elsie Kingsley, Dave Marshall, Truda Marson, Dorothy Mason, Pauline Parker, Gwen Phillips, Wallace Pindell, Clarice Roma, Sylvia Rosenberg, Jill Ogden, Carolina Scott, Richard Stuart, Wallace Warner, Gaunt West, Mildred Wilson.

Corrigan performed under his other stage name of Ray Benard (see previous entry in this section).

⎯WAAAY OFF BROADWAY⎯

THEATRE Dick Robison, Executive Producer

KEN GASTON

presents

HUSTLERS

a new erotic comedy by A. J. Kronengold

featuring

WARREN PARKER

and

EVE ADAMS   DAVID CARGILL   JIM FABER

GARY FAGA   CASSIE FULLER

SONNY LANDHAM ⸺

SUSAN VALENTINO   DENNIS WALSH

Scenery & Lighting by ROBERT FEDERICO	*Stage Manager* BRUCE DE LUCA	*Costumes by* FABER INC.
General Manager NICHAEL WOODS	*Production Coordinator* MARSHALL BALLOU	*Photography by* RON SCHUBERT

produced in association with

MARK SEGAL

Directed by

CRASH CORRIGAN

55 K Street, SE · (202) 488-1207
Washington, D.C. 20003

464

Hustlers

Produced in January and February 1975. Play by Ken Gaston writing as A. J. Kronengold. *Directed by* Crash Corrigan; *produced in association with* Mark Segal; *scenery and lighting by* Robert Federico; *stage manager*, Bruce De Luca; *costumes by* Faber Inc.; *general manager*, Nichael Woods; *production coordinator*, Marshall Ballou; *photography by* Ron Schubert.

Cast:

Warren Parker	. . . . .	Roger De Jonge
Susan Valentino	. . . . .	Janine
Eve Adams	. . . . .	Carrie
Cassie Fuller	. . . . .	Fruitfly
David Cargill	. . . . .	The Johns
Jim Faber	. . . . .	Cory
Sonny Landham	. . . . .	Cash
Dennis Walsh	. . . . .	K. C. Starr
Gary Faga	. . . . .	Terry Bloomingdale

Synopsis:
The action of the play takes place during a 72 hour period of time, on 8th Avenue (the hustlers' district) of New York City. The play takes place on the street, in a Bickford's Restaurant, and in Roger De Jonge's walkup tenement apartment.

Production Notes:
The play was performed in at least three cities: New York City, Boston, and Washington D.C. From the Author's Note in the playbill: "8th Avenue in New York City is a melting pot of every hustler, pimp, prostitute, drag queen, John and everything else. There was a Bickford's Restaurant where these people used to hang out. The hustlers who worked this Bickfords were generally runaways, in New York for the first time, or regular Boys of the Night. Their Johns affectionally used to call them "Bickford Babies".

For the most comprehensive and accurate information on the Ray "Crash" Corrigan Movie Ranch, also known as Corriganville, The Lone Ranger Ranch at Corriganville, Hopetown, and Corriganville Park, you need to pick up a copy of our definite history on the ranch.

CORRIGANVILLE
MOVIE RANCH

Schneider

Corriganville Press

CORRIGANVILLE

HOME OF WESTERN STARS
HOME OF WESTERN PICTURES

The Definitive True History of the
Ray "Crash" Corrigan Movie Ranch

by Jerry L. Schneider

Have you read our first book on the Western Movie Locations? If not, pick one up.

WESTERN
Movie Making
LOCATIONS

Vol 1 Southern California
Jerry L. Schneider